ABSOLUTE BEGINNER'S GUIDE

TO

Microsoft® Office

PowerPoint® 2003

Read Gilgen

800 East 96th Street,
Indianapolis, Indiana 46240

Absolute Beginner's Guide to Microsoft® Office PowerPoint® 2003

International Standard Book Number: 0-7897-2969-5

Library of Congress Catalog Card Number: 2003103661

Printed in the United States of America

First Printing: October 2003

06   05   04   03   4   3   2   1

Trademarks

All terms mentioned in this book that are known to be trademarks or service marks have been appropriately capitalized. QUE Publishing cannot attest to the accuracy of this information. Use of a term in this book should not be regarded as affecting the validity of any trademark or service mark.

Warning and Disclaimer

Every effort has been made to make this book as complete and as accurate as possible, but no warranty or fitness is implied. The information provided is on an "as is" basis. The author and the publisher shall have neither liability nor responsibility to any person or entity with respect to any loss or damages arising from the information contained in this book.

Bulk Sales

QUE Publishing offers excellent discounts on this book when ordered in quantity for bulk purchases or special sales. For more information, please contact

U.S. Corporate and Government Sales
1-800-382-3419
corpsales@pearsontechgroup.com

For sales outside of the U.S., please contact

International Sales
1-317-428-3341
international@pearsontechgroup.com

Associate Publisher
Greg Wiegand

Acquisitions Editor
Stephanie McComb

Development Editor
Mark Cierzniak

Managing Editor
Charlotte Clapp

Project Editor
Matthew Purcell

Copy Editor
Kitty Jarrett

Indexer
Mandie Frank

Proofreader
Juli Cook

Technical Editor
Jason E. Moore

Team Coordinator
Sharry Gregory

Interior Designer
Anne Jones

Cover Designer
Dan Armstrong

Page Layout
Kelly Maish
Julie Parks

Contents at a Glance

Table of Contents

About the Author

Read Gilgen has taught and written extensively on DOS, Windows, word processing, and presentation software since the early 1980s and has been writing for Que since 1991. He is director of Learning Support Services at the University of Wisconsin, where his primary interests are instructional and foreign language technology. He has recently taught advanced courses on PowerPoint in the United States and Japan. He is a contributing author to the PowerPoint sections of Que's *Special Edition Using Office 97* and *Special Edition Using PowerPoint 2000*.

Dedication

To my wonderfully supportive wife, Sue, an artist in her own right, who puts up with being a book widow while I work on these projects.

Also to my early-morning kids, the next generation, who continually inspire me to find better ways of communicating and who make teaching worthwhile.

Acknowledgments

Many people work hard and in concert to bring a book like this to the light of day. To them I express my gratitude.

Having worked with Stephanie McComb on other projects, I was delighted to work with her again. She has a down-to-earth sense of what has to be done, and with good cheer she brings everyone together.

Thanks also to the fine folks at the Microsoft PowerPoint newsgroup who, probably unbeknownst to them, provided insight, background, and answers.

My appreciation also to the many faculty, students, clients, and colleagues who allowed me, at their expense, to learn the ins and outs of PowerPoint, and to discover what works and what doesn't. This is a richer book because of the experiences I've gained from their real-life forays into the world of PowerPoint.

Thank you to the editorial team who worked on the book, including Mark Cierzniak, Jason Moore, Matt Purcell, Kitty Jarrett, Mandie Frank, and Juli Cook.

We Want to Hear from You!

As the reader of this book, *you* are our most important critic and commentator. We value your opinion and want to know what we're doing right, what we could do better, what areas you'd like to see us publish in, and any other words of wisdom you're willing to pass our way.

As an associate publisher for QUE Publishing, I welcome your comments. You can email or write me directly to let me know what you did or didn't like about this book—as well as what we can do to make our books better.

Please note that I cannot help you with technical problems related to the topic of this book. We do have a User Services group, however, where I will forward specific technical questions related to the book.

When you write, please be sure to include this book's title and author as well as your name, email address, and phone number. I will carefully review your comments and share them with the author and editors who worked on the book.

Email: feedback@quepublishing.com

Mail: Greg Wiegand
Associate Publisher
QUE Publishing
800 East 96th Street
Indianapolis, IN 46240 USA

For more information about this book or another QUE Publishing title, visit our Web site at www.quepublishing.com. Type the ISBN (excluding hyphens) or the title of a book in the Search field to find the page you're looking for.

Introduction

Unless you've led a cloistered life over the past few years, chances are good that you've seen a PowerPoint slide show. From the corporate boardroom to the university classroom, or even at your neighborhood church, PowerPoint is being used to visually communicate to audiences everywhere.

Used properly, PowerPoint can be a great tool to help you communicate, persuade, inspire, motivate, convince, and educate. And that's what this book is all about—helping you use PowerPoint as a tool in support of what you do. Let's get started.

Who This Book Is For

This book is for you if you're new to PowerPoint or if you've already dabbled with it and want to know a bit about what you're doing. I assume that you have absolutely no prior knowledge of PowerPoint, although I'm quite sure you're pretty smart about a lot of other things. In this book I try to match PowerPoint smarts with your smarts to come up with a winning combination.

However, this book doesn't dwell only on the basics. In these pages you'll find dozens of practical suggestions, tips, and even cautions that are useful for both new and experienced PowerPoint users.

This book is targeted to those using PowerPoint 2003 in Microsoft Office 2003. However, if you're still using PowerPoint 2002 in Office XP, you'll find that nearly everything included here still applies.

The PowerPoint Program

If you have the Microsoft Office suite installed on your computer, you might have used Word or Excel, but you might not have realized that you probably also have PowerPoint. If you look for the program and don't find it, you might need to install it, or you might have the Small Business Edition of Office, which unfortunately doesn't include PowerPoint. In this case, you need to upgrade your version of Office or purchase PowerPoint separately.

Some Key Terms

To use PowerPoint effectively, you need to know the basic terminology used for common mouse actions:

- *Point*—Move the mouse to move the onscreen pointer. The mouse pointer changes shape, depending on where it's pointing.

- *Hover*—Move the mouse to a location and wait a second before you do anything else. When you hover, often a short description of that location, menu, or button appears to let you know what happens if you click there.

- *Click*—Press and release the mouse button once. You use a single click to select menu items, to activate toolbar buttons, to select onscreen objects, and to perform other tasks.

- *Double-click*—Press and release the mouse button twice, quickly, and without otherwise moving the mouse. This often has the effect of selecting and also executing, for example, selecting *and* opening a file.

- *Right-click*—Press and release the *right* mouse button. You most often right-click to get a context menu of choices that apply to whatever you're pointing at. If you're left-handed and you've changed your primary mouse button to the right side, you have to mentally translate to the left side when we tell you to right-click.

- *Drag and drop*—Point at an object, hold down the mouse button, drag the pointer across the screen, and release the mouse button. Dragging is most often used to move objects from one part of the screen to another.

- *Object*—Things such as text objects (boxes that contain text), graphic objects (clip art, drawings, or photos), and multimedia objects (audio or video clips) that you can use in a slide show. Unlike a word processing program that deals with sequential text, PowerPoint helps you create and rearrange objects spatially onscreen.

Things to Keep in Mind

One of the great things about using PowerPoint is that you can customize many of its features to work the way you want to work. That can also mean, however, that your program and screen might not look exactly the same as the way it looked when you first installed it. Nevertheless, this book has to make certain assumptions about the way PowerPoint looks, which you should keep in mind as you view figures and work through steps described in this book:

- Typically, you can access PowerPoint features in more than one way. For example, you can select a feature from a menu, from a toolbar button, from a context menu, or by using a keystroke. I try to mention the most common approaches and to vary the approaches I describe to get you used to various options. I cannot cover every method every time, so you should experiment a bit if you think there might be an easier or quicker way to do something.

■ Your PowerPoint screen very likely will look different from those shown in the figures in this book. I have tried to crop out those parts of the screen that are irrelevant, but if you see something that seems out of place, don't let that distract you. Look for what's being described.

■ Although I try to use fonts, clip art, designs, and other elements that you're likely to find with your version of PowerPoint, don't worry too much about replicating exactly what you see. If you have a favorite picture, use that instead of what is shown in an illustration. If you like a different font, use it.

How to Use This Book

This book is divided into six parts, each of which deals with a different theme. Although the first part is fundamental to your learning to use PowerPoint, all the others can be used as needed. If something comes up that is covered in another chapter, earlier or later in the book, I try to provide a cross-reference to make it easier for you to find information you might have skipped over.

Part I, "Getting Started with PowerPoint," is a basic introduction to PowerPoint and a how-to for everything required to create a basic slide show. This part takes a somewhat unusual approach in that it has you create a basic slide show first, in Chapter 2, "PowerPoint Quickstart," and then Chapter 3, "PowerPoint Basics," takes you on a tour of PowerPoint. If you're brand new to PowerPoint, you should consider going in sequence through the chapters in Part I. Even if you know something about PowerPoint, you might want to read Chapter 1, "What's the Point?" which talks about why, or why not, to use PowerPoint.

Part II, "Creating Slide Show Content," isn't necessarily sequential, but it does include most of the essential tasks you're likely to need. Chapter 4, "Organizing a Presentation," helps you understand why and how to organize a PowerPoint presentation, including the use of PowerPoint's outline feature. Chapter 5, "Working with Text Objects," focuses on text objects. Chapters 6, "Working with Graphic Objects," and 7, "Creating Drawing Objects," deal with graphic images and drawing objects. Chapter 8, "Organizing Information by Using Tables," shows you how to use tables, and Chapters 9, "Presenting Numbers by Using Data Charts," and 10, "Using Diagrams and Organization Charts," talk about data charts, diagrams, and organization charts.

Part III, "Making a Slide Show Active and Interactive," shows you how to make a slide show more than a series of still images. In Chapter 11, "Animating Slide Show Objects," you learn to make things move on slides. Chapter 12, "Letting Action

Settings Work for You," describes how you can get PowerPoint to link to other slides or to actions you specify, and how you can make a slide show an interactive, nonlinear presentation.

Part IV, "Preparing and Presenting a Slide Show" helps you get a show ready for presentation to an audience. Chapter 13, "Preparing a Slide Show for Presentation," describes ways to polish up your slides, and Chapters 14, "Preparing to Make a Presentation," and 15, "Making a Presentation," show you how to set up a slide show and prepare both yourself and the room for the actual presentation. Chapter 16, "Learning the Elements of Effective Presentations," summarizes in one place many of the elements of effective presentations that are scattered throughout the book.

Part V, "Making a Slide Show Available in Print and on the Web," describes various ways of getting a slide show in a format that the audience members can take with them. Besides the typical printing options described in Chapter 17, "Printing a Presentation," Chapter 18, "Publishing to the Web," explores how to quickly and easily turn a slide show into a Web page.

Part VI, "Beyond the Basics," helps you learn some useful, but perhaps not immediately needed, skills. Chapter 19, "Adding Multimedia Elements," explores adding audio and video objects to a slide show. Chapter 20, "Customizing PowerPoint," shows how to customize PowerPoint menus and toolbars and how to create custom design templates. Chapter 21, "Looking Beyond the Basics," gives you a nudge toward using additional features that are truly beyond the scope of a basic book, including network-based slide presentations and using macros or other programmed add-ins. This chapter also lists several places you can go for additional help.

I love watching a good PowerPoint presentation. I groan when I have to sit through a bad one. I hope what I've presented here will help you to become the kind of presenter that I and others will love to listen to.

Conventions Used in This Book

This book explains the essential concepts and tasks in an easily digestible format. At the beginning of each chapter is a bulleted list of *In This Chapter* highlights that provides you with a framework for what you are about to learn. At the end of each chapter, under the heading *The Absolute Minimum*, you can review the main points covered in the chapter.

In addition, several icons appear throughout the book to direct your attention to a *note* that provides more detailed information, a *tip* that can help you perform a step more efficiently, or a *caution* to help you steer clear of a potential problem. Following is a brief description of each icon:

note

Notes provide additional information about the subject matter covered in a particular section. You can safely skip these notes and still learn the basics.

tip

Tips provide an insider's guide to a particular concept or task. Look for the tip icon to learn useful shortcuts that show you how to perform a task more efficiently.

caution

Cautions point out common user errors and problem areas to help you avoid the mistakes that hundreds of other users have already made. To avoid trouble and stay on the right track, read the cautions.

PART I

GETTING STARTED WITH POWERPOINT

1

WHAT'S THE POINT?

Unless you've led a cloistered life over the past few years, chances are good that you've seen a PowerPoint slide show. From the corporate boardroom to the university classroom to the neighborhood church, PowerPoint is being used to visually communicate information that not long ago would only have been spoken or, at best, supplemented with printed handouts.

Like everyone else, you too want to "do" a PowerPoint slide show. After all, how hard could it be? Besides, you want to keep up with the rest of the world. So you've decided it's about time to learn how to use this nifty program. This book is here to help, whether you're brand new to computers or an experienced computer user adding PowerPoint to your repertoire of useful tools.

This chapter provides the information you need to decide whether you should learn to use PowerPoint. Is this program the greatest thing to come along since the computer was invented, or is it just going to complicate your life? Can you really use PowerPoint effectively, or will it get in the way of your doing what you already do so well? I come to this topic with a fair amount of everyday experience, painfully aware of the challenges and pitfalls you'll encounter but confident that once you learn what PowerPoint is and does, you'll also come to the conclusion that PowerPoint can be a great tool. Used properly, PowerPoint can help you communicate, persuade, inspire, motivate, convince, and educate.

What PowerPoint Does

PowerPoint was originally created to make it easier to print overhead transparencies. With the advent of the data projector, it also became possible to project images directly from the computer, and thus PowerPoint evolved to take advantage of a whole new world of presentation possibilities. Today, with PowerPoint you can design computer-based *slide shows* that easily exceed the capabilities of the standard 35mm slide shows of yesteryear. For example you can do the following:

- Use bulleted or numbered lists of text to summarize important points
- Use charts and diagrams to visually represent facts and figures
- Use graphics or pictures to illustrate things that are otherwise difficult to describe
- Use animations to illustrate processes or concepts or to gradually add information (such as bullets or figures) to a slide
- Add sound or video to give lifelike realism to slides, without having to fumble with video or tape players
- Quickly publish information to the Web

Last, but not least, you can still *print* overhead transparencies.

note

One of the great advantages to working with an electronic slide show is that, unlike with traditional slide shows, you can make changes right up until you make your presentation. Although you're always well prepared far ahead of your presentation, if you're quick, you could add slides that respond to what other speakers on the program have said.

Exploiting the Visual Side of Communication

PowerPoint is a communication tool, but it's also quite different from word processing programs you're likely familiar with. In Word, for example, the focus is the written word. Graphics and formatting are available merely to enhance the written word. Motion, interactivity, or *multimedia* elements (such as sound and video) aren't typically found in Word documents.

PowerPoint, on the other hand, is a visual tool. Yes, you use words in PowerPoint. But the combination of graphic designs, colors, and visual layouts are as important as the words you use. The visual pictures you create may not be worth the proverbial thousand words, but then again, they just might be (consider Figure 1.1).

FIGURE 1.1

A well-conceived PowerPoint slide can communicate as much information as, if not more than, several paragraphs of carefully worded text.

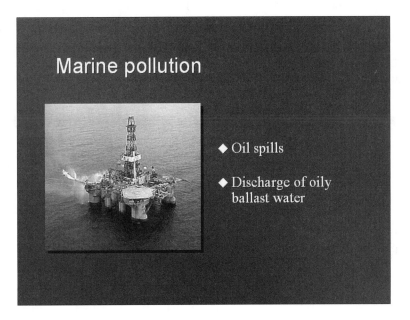

The challenge you'll have as you begin creating PowerPoint slide shows is to think visually, not verbally. One way you can learn to do this is to observe television commercials or billboard signs. Note how few words they use. Instead, the producers try to capture your attention with graphic images, sometimes presented in very unusual ways. You need to try to determine what it is about an effective ad that captures your attention. Further, you should see if you remember what the ad is all about 15 minutes, an hour, or a day later. The same kinds of things that make ads both interesting and memorable are what you'll want to use in your own PowerPoint shows.

Overcoming Linear Word Processing Concepts

Back in high school you learned that before you write an essay, it's a good idea to outline your thoughts. Unfortunately, most of us ignore that advice and simply move forward, writing documents from beginning to end. The path between sometimes wanders, but generally it is relatively straight, or *linear*.

A highly structured, linear approach can work well in some presentations. For example, if you're reporting your company's earnings for the last quarter, and you've been given six minutes to do so, you don't have a lot of time for side trips. But if you're making a presentation where you expect feedback, questions, or interaction with the audience—as in nearly any teaching or training situation—being tied to a strictly linear presentation could spell disaster because such presentations rarely follow a strictly linear path.

Fortunately, PowerPoint allows you to organize material in such a way that you can jump from one topic to another and back again. You can skip topics or have additional topics available just in case they're needed. But you can still stick to a hard-hitting, linear approach if that's called for.

For example, if you're teaching a workshop on how to maximize investment earnings, you might have half a dozen topics, all of which are equally valid. However, some of the topics might be of more interest to the audience than others. You need the flexibility to deal with selected topics in any order and even to skip topics if interest or time constraints make it necessary to do so.

➩ For information on creating a nonlinear presentation, see **p. 221**.

Assessing the Power of PowerPoint

Ultimately, you have to determine whether PowerPoint will function as a real tool in support of whatever your task is. If you're a teacher, can it help you teach better? If you're a motivational speaker, can it help you motivate better? If you're a church music director, can it help you get your congregation to sing better?

Because it takes a lot of time and energy to become proficient with PowerPoint, you certainly don't want to go to a lot of effort, only to find that PowerPoint can't help you. You should therefore start small and resist the temptation to try to do everything all at once. You should try a few things that you think will work and see what happens. As you become more comfortable using PowerPoint, you can try more features until you find yourself wondering how you ever lived without PowerPoint.

How Effective Is PowerPoint?

If you listen to PowerPoint proponents or to its detractors, you could be convinced that it's a panacea, with the potential for brining world peace, or the embodiment of evil itself, contributing to the delinquency of minors and turning corporate minds into mush. So what's the real story?

What's Behind an Effective Presentation

An effective presentation is one that communicates ideas, teaches concepts, or convinces or motivates listeners. Obviously, such presentations can happen without PowerPoint. And that's the point. In my experience, if you're already a good teacher, PowerPoint can help you teach more effectively. If you're a poor teacher, more likely than not PowerPoint will only make that more obvious. But that's why you're here—you're already good and you want to find ways to do your job even better.

The following is not an exhaustive list, but it describes some key elements for any engaging presentation:

- Know what the purpose is for your presentation. Do you want to entertain or inform, motivate or convince, provide facts or stimulate creative thinking? If you don't know what you want to accomplish, your audience won't either.

- Organize yourself. Creating a plan or roadmap is crucial if you want to reach a target destination. Using an outline can help you show the big picture (major topics) and make sure the small picture (subtopics) is covered as well. If you don't know what you want the audience to know, chances are it won't end up knowing it.

- Practice your presentation. Know where you'll stand and when and how you'll move, what visual materials you'll use, and how you'll interact with the audience. You have to be comfortable with your presentation, or the audience certainly won't be.

- Capture the audience's interest. What can you use to grab people's attention and get them thinking along with you? How can you add fuel when the fire of interest is flickering? Can you use a story, an illustration, or some humor to keep them with you? Even the most important information can go unlearned or unnoticed if you don't get the audience's attention and keep it.

- Keep it relevant. Talking about critical success factors to third graders works no better than using exploding spiders in the boardroom to illustrate the need to lay off employees. Likewise, don't let merely interesting facts obscure what you really want the audience to know.

■ Try to assess whether the presentation has worked. Use overviews at the beginning and summaries at the end so that it's clear to the audience members what they *should* have learned. Look for ways to get them to tell you what they learned.

None of these elements require the use of PowerPoint. However, PowerPoint might make it easier to pull them off. You should try to keep this in mind as you explore PowerPoint.

⇨ For more details or a summary of effective presentations, see **p. 289**.

Can PowerPoint Make Presentations Less Effective?

Earlier in this chapter I asked you to consider successful TV or print ads. You have probably noticed that not all commercial ads get the job done. Likewise, things that don't work in an ad probably won't work in PowerPoint either. What was the purpose of the ad? Was the presentation too "cute" so that you remember the cuteness but not the product? Were you distracted by poor design, clashing colors, extraneous music or sounds? Was the screen filled with too much text, not allowing you to read it all, or worse, making you not care to read it?

Once again, if you work at being an effective presenter, PowerPoint will help. If you don't, PowerPoint will likely magnify your shortcomings.

POWERPOINT 101

I once heard a story about a campus English professor who used PowerPoint to illustrate a lecture on Mark Twain. The opening slide read: "Mark Twain wrote..." When the professor tried to advance the slide, nothing happened. He and several technology-oriented students worked for 15 minutes before they fixed the problem, whereupon the professor proudly stated, backed up by flying, flaming text and a ricocheting bullet sound effect: Huckleberry Finn! The student who reported the incident opined that many professors seem to be majoring in PowerPoint 101, not in the subject they're trying to teach.

Another, more recent, phenomenon also makes it difficult to use PowerPoint effectively. Because PowerPoint has been used so poorly in many presentations, some audience members automatically think, "Oh no. Here comes another boring PowerPoint lecture. Turn off the lights and put me to sleep!" You need to be doubly effective if you want to overcome this conditioned negativity.

On the other hand, enough people have seen good presentations that they often expect you to use the technology available to you. If you don't, you have to rely on your charisma (and we don't all have that) if you want to capture and keep their attention. Likewise, the "MTV Generation" knows what it likes and expects to see a little pizzazz in any presentation.

PowerPoint in the Real World

Hopefully, I've convinced you by now that PowerPoint *can* be a powerful tool to increase your effectiveness in making presentations. But let's talk about a few real-world, practical examples that might get you thinking about how PowerPoint will work specifically for you.

Improving Business Presentations

PowerPoint, as a presentation tool, has evolved primarily in support of business presentations. Chapter 3, "PowerPoint Basics," provides a discussion of the AutoContent Wizard, which includes several predesigned templates for such things as recommending a strategy, conducting a company meeting, providing a financial overview, and presenting a marketing plan.

At a minimum, PowerPoint can improve these types of presentations primarily because you have to organize yourself better than if you were to present off-the-cuff. Further, you can visually present key points with text (usually bulleted summaries) or with graphic images. In addition, you can use data charts, organization charts, or diagrams to visually depict numbers, dollars, percentages, and more.

Suppose you're presenting information to a busy corporate executive. Do you want to waste his or her time trying to explain last quarter's sales figures, or might you make a better impression by using a graph to quickly summarize how things went in each region? Consider, for example, the difference between Figure 1.2 and Figure 1.3. Technically, the first is more thorough, presenting all the numbers. However, the second is much more likely to be remembered because it visually shows how quickly the East region is growing, while the West region is slowly declining.

Imagine trying to convince a prospective client that your product is the best on the market. With PowerPoint, the client doesn't have to rely only on what you say, but you can show pictures of the product, illustrate test results, show rate of return figures with graphs, or include video clips of user testimonials.

FIGURE 1.2
Too much
numeric infor-
mation can be
confusing to an
audience.

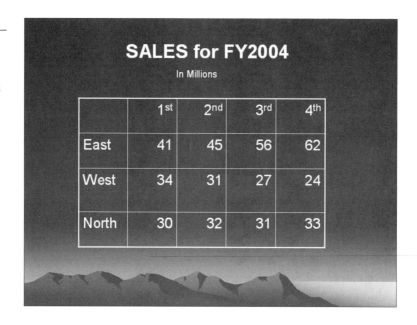

FIGURE 1.3
Graphs can
make compli-
cated data
easier to
understand.

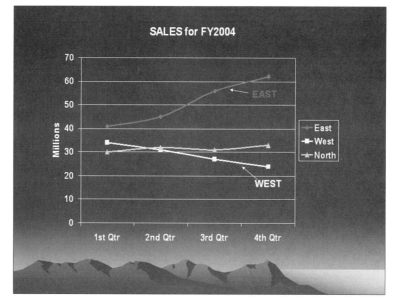

Enhancing Teaching Presentations

Although PowerPoint is often identified with business, it has also found a home in schools, universities, and training centers. Indeed, PowerPoint can be utilized in education settings in ways probably never envisioned by its designers.

Consider, for example, the following figures. Figure 1.4 is the kind of illustration you find in a text book, and although it's technically complete, a student viewing such a figure in a classroom is easily overwhelmed by the amount of information it contains. It is difficult to quickly read and sort the information. If you remove all the labels and add simplified versions of them progressively (see Figures 1.5 and 1.6), the student can more quickly understand the illustration. In addition, your verbal explanations become more important to the student. The textbook version can then be used as a review and reinforcement instead of as the initial source of learning.

FIGURE 1.4

Illustrations that may be appropriate for a textbook often contain too much information to be useful as a PowerPoint slide.

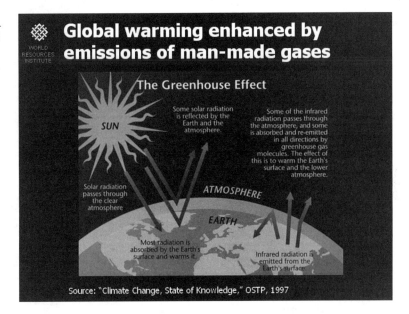

FIGURE 1.5

You can edit illustrations to remove confusing information.

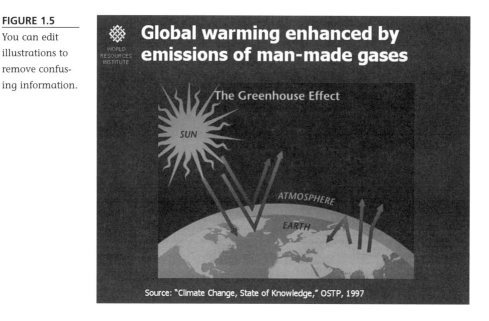

FIGURE 1.6

You can progressively add simplified labels as you discuss an illustration.

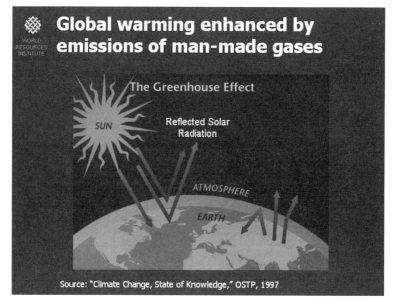

As another example, an art object can be presented by adding labels and arrows, by adding text quotes from the artist, or by placing similar objects side-by-side for comparison. Or a written poem might be accompanied by the recorded voice of the author reading it (see Figure 1.7).

FIGURE 1.7

You can use a multisensory approach to learning: text, illustration, and recorded sound.

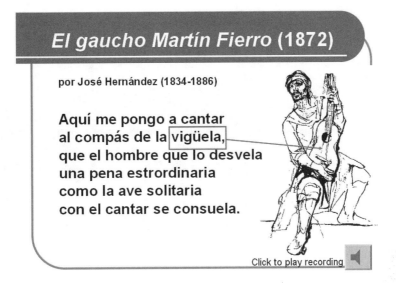

For details on how to illustrate and animate slides, see **p. 123** and **p. 197**.

You might want to direct your students' attention to a Web site for additional information related to your lecture. By using an action setting, you can *link*—that is, jump—to your Web browser and go to the site during class.

For more information on creating hyperlinks and action settings, see **p. 221**.

Finally, before class, you might publish your slide lecture to the Web so students can preview it. They might also print the slides and use them to take notes.

For details on publishing a PowerPoint slide show to the Web, see **p. 319**.

Unique Uses for PowerPoint

The ways you use PowerPoint are generally limited only by your imagination. Consider, for example, the following situations that can be illustrated by PowerPoint slides:

- Your daughter's high school swim team has just won the state championship. You could prepare a slide show that includes scanned or digital photos of meet highlights, play the school's fight song, or reveal the winners of the team awards (see Figure 1.8).

FIGURE 1.8

You can use a slide to progressively reveal team award winners.

■ A funeral service might include a visual tribute to the deceased, with appropriate background music along with photos, quotes, and life statistics (see Figure 1.9).

FIGURE 1.9

PowerPoint slides can tastefully deliver a eulogy with more impact than words alone.

■ You want to advertise an upcoming garage sale. Using PowerPoint's powerful graphics tools, you create and print attention-getting flyers (see Figure 1.10).

FIGURE 1.10

You can use PowerPoint as a tool to create printed flyers.

■ A church worship service might be enhanced by projecting the order of service, including words to hymns or prayers, scripture quotes, visual representation of scripture stories, and so on (see Figure 1.11).

FIGURE 1.11

PowerPoint can find a place in worship services.

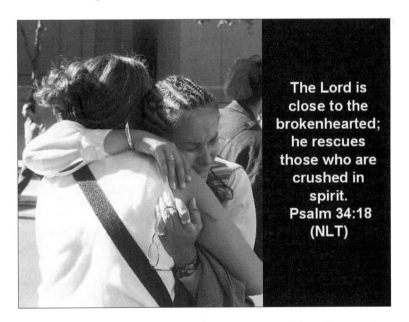

Although you can probably justify learning PowerPoint based on its usefulness for your work, you'll find it useful and appropriate for many other situations as well.

What's New in PowerPoint 2003

Most of what's new in PowerPoint 2003 is found behind the scenes—processes and features that make it easier to share PowerPoint slides and work on them in a variety of environments.

If you're brand new to PowerPoint, none of this makes any difference because it's all new to you. But if you've used earlier versions of PowerPoint and are looking for what's new, here's the list:

- *Updated viewer*—The viewer enables you to display a PowerPoint slide show without having PowerPoint installed. This new viewer provides higher-fidelity output and better support for graphics, animations, and media. The viewer can be downloaded from Microsoft's Web site and can be used on Windows 98 or later.

- *Package for CD*—You can package a slide show along with the viewer and write it directly to a CD. You can then play the slide show directly from the CD, even if PowerPoint isn't installed on the computer you use to play the show.

- *New slide show navigation tools*—The subtle menu button that displays at the lower left during a slide show presentation has been expanded, making it easier than ever to navigate or to use the pen and annotation features.

- *Improved slide show annotations*—You can make annotations directly on the slide show and then keep the annotations for future reference.

- *Smart tags*—Formerly available only in other Office applications, smart tags can be used to initiate actions for which you'd typically open other programs. Advanced users and information technology staff may especially find this feature quite useful.

- *Workgroup features*—If you work in a networked environment and collaborate with others on PowerPoint slide presentations, you can take advantage of several new features from the Office 2003 suite that help manage documents and protect information.

- *Additional features*—Additional features of PowerPoint 2003 include support for tablet PCs and the Research task pane, including a thesaurus.

Whether or not you're new to PowerPoint, this book will help you with the mechanics of PowerPoint. More importantly, it will also show you real-life context and experiences that will help you use PowerPoint effectively. And, after all, *that's* the point!

THE ABSOLUTE MINIMUM

If you've been somewhat hesitant or unsure about using PowerPoint, I hope you're convinced that it can be a powerful tool to enhance your communication and presentation skills.

In this chapter, you have learned the following:

- PowerPoint can be a powerful tool to help you make effective presentations.

- There can and should be a point to using PowerPoint. Although some people might use PowerPoint poorly, you can consciously choose the right elements and procedures to enhance rather than detract from you presentation.

- PowerPoint can be used not only for business presentations but also as a powerful teaching tool.

- There are many unique uses for PowerPoint, such as posters, handouts, Web pages, and more.

- PowerPoint 2003 is not dramatically different from other versions, but certain new features increase its power and versatility.

In Chapter 2, "PowerPoint Quickstart," you'll learn how to create a basic slide show, how to save and print it, and how to make a presentation.

IN THIS CHAPTER

- Jump right in and create a simple slide show
- Learn various ways to view and work with slides
- Understand the basic elements of a slide
- Learn how to present a slide show

2

POWERPOINT QUICKSTART

In Chapter 1, "What's the Point," you learned just what PowerPoint can do for you and some of the things you'll need to watch out for. Enough introduction, you say! Hopefully you took at least a little time with Chapter 1, but now you're ready to jump right in to using PowerPoint.

Typically, beginning books tell you all about the screen, the menus, how to get help, and so on—you know, more stuff to make you wait even longer to use PowerPoint. All that *is* important, but you're going to try something a little different in this book. You're going to jump in, poke around, and create a simple slide show. By doing so, you'll see how really easy it can be to use PowerPoint. Then you'll go back and learn everything you need to understand what you're dealing with.

Creating Your First Title Slide

It might seem obvious, but before you can create your first slide, you have to start up PowerPoint. You can do so in a variety of ways: from the Start menu, from a desktop icon, or from the Taskbar.

PowerPoint starts in Normal view, with a blank title slide staring at you. All you have to do is click where it says to click and type the text you want to include. For example, to add information to the title slide, follow these steps:

1. Move the mouse pointer to the title place-holder—the area that says "Click to add title"—and click. PowerPoint opens a text edit box, surrounded by hash marks (see Figure 2.1), and displays a blinking *insertion point* (the vertical blinking line that appears to show you where the text you type is to be inserted).

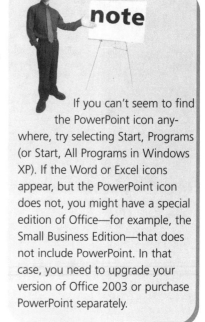

note

If you can't seem to find the PowerPoint icon anywhere, try selecting Start, Programs (or Start, All Programs in Windows XP). If the Word or Excel icons appear, but the PowerPoint icon does not, you might have a special edition of Office—for example, the Small Business Edition—that does not include PowerPoint. In that case, you need to upgrade your version of Office 2003 or purchase PowerPoint separately.

FIGURE 2.1

A box surrounded by hash marks means you're able to add or edit text in the placeholder box.

Blinking insertion point

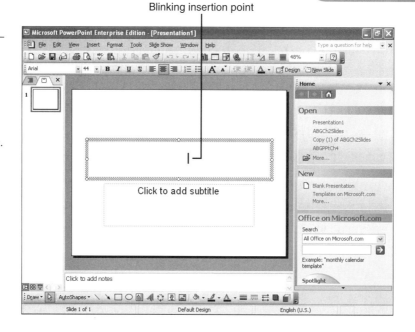

2. Type the title (for example, `I Want You to Know`). Use uppercase or lowercase characters as you want them to appear in the title.

3. Click the subtitle placeholder—the area that says "Click to add subtitle."

4. In the subtitle box, type your name.

5. Click anywhere on the slide outside both placeholders.

You now have your first title slide (see Figure 2.2).

FIGURE 2.2

Clicking any-where on the slide outside the placeholder boxes deselects the boxes and shows your text nearly as it will appear when you play the slide show.

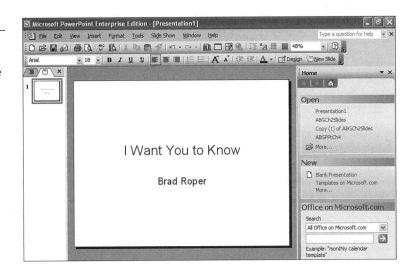

Adding Slides

Creating your first title slide was pretty easy, but now what? You probably need more than just a title slide, so choose **I**nsert, **N**ew Slide (or press Ctrl+M). PowerPoint adds a new *bullet slide* to the slide show (see Figure 2.3).

Bullets, which are the dots or icons at the left of the text, help viewers see the major topics. You could use a numbered list instead of a bulleted list, but generally, bullets do the trick.

At this point you can go ahead and add text to the title placeholder (for example, `About Me`).

To add items to a bulleted list, you follow these steps:

1. Click the bulleted text placeholder. PowerPoint opens a text editing box, with the insertion point following the first bullet (see Figure 2.4).

FIGURE 2.3

When you add a slide to a slide show, by default, PowerPoint creates a bullet slide that also includes a slide title.

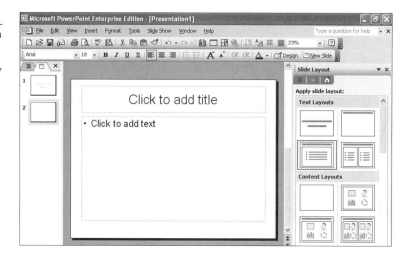

Blinking insertion point

FIGURE 2.4

Bulleted text placeholders are really text boxes, formatted in the bullet style.

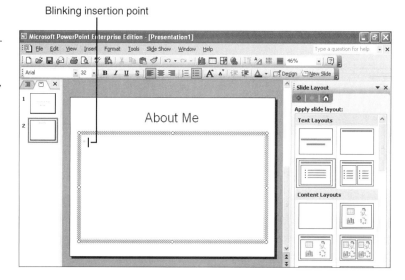

2. Type the text of the first bullet (for example, your age, where you're from, your profession).

3. Press the Enter key. PowerPoint ends the first bulleted line and adds a second one (see Figure 2.5).

4. Continue typing items in the list, until you have three to five items.

5. Click anywhere on the slide outside the placeholders to close the bulleted text placeholder.

FIGURE 2.5

Bullet text is easy to enter, and you just press Enter to get a new bullet.

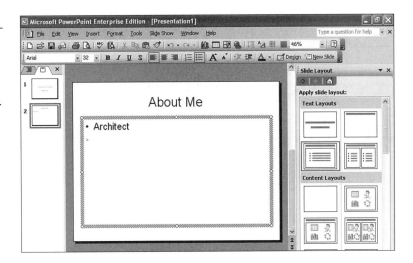

If you want to go back and edit a title or text box, you just click the box and then make any changes you want.

If you accidentally add a bullet you don't want, just press the Backspace key twice, and PowerPoint erases the bullet and returns you to the right side of the preceding bullet.

⇨   For more information on creating good, powerful bullets, see **p. 76**.

If you'd like, you can insert a couple more slides (`My Work` or `My Hobbies`, for example). Then you should insert a final slide.

In the title placeholder of the final slide, you should type `The End`. Don't worry right now about the blank bulleted text placeholder. When you view the slide show, it won't be visible.

caution

A typical temptation for beginning PowerPoint users is to put lots of text or lots of bullets on a slide. Keep your bullets short and to the point and don't make lists of bullets so long that you confuse or lose your viewers.

It's important that you get in the habit of saving your work on a regular basis. There's nothing more painful than putting a lot of creative energy into building a slide show, only to lose it because something happens before you save it. One way to save a slide show is to just choose **F**ile, **S**ave and then click **S**ave. PowerPoint saves the file with a generic filename, such as `Presentation1`. Later you'll learn more about PowerPoint filenames and how to save and retrieve them. From time to time, I'll remind you to save your work. To do so, you can choose **F**ile, **S**ave, you can click the Save icon on the toolbar, or you can simply press Ctrl+S (my favorite…it's quick and easy).

⇨ For more information on saving, retrieving, and managing PowerPoint files, see **p. 53**.

Working with PowerPoint Views

Until this point, we've been working in PowerPoint's Normal view (refer to Figure 2.1). In the center of Normal view is a large version of the slide you're working on. At the left is either an outline of the text of the slide show or *thumbnail* or miniature versions of the slides in the slide show (see Figure 2.6). To see the thumbnail list, click the Slides tab at the top of the column. To see the text, click the Outline tab at the top of the column.

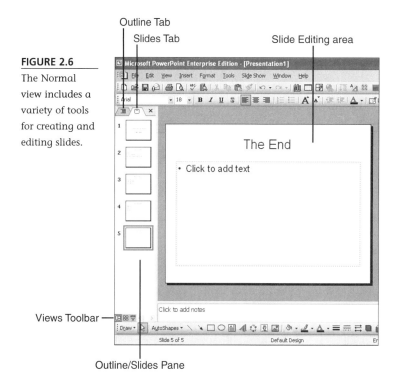

FIGURE 2.6

The Normal view includes a variety of tools for creating and editing slides.

Depending on the features you've been working on, the right side of the Normal view might display certain options and helps, although that is not necessarily part of the Normal view. And of course, as always in PowerPoint, there are various menus and toolbars.

There are two other views besides the Normal view:

- *Slide Sorter view*—To open this view, choose **V**iew, Sli**d**e Sorter, and PowerPoint displays a page of *thumbnails* (miniature pictures) of slides—at least as many as fit on the screen (see Figure 2.7). Double-click a slide to return to the Normal view of that slide.

FIGURE 2.7

You can see a whole range of slides at a time, and easily rearrange them in the Slide Sorter view.

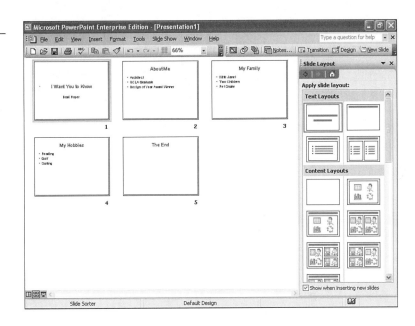

- *Slide Show view*—To open this view, choose **V**iew, Slide Sho**w** or press F5. This view allows you to view the slide as it will appear when you play the slide show, starting with the first slide (see Figure 2.8). To return to your Normal or Slide Sorter view, simply press the Esc key.

FIGURE 2.8

The Slide Show view takes up the whole screen and lets you preview how a slide will look when you play the slide.

I Want You to Know

Brad Roper

You may have noticed a short bar with some tiny icons down at the lower left of your screen (refer to Figure 2.6). These are the view buttons found on the Views toolbar. Click them to quickly go to the Normal, Slide Sorter, and Slide Show views.

tip

If you want to preview only the slide you're working on, from the current slide, click the Slide Show button on the Views toolbar at the lower left of the screen and then press Esc to return to your editing.

Moving from Slide to Slide

As you create and edit a slide show, you'll often need to move quickly from one slide to another. PowerPoint makes it easy to do this, using either the mouse or the keyboard. The different methods for moving to another slide in the Normal view include the following:

- Click the outline or thumbnail slide to the left of the slide editing screen. PowerPoint immediately jumps to that slide.

- Using the scrollbar at the right of the slide editing screen, click the scroll box to display which slide you're on and how many slides are in the slide show. Drag the scroll box up or down, and PowerPoint tells you which slide you'll be at when you release the mouse button.

- At the bottom of the scrollbar are an up double-pointed arrow and a down double-pointed arrow. Click the up arrow to move up one slide, and the down arrow to move down one slide.

- On the keyboard, press Page Up to go up one slide or Page Down to go down one slide.

In the Slide Sorter view, simply scroll up or down and then double-click the slide you want to go to, and PowerPoint returns to the Normal view for that slide.

In either view—Normal or Slide Sorter—you can press Ctrl+End to go to the end of the slide show or Ctrl+Home to go to the beginning.

Understanding the Elements of a PowerPoint Slide

PowerPoint slides are conceptually quite different from spreadsheets or word processing documents with which you may already be familiar. The following sections take a look at some of the elements that make up a typical PowerPoint slide.

Choosing Design and Background Elements

The slide show you've been working on in this chapter looks pretty plain at this point, with its white background and black text. You probably want something a little more interesting. What you're looking for is the *design layer* of the slide. Fortunately, PowerPoint comes with dozens of predefined design templates. To select a design template, follow these steps:

1. Choose F**o**rmat, Slide **D**esign. PowerPoint displays several design template thumbnails at the right of the screen (see Figure 2.9). The list that appears varies, depending on what you or someone else has used recently.

FIGURE 2.9

PowerPoint's predefined design templates enable you to create stunning and effective presentations with very little effort.

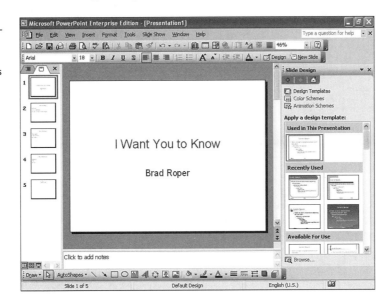

2. Scroll through the list of design templates until you find one you like. Click a design template to apply that design to your entire slide show (see Figure 2.10).

A design template changes several different elements of your slides, all coordinated to create an attractive and functional effect. Templates typically consist of these elements:

- A title master, used only on title slides, that consists of a graphic background, designed to work with the size and placement of the slide's title.
- A slide master, used on all slides except title slides, is similar to the title master but is designed to work with a variety of slide layouts.
- A font style that has specific default font sizes for titles, bullets, and other text you may add.
- An overall color scheme, including font colors, shading, background colors, and other properties that coordinate well with the colors of the design.

FIGURE 2.10

A design template coordinates colors, sizes, fonts, and layouts so you don't have to.

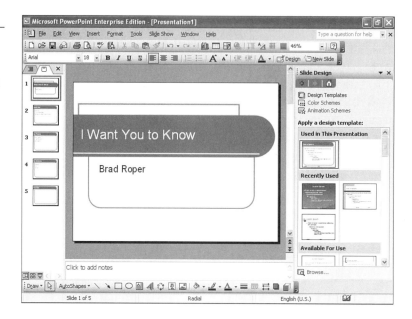

If you don't like the effect of a design template you chose, you can select another. Although you can modify a design template, or even create your own, it's usually best to use those that come with PowerPoint until you become comfortable with PowerPoint and until you've had a chance to develop a sense of what works and what doesn't work in design templates.

Communicating by Using Objects

Unlike a word processing document that relies on strings of words to convey a message, PowerPoint slides consist primarily of several objects, placed onscreen in such a way as to communicate a message visually. Slides can contain few or many objects, depending on what you're trying to accomplish.

Consider the slide shown in Figure 2.11. How many objects do you think the slide contains? Depending on how you look at it, you might say anywhere from two objects to five or more. However, objects are only items that can be selected, added, deleted, or moved as a unit. For example, you cannot select the blue bar or the frame around the bullets because they're part of the design layer. Objects can include the following:

FIGURE 2.11

In PowerPoint
you create and
edit objects on a
slide, but you
can't directly
select or edit ele-
ments of the
design layer.

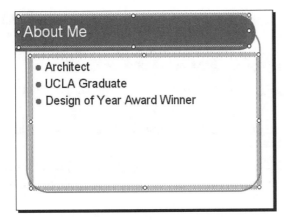

- Title placeholders
- Bulleted text placeholders
- Chart or diagram placeholders
- Text boxes
- Graphic images (for example, clip art, photos, drawings)
- Multimedia placeholders (for example, video clips, audio clips)

If you click an object, the object's frame appears, indicating what it is that you're working with. Note that in Figure 2.11 the only two objects onscreen are selected: the title placeholder and the bulleted text placeholder. The other graphic images and lines are part of the design layer and thus are not slide objects.

Organizing the Layout Structure

When you created your first slide show, you may have noticed that the organization of the first and second slides was different. This organization of objects is called the *layout* of the slide in that it determines where such things as the title, bullets, or other objects normally reside, and it provides placeholders for those objects. A title placeholder, for example, reserves the location and space for a title; until you actually add text to the title placeholder, no title appears when you play the slide. The location of layout placeholders is determined initially by the design template that is applied, but ultimately you can choose any layout you want or move or remove objects from a layout that doesn't quite meet your needs.

By default, PowerPoint applies the Title Slide layout (title and subtitle) to the first slide in a slide show and the Title and Text layout (bullets) to all subsequent slides. Suppose, however, that you want to change a slide to include two columns of bullets. To change the layout of a slide, follow these steps:

1. Go to the slide you want to change (for example, the "My Hobbies" slide in your slide show).

2. Choose F**o**rmat, Slide **L**ayout. PowerPoint displays a list of layout types at the right side of the screen.

3. Scroll through the list until you find the layout you need (for example, the Title and 2-Column Text layout) and click the layout to apply it to the current slide.

PowerPoint presents you with the initial objects required for the layout you've chosen (see Figure 2.12).

FIGURE 2.12

Layout options give you predefined arrangements of text and content objects.

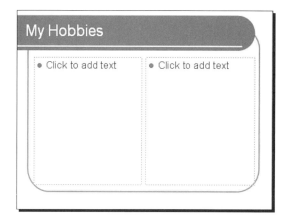

Layout options are grouped as follow:

- *Text layouts*—Nearly all slide layouts include at least a title placeholder. Text layouts include text-only combinations.

- *Content layouts*—Content layouts include slides with placeholders for more than just text: charts, diagrams, tables, or images, in a variety of arrangements. You can also choose a blank slide layout that contains no objects.

- *Text and content*—You can select combinations of text and content placeholders.

- *Other layouts*—Other layouts include specific content types—for example, a table or a data chart instead of multicontent placeholders found in the other groups of layouts.

Layouts provide predefined placeholders that also coordinate with your design layer. However, until you actually fill the placeholders with something, they remain invisible when you play a slide show.

Adding Objects to Slides

Placeholders are just one type of object. You can also add other objects to complement them. For example, you might want to add a text label and an arrow to draw the audience's attention to something important onscreen (see Figure 2.13).

FIGURE 2.13

You aren't limited to predefined layouts: You can add text or graphic objects that help present your message.

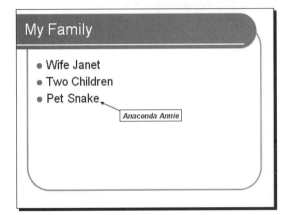

The kinds of objects you add, and especially what you do with them, is limited only by your creativity and imagination. Some of the most common types of objects include the following:

- *Text objects*—You can add small or large amounts of text. You can rotate text, highlight it, or animate it for different effects.

- *Graphic objects*—You can add graphic objects, including clip art images, images from the Internet, drawings you create yourself, or scanned images, including photos. You can determine the size, location, rotation, and often the colors of such objects.

- *Content objects*—You can add content objects, including data and organizational charts, diagrams, tables, and multimedia elements. You can use layouts to add content objects, and you can also add such objects to any slide, placing them wherever you want.

To add an object to a slide, simply use the menu or toolbars to select and insert the object. For example, to add an arrow to draw the viewer's attention to one of your bullet points, follow these steps.

1. Choose **I**nsert, **P**icture, **A**utoShapes. PowerPoint displays the AutoShapes palette. Click the Lines button to see the extended palette of line types (see Figure 2.14).

FIGURE 2.14

One way to add graphic objects is to use the AutoShapes palette.

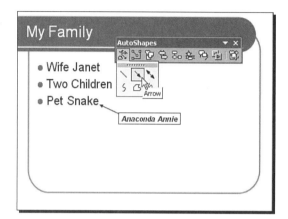

2. Click the type of arrow you want to insert (for example, the single-headed arrow). The mouse pointer changes to crosshairs (a large plus sign).

3. Move the mouse pointer to where you want the arrow to start.

4. Click and drag the mouse pointer to where you want the arrowhead to point.

5. Release the mouse button to insert the arrow.

6. Close the AutoShapes palette by clicking its Close button.

Don't worry yet about the details of adding a drawing object. At this point, you can just congratulate yourself on a job well done. Other chapters explore in detail how to add all sorts of objects. The important thing to know at this point is that you can add a variety of objects to help you visually communicate just about any message.

Making a Presentation

The point of creating a slide show is to show it! Although your initial creation may not win any awards for powerful communication, it will allow you to learn how to make a presentation.

Other chapters explore how to make *effective* presentations, but for now you simply need to learn how to start a show, how to advance slides, and how to end a show.

Starting and Ending a Slide Show

Starting and ending a slide show is quite simple. To start a slide show, you choose Sli**d**e Show, **V**iew Show or press the F5 key. PowerPoint jumps to the first slide in the show and displays it full screen, without menus or other distractions (refer to Figure 2.8).

If you see icons in the lower-left corner of the screen, or if you see the mouse pointer, it's because you've moved the mouse. These icons do have a purpose, which we'll explore later, but if you let the mouse lie for a moment, these distractions disappear.

Remember that if you want to begin the slide show with the current slide, or if all you want to do is preview the current slide, from the current slide, you click the Slide Show button on the Views toolbar at the lower left of the screen.

To end a slide show immediately, press the Esc key. PowerPoint returns you to the editing view you had selected when you started playing the show.

You can also simply advance to the end of the show. By default, PowerPoint shows a blank, all-black screen after the last slide in a slide show. At that point, if you advance one more time, or press Esc, PowerPoint automatically returns you to the editing screen.

⇨   For details on playing a slide show, see **p. 253**.

Advancing Slides in a Slide Show

There are at least four basic and simple ways to advance a slide after you've started a slide show:

- Click the primary mouse button (usually the left button).
- Press the spacebar.
- Press the Page Down key.
- Press the down-arrow key or the right-arrow key.

Each time you perform one of these actions, PowerPoint immediately advances to the next slide. You can also change how the slides change by modifying slide transitions to include various visual and sound effects.

⇨   For details on adding transitions to slides, see **p. 244**.

You should also be aware that these actions advance a slide show to the next slide, unless the slide contains animations, in which case the show advances only to the next scheduled action.

➪   For more information on animating slides, see **p. 197**.

tip

Advancing slides is easy. But what happens if you accidentally go too far? The easiest way to back up is to press the Page Up key, the up-arrow key, or the left-arrow key.

THE ABSOLUTE MINIMUM

In this chapter, you jumped right in and created a simple slide show, utilizing the basic functions you'll need for creating any presentation. You also did the following:

- You learned how to create and add slides.
- You found out how to view slides in various ways that help you develop a slide show.
- You discovered the basic building blocks of a PowerPoint slide: designs, layouts, and objects.
- You learned how to show a slide show.

In Chapter 3, "PowerPoint Basics," we'll step back and talk about the basics of the PowerPoint program itself—how to understand the PowerPoint layout, how to use the various menus and toolbars, and how to save, retrieve, and print PowerPoint slides.

3

POWERPOINT BASICS

In Chapter 2, "PowerPoint Quickstart," you moved full-steam ahead into creating your first slide show. You probably saw lots of things you couldn't easily identify, and you may have wondered just what they were for. This chapter steps back and talks about the PowerPoint program itself, including its tools, helps, and procedures, so that you can be prepared to take full advantage of what PowerPoint has to offer.

Finding Your Way Around the PowerPoint Screen

In some ways PowerPoint looks like a lot of other Windows-based programs. That's to be expected because one of the purposes of Windows is to create a common user interface. But PowerPoint also uses a lot of unique tools, and its editing and other screens are unique to the tasks you need to accomplish.

When you first start PowerPoint, it comes up in the Normal view (see Figure 3.1). Some of the menus and toolbar items are probably familiar to you. Other elements, however, may be new to you. We're not going to explore everything in this chapter, but we will take a look at things that are likely to be useful to you not only as you get started but also as you later apply some of PowerPoint's more complex features.

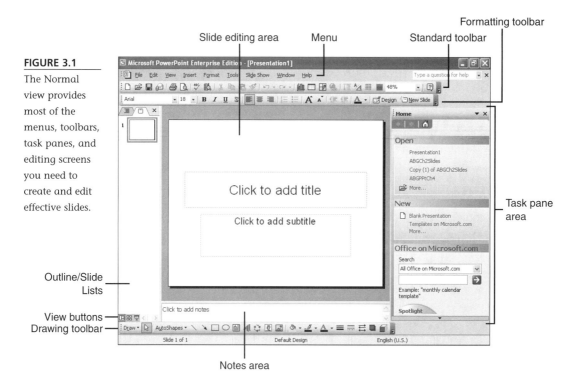

FIGURE 3.1
The Normal view provides most of the menus, toolbars, task panes, and editing screens you need to create and edit effective slides.

When you open PowerPoint, you find four distinct types of areas (refer to Figure 3.1): menus; toolbars; work, or editing, areas; and task panes.

Exploring Menus and Toolbars

In some ways, menus and toolbars are likely to be familiar to you. However, if you're coming from another type of operating system, for example, or from another program, the way Windows and Microsoft Office use menus and toolbars might be a bit confusing.

You're probably familiar with menus that are organized from **F**ile on the left to **H**elp on the right. You can choose **E**dit to see a relatively short list of options. If you hover the mouse over a menu long enough, the list expands to include all the options found there. Or you can expand a menu more quickly by clicking the double down arrows at the bottom of the menu list. As you use menu items, they appear immediately, but items that you haven't ever used don't appear unless you click the double arrows. Some folks like this approach; others don't.

➡️ If you don't like the way menus or toolbars work in PowerPoint, you can change them. To find out how, see **p. 371**.

By default, PowerPoint displays three important toolbars. The Standard and Formatting toolbars appear at the top, beneath the menu bar. The Drawing toolbar can be found at the bottom of the screen (refer to Figure 3.1). If you're not sure what a button represents, you can simply hover your mouse pointer over it, and PowerPoint displays a *ScreenTip*—a label that names or describes the button's function.

A toolbar button may have a drop-down arrow at its right. You can click this arrow to choose from an expanded palette or menu of choices. Choosing a different option often changes the default choice displayed on the button. The next time you click the button, you get your most recent choice (for example, green text instead of black).

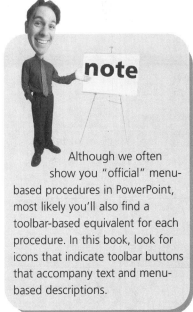

note

Although we often show you "official" menu-based procedures in PowerPoint, most likely you'll also find a toolbar-based equivalent for each procedure. In this book, look for icons that indicate toolbar buttons that accompany text and menu-based descriptions.

Understanding Task Panes

Yes, I spelled *panes* correctly, even if sometimes knowing what to do with them can certainly be a pain. In the Windows environment, the smaller divisions of the large window are called panes. In Figure 3.2, the task pane is the section at the right that looks like a mini-browser, complete with back, forward, and home buttons.

FIGURE 3.2

The task pane changes depending on the task you're working on.

Task pane options   Task pane menu

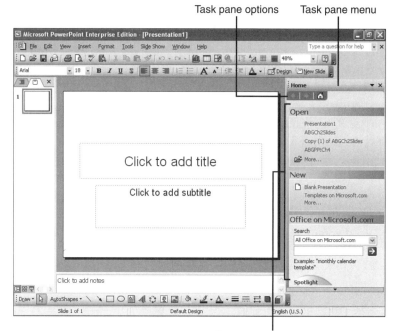

Task pane navigation bar

When you first start PowerPoint, the Home task pane appears, and you can do the following:

- Quickly open presentations you have recently worked on or browse for and open any presentation on your computer or on your network.

- Start a new blank presentation, a new presentation based on PowerPoint's templates, or a presentation using templates you can find at the Microsoft Web site.

- Search for help or get other information at Microsoft's Web site.

Click the task pane menu bar to see a list of the PowerPoint task panes that are available (see Figure 3.3). Some of these you can choose yourself, but many of them automatically appear when you begin a certain activity. For example, when you insert a new slide in a slide show, PowerPoint automatically displays the Slide Layout task pane, assuming that you want to choose a layout before you add content to the slide.

You'll find that task panes often replace what you used to find in dialog boxes. For example, in earlier versions of PowerPoint, you select a design or layout from a dialog box; now you do that from a task pane.

FIGURE 3.3

PowerPoint groups related tasks together in task panes, making it easy for you to use the tools you need.

You can use the task pane navigation bar to return to the Home task pane or to go back or forward among task panes you have recently used.

I won't take time now to describe each task pane. Rather, I do that as you use them.

Using Context Menus

One extremely helpful method for quickly accessing a needed feature is to use context menus. These menus pop up when you click the secondary mouse button while hovering over an item. Typically, the secondary mouse button is the right mouse button. Therefore, this text talks about clicking the right mouse button, or *right-clicking*. If you've switched your buttons because you're left-handed, you need to translate right to left.

Suppose you are ready to put the final touches on a slide. If you right-click a text *placeholder* (for example, a title box), you get a menu that provides editing and wordsmith tools, as well as options for animating the placeholder and doing other tasks (see Figure 3.4). On the other hand, if you right-click the slide toward the edges, outside the placeholders, you get a shorter context menu that lets you choose design, layout, slide transition, and other options.

tip

You can save untold amounts of time by learning to use context menus, not only in PowerPoint but in nearly all Windows programs. Simply right-click while pointing at what you want to change, and usually a context menu pops up, offering features that relate specifically to what you're pointing at.

FIGURE 3.4

Access context
menus by right-
clicking on an
area of an object
that you want to
modify.

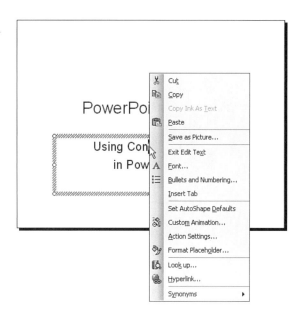

After you bring up a context menu, you can move the mouse pointer to the menu item you want and click the left mouse button to choose it.

Finding Help

When was the last time you opened a manual? Oh, right. You've got this book open! Well, besides this one? Some time ago, software makers decided that providing printed manuals was just too expensive. Instead, they now provide extensive Help screens built into their programs or give you links to online sources where you can find the help you need. Some of us still prefer books, but if you don't have one handy, you can use PowerPoint's built-in Help.

To get PowerPoint help, start by choosing **H**elp, Microsoft PowerPoint **H**elp or simply pressing F1. PowerPoint displays the Microsoft Office Help task pane (see Figure 3.5). In this pane you can browse the Table of Contents of the online Help tool, or you can type a simple question or keyword in the Search box and click the Start Searching button to search Microsoft's help database.

PowerPoint—indeed, Office 2003—comes with a cutesy Office Assistant. Fortunately, the Office Assistant isn't quite as obnoxious as it was in earlier versions of Office. The Office Assistant pops up when you choose to use a wizard and also at unexpected times. If you don't like it, you can right-click the Office Assistant and choose Hide. Or you can let the Office Assistant teach or help you. It's your choice.

FIGURE 3.5
PowerPoint
provides nearly
everything,
except a printed
book, to help
you.

Task pane menu

Task pane navigation bar

Task pane options

For information on how to get help from other PowerPoint users, as well as from other Internet resources, see **p. 382**.

Starting with a Template

Now that you've become familiar with the layout of the PowerPoint screen, you're ready to explore a wider range of possibilities in designing PowerPoint presentations.

In Chapter 2 you started with a blank presentation so you could see how to put together a simple slide show. You added text and even changed the overall slide design. Knowing that most of us are neither accomplished artists nor experienced presenters, the PowerPoint folks have created a variety of slide shows and formats to help us start out on the right foot. These predesigned shows are *templates*; all you have to do is fill in a little information, and PowerPoint does the rest. Well, mostly.

Using the AutoContent Wizard

The most fully developed templates are those found in the AutoContent Wizard. When you first start PowerPoint, the Getting Started task pane offers the choice of opening an existing presentation or creating a new one. Click Create a New Presentation to access the New Presentation task pane (see Figure 3.6). In the New area, you can choose from Blank Presentation (as you did in Chapter 2), a design template, the AutoContent Wizard, or a template from the Microsoft Web site.

FIGURE 3.6

The New Presentation task pane provides several options for creating a new presentation, including the AutoContent Wizard.

If you click From AutoContent Wizard, PowerPoint displays the AutoContent Wizard dialog box. Click **N**ext to get started (see Figure 3.7).

FIGURE 3.7

The AutoContent Wizard leads you through the steps required to prepare presentations with specific content.

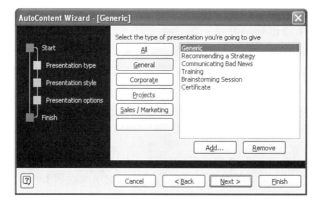

The first step is to select a presentation type. You'll notice right away that most of the presentations are geared for the corporate world. You can choose from various categories, or you can select **A**ll to see all the templates you can choose from. When you find the one you want, select it and then click **N**ext.

The second step is to choose the presentation style. Typically, you'll be making an onscreen presentation, but you can also create a presentation targeted for the Web, for printed overhead transparencies, or for 35mm slides. Stick with the onscreen presentation for now. After you select it, click **N**ext.

The third step (see Figure 3.8) is to choose certain basic options, which include the following:

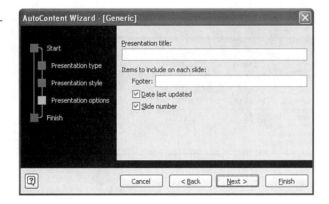

■ You can add the title of your presentation here, or you can add it later.

■ You can add a footer, which is text that appears at the bottom of each slide. An example might be your company, university, or department name.

■ By default, PowerPoint automatically generates the date your slide show was last updated (that is, saved) and places it at the bottom of each slide. Uncheck the Date Last Updated check box if you don't want this information on your slides.

■ PowerPoint assumes that you want slide numbers. Uncheck the Slide Number check box if you don't.

After you make your choices, click **N**ext, and then on the final wizard screen, click **F**inish. PowerPoint displays the title slide with the options you chose, and it also closes the task pane and displays an outline with predefined text to the left of the slide (see Figure 3.9).

You can scroll through the outline to get a sense of suggested elements for a success-ful presentation on the topic you chose. For example, if you chose a marketing plan, you see slides showing market summary, production definition, competition, and so on. You may or may not use all the sample slides, and you'll likely add others.

FIGURE 3.9

The AutoContent Wizard gets you started, but you have to fill in the details yourself by changing the generic content.

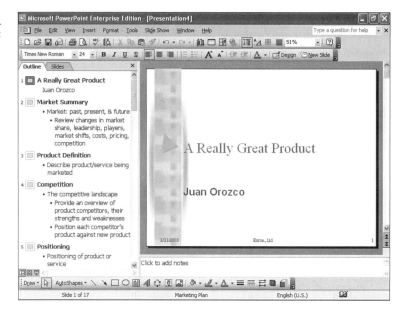

In any case, you'll certainly want to change the text in the sample slides. To change a slide's text content, you follow these steps:

1. From the left side of the screen, select the slide that you want to change (for example, Product Definition).

2. Change the title so it's a little less generic. For example, instead of Product Definition, you might use the real name of the product you want to market. To change the title, click the title placeholder and then edit the text as you would any word processing text.

3. Change the bullet items by clicking the bulleted text placeholder, deleting what's there, and adding your own bullets.

Repeat these steps for the other slides until you've inserted your marketing information into the template.

You can also delete slides or slide information. To delete information from a slide, simply click the object you want to remove (for example, a graph or graphic image) and press Delete. To delete an

tip

You can use Undo to reverse nearly anything. But Undo is not only a tool that you use to correct mistakes. Because creating PowerPoint slides is akin to an artistic experience, consider the Undo tool as a way to try things out. You can do, undo, and do again until you get just what you want.

entire slide, click the slide icon in the outline area at the left and press Delete. PowerPoint does *not* warn you that you're about to lose an entire slide. If you accidentally delete a slide, simply click the Undo button on the toolbar.

So how useful are the templates from the AutoContent Wizard? It depends on how much experience you already have in designing presentations. If you're just beginning, these templates can be a good way to learn about the fundamental components of a good presentation. But if you're more experienced, more likely than not you'll find these templates somewhat limiting.

Starting with a PowerPoint Design Template

If you're not satisfied with the content or approach of the AutoContent Wizard's templates, you might want to start by choosing a design template that matches the mood or tone of your presentation. You can then add whatever content slides you want to present, in any sequence you want.

➪   To learn more about planning and organizing a slide show, see **p. 65**.

To create a new presentation using a design template, simply start PowerPoint and click the Slide Design button on the Formatting toolbar. PowerPoint displays a gallery of designs that include coordinated colors, fonts, and layouts (see Figure 3.10). Scroll through the gallery to find a design you think you'd like and click the design to apply it to your slide show.

FIGURE 3.10

PowerPoint provides a variety of designs that can reinforce the tone and content of a presentation.

You can change the design any time, even after you've created an entire slide show. However, by default PowerPoint changes the design for all slides in the presentation, and changes in fonts and colors may make it necessary to edit the slide show to make text and other objects fit the new layout. For example, a title that fits nicely in one design layout might be too long for another. If possible, try to select a design that you'll stick with for the entire presentation.

You can, however, apply a design to just a single slide in a slide show. To do so, simply go to the slide you want to change and then click the right side of the design in the gallery to get a menu of choices (see Figure 3.11). Click Apply to **S**elected Slides if you want to change just this slide, but not the rest of the slide show.

caution

Just because you *can* use a feature in PowerPoint doesn't mean you *should* do so. For example, design templates are intended to give a consistent look to an entire slide show. Changing the design every few slides can be quite distracting, drawing attention to the slide designs instead of to the content you're trying to present. Choose a design and stick with it, unless you have a compelling reason to change it.

FIGURE 3.11

Although you usually use only one design in a slide show, you can also change the design for selected slides.

Starting with a Blank Slide Show

In Chapter 2 you created a slide show that starts with a blank design. Although you should stick to basics as you learn PowerPoint, a blank slide show is going a bit too far.

Nevertheless, there are times when you simply don't need a slide design. For example, if you're displaying photos or screen shots that take up the whole screen, the design won't be seen anyway.

Some advanced users start with a blank screen so that they can create their own custom designs. Creating your own design, however, can be extremely time-consuming, and you also need to have a fair amount of graphics design experience to make a custom design work.

➪ If you think you'd like to create your own design template, see **p. 358**.

Saving and Retrieving a PowerPoint Presentation

Saving PowerPoint presentations is pretty straightforward. The trick is to use names that you can find later and also to remember where you saved your presentations.

Saving a Presentation

In Chapter 2, you saved a file with the generic `Presentation1` filename. That name won't be very helpful later, when you're trying to find the presentation on the Capital Building Program. To save a file with a meaningful name, follow these basic steps:

1. Choose **F**ile, **S**ave. If this is the first time you've saved the file, or if you choose **F**ile, Save **A**s, the Save As dialog box appears (see Figure 3.12).

FIGURE 3.12

When you save a presentation, be sure to remember not only the name of the slide show but also the location where you save it.

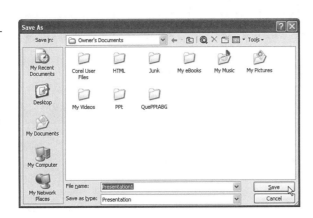

2. Note the location in the Save **I**n box, for example, Owner's Documents (in Windows XP).

3. In the File **N**ame box at the bottom of the dialog box, a generic presentation name appears and is highlighted. Over that name, start typing a name for your presentation (for example, `Capital Building 2005`). The new presentation name replaces the generic name.

4. Click **S**ave. PowerPoint saves the file with the name and in the location you chose, and it closes the dialog box.

You can tell whether saving the file worked by looking at the title bar at the top of the screen. PowerPoint displays the name you chose in brackets. If your Windows setup allows you to see filename extensions, you'll also notice that `.ppt` has been appended to the filename. That simply means that it's a PowerPoint file, making it easier for you and for Windows to identify the file.

Finding and Opening a Presentation

Saving a file is easy. Finding a file is sometimes a bit more tricky. But when you do find it, opening a file is also simple.

If you've worked on a presentation recently, chances are that you can quickly open the file from the **F**ile menu. To do so, choose **F**ile, look at the bottom of the menu to see if your file is listed, and if it is listed, simply select the filename to open it.

If it's been a while since you worked on the presentation you want to open, or if you've worked with several other presentations in the meantime, the name might not appear at the bottom of the **F**ile menu. In that case, you must use the Open dialog box. To open a file using this method, follow these two easy steps:

1. Choose **F**ile, **O**pen. PowerPoint displays the Open dialog box (see Figure 3.13).

FIGURE 3.13

Retrieving a file from a computer is called opening a file.

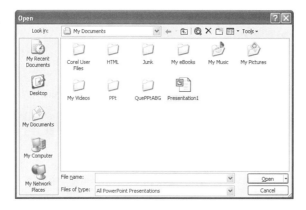

2. Look for the name of the file you want to open. When you find it, click it once and then click **O**pen. Or, you can double-click the filename to open the file.

If you don't see the file you want to open, you need to check whether there's a folder that might contain the file. To do so, you double-click the folder name to move inside that folder. Most of the time this suffices. But once in a while, you might have a difficult time finding a file, even when you're sure you saved it. One reason might be that you have several files, and you've just forgotten the filename, or you have several filenames that are similar to one another. One method for finding files in this situation is to sort them by date, which helps you find files based on when you last worked on them. To sort files by date, follow these steps:

1. Choose **F**ile, **O**pen to display the Open dialog box (refer to Figure 3.13).

2. Click the drop-down menu to the right of the Views button on the toolbar. PowerPoint offers several options for how you can view files.

3. Choose **D**etails. PowerPoint lists all the files in alphabetical order, and it also shows their sizes and the dates they were last modified.

4. Click Date Modified at the top of the list to sort the files in ascending order (that is, oldest first). Click Data Modified again to list the files in descending order (that is, newest first).

You can then search this list of files, and when you find the one you want, you can double-click it to open it.

If you've simply misplaced a file and really have no idea where it is, you can use PowerPoint's Search feature to find it. To search for a lost file, follow these steps:

1. Choose **F**ile, **O**pen.

2. Click the Too**l**s button on the toolbar and then choose **S**earch. PowerPoint displays the File Search dialog box (see Figure 3.14).

FIGURE 3.14

If you don't remember where a file is, you can use the Search tool to find it.

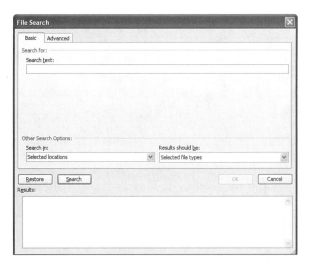

3. In the Search **T**ext box, type a word or words that you know are in the presentation. Try to use relatively unique words, such as a proper name, instead of common words, such as *presentation*.

4. By default, PowerPoint searches your entire local hard drive. From the Search **I**n drop-down menu, specify exactly where you want PowerPoint to look.

5. By default, PowerPoint also searches for any Office documents. If you want to look only for PowerPoint files, click the Results Should **B**e drop-down menu and uncheck all but the PowerPoint Files option.

6. When you're ready to begin the search, click **G**o. PowerPoint searches your computer and displays a list of the files it finds.

7. Hover your mouse over each filename to see the exact location of each file and the date and time it was last modified. When you find the file you want, double-click it to go to its location and then click **O**pen to open the file.

Saving, finding, and opening files are some of the most mundane tasks you'll perform in PowerPoint. They might not be glamorous tasks, but learning to manage files can save you untold time, allowing you more time to enjoy working with PowerPoint.

Printing Slides from a Presentation

Generally, your objective in preparing a presentation is to show it to an audience as a slide show. But PowerPoint was originally designed as a means of creating and printing overhead transparencies. Indeed, printing is an often overlooked but useful PowerPoint feature. It's also one of the most abused and poorly used features. Let's talk about *how* first, and then you can watch me rant and rave at the end of this section.

With PowerPoint, you can print the following:

- Copies of a slide or slides
- Overhead transparencies, in black and white or in color
- Handouts that contain from one to nine slides per page
- Speaker notes
- An outline of a slide show's text

Of course PowerPoint provides several options for printing all these things.

Selecting a Printing Method

PowerPoint offers several ways to print slides. To print a slide or slides, you follow these steps:

1. Choose **F**ile, **P**rint or press Ctrl+P. PowerPoint displays the Print dialog box (see Figure 3.15).

FIGURE 3.15

You use the Print dialog box to select print options, to preview a print job, or to print a slide show.

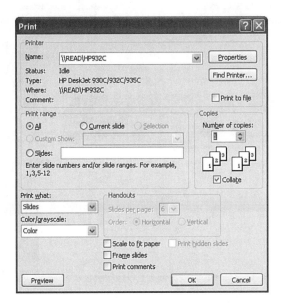

2. Make sure the proper printer is selected.

3. Select which slides you want to print: all, only the current slide, or specific slides (for example, see the sample page ranges given in the Print dialog box).

4. Set the number of copies and how you want multiple copies stacked.

5. By default, PowerPoint prints all the slides in the slide show, in their natural color if you have a color printer or in *grayscale* (that is, shades of gray) if you don't. You can force color slides to print in grayscale or pure black and white by choosing from the Color/**G**rayscale drop-down list box.

6. Click OK to print your selection.

Another useful approach to printing is to preview the print job so you can see what it will look like before you waste paper and ink. Many of the printing options you normally use can also be accessed in the Print Preview screen. To preview before printing, follow these steps:

1. Choose **F**ile, Print Pre**v**iew, or click the Pre**v**iew button in the Print dialog box (refer to Figure 3.15). PowerPoint displays the current slide in the Print Preview screen (see Figure 3.16).

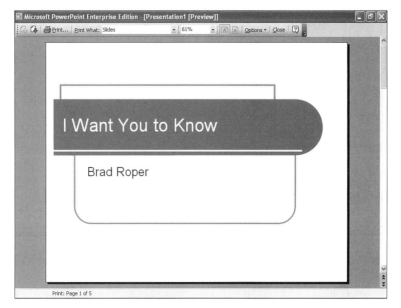

2. On the Print Preview toolbar, choose what you want to print, along with other options, such as color and grayscale.

3. If you're ready to print the entire slide show, click the **P**rint button. Or, to cancel Print Preview and return to the slide show, click **C**lose. If you want to print only selected slides, you must use the Print dialog box, not Print Preview.

You can create attractive and useful handouts, outlines, or speaker notes by sending a slide show to Word. The trick here is to forget the word *print* and instead follow these steps:

1. Choose **F**ile, Sen**d** To, Microsoft **W**ord. PowerPoint displays the Send to Microsoft Word dialog box (see Figure 3.17).

FIGURE 3.17

The Send to Microsoft Word feature can help you create useful handouts.

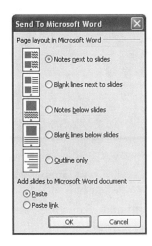

2. Choose the page layout you want. For example, you can specify small versions of slides with speaker's notes beside or below them or accompanied by blank lines. You can also choose to send the outline only.

3. Click OK. PowerPoint sends the slide show to a Word document in the format you selected (see Figure 3.18).

FIGURE 3.18

When you use the Send to Microsoft Word feature, your slides become images in a Microsoft Word document.

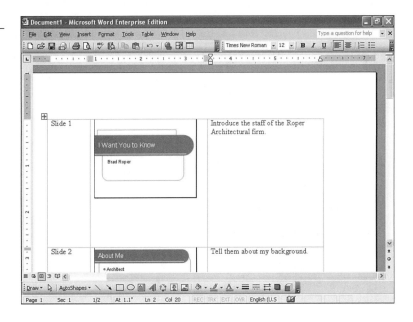

At this point you're in Word, and you can edit, save, or print the resulting Word document. To return to PowerPoint, you simply close Word or click the PowerPoint button on the Windows taskbar.

To Print or Not to Print?

I said I would rant and rave, but I really won't. However, I do hope you'll learn something that will help you be more effective *and* save a tree or two.

First, consider why you want to print a slide show. There are good reasons to do so, but they rarely involve providing the audience with handouts. If you've ever attended a presentation and been given the complete slide show, one slide per page, you understand that this is usually a waste of paper. Some presenters even hand out the pages prior to the slide show. In that case, why present the slide show at all? Turn off the lights and let me take a nap!

If you want to provide handouts, choose one of the options of printing several slides per page. Or even better, use the Send to Microsoft Word feature and then add your own comments to the thumbnail versions of the slides or provide a place for the audience members to add their own comments.

An even better, more environmentally friendly method for providing handouts is to post the slide show on the Web as a Web-based presentation (see Figure 3.19).

FIGURE 3.19

Publishing a slide show to a Web page can make a presentation readily accessible without wasting paper.

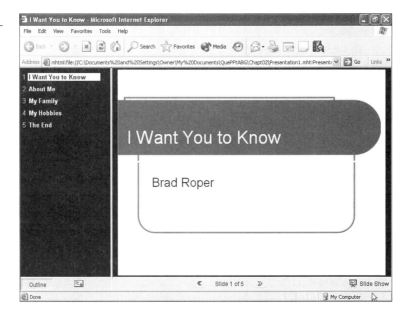

⇨   To learn more about publishing a slide show to the Web, see **p. 319**.

Second, consider the ways printing might be of value beyond providing handouts. The primary use, in my book, is to prepare overhead transparencies of key slides so that in case your equipment fails, you can at least use an overhead projector to show them. And if you don't have an overhead projector, or if the power fails, you can hold up the printed overheads for all to see. That's not ideal, but it's much better than trying to fill your time with a soft shoe routine!

Another use for printing is to create and print single-slide posters, signs, or flyers.

In short, designing and presenting a slide show is only part of the total presentation. Learning to create useful printed materials is another important part.

THE ABSOLUTE MINIMUM

Understanding the basic elements of the PowerPoint program and its procedures can make using the program much easier. In this chapter, you did the following:

- You learned how to find your way around the PowerPoint screen.

- You explored the use of templates to automate the creation of a PowerPoint slide show.

- You learned how to save and how to find and open a PowerPoint presentation.

- You learned why, when, and how to print a presentation.

In Chapter 4, "Organizing a Presentation," you'll learn how to plan and organize a presentation, including how to use the outline feature.

PART

CREATING SLIDE SHOW CONTENT

4

Organizing a Presentation

Unless you're already an experienced teacher or public speaker, you may not be aware of the importance of sizing up the audience before you even start preparing a presentation. If you don't know who you're speaking to—what they want to know or what will keep their interest—it makes little sense to jump in and create a slide show. Sure, you might prepare something entertaining, but will the folks in the audience walk away better informed or motivated than they were before you spoke to them?

On the other hand, when you know who your audience is, selecting the right elements and organizing your presentation becomes a much easier task. This chapter explores the process of organizing appropriate and effective presentations.

Focusing on the Audience

Sometimes it's easy to know who your audience is. You may have already taught or presented to the people in this audience before, or these people might have the same professional experience and background as you. Sometimes, however, you face groups that say they want to hear you talk about a certain subject, but then you find out that their ideas of what they asked for doesn't quite match your ideas of what needs to be presented.

So how do you determine who your audience really is? These are some of the characteristics to consider:

- *Age*—Are you presenting to children, teens, young professionals, or seasoned veterans? Speaking down to young adults can be as disastrous as speaking over the heads of children.

- *Experience*—What experience do members of the audience have with what you'll be talking about? If it's a technical presentation, how much background do you have to cover before the audience can understand? How much "shorthand" (terminology that assumes prior knowledge) can you use?

- *Interest*—Why are the audience members there? Are they eager students or lumps of unmotivated humanity? Are they team members interested in success or skeptical outsiders looking to be convinced?

- *Motivation*—What's in it for the audience members? Do their grades depend on what you say? Does their financial future rest on the quality of the information you give them? Will chances for their success be enhanced by your presentation?

- *Technology background*—Are they from the old school, expecting verbal presentations more than snazzy charts and pictures? Or have they experienced lots of visual programs and therefore expect the quality of your presentation to match their experience? Are they, as some have called them, the "MTV Generation?"

- *Familiarity*—Are these people you know, and might they cut you some slack as a result? Or are they total strangers, who may or may not be willing to give up their time unless what you have to say is really worth it? Conversely, are they so familiar with you that they don't afford you the courtesy you deserve, feeling free to interrupt or divert the presentation?

- *Your background*—Are you the kind of expert or authority who commands respect even before you start? Or are you an unknown who has to establish your credibility before the audience will put stock in what you say?

As you can see, this partial list underscores the complex nature of determining who your audience is. One type of presentation definitely won't work for all audiences. Understanding your audience first determines what and how you prepare and is a key factor in your success or failure.

What's the Purpose of the Presentation?

After you figure out who your audience is, you then have to determine why you're making the presentation. Perhaps it seems obvious to you, but consider this: Even if you know what you're presenting (for example, a business plan), do you know why? Is it to convince your audience (for example, senior management)? Is it to inform and motivate (for example, your co-workers or subordinates)? Is it to assuage stockholders? Knowing the subject is great, but knowing why you're presenting it is important as well.

Determining What Text to Use

Determining the textual content of a presentation is as much art as it is formula. PowerPoint is designed more to summarize or suggest ideas or topics than it is to fully describe them in excruciating detail. Consider, for example, the bullet points in Figure 4.1. Do you think the bullets on the left or the ones on the right are more effective? Although the bullets on the left provide more detail, viewers are more likely to remember the bullets on the right.

FIGURE 4.1

The bullets on the left are too detailed to be effective.

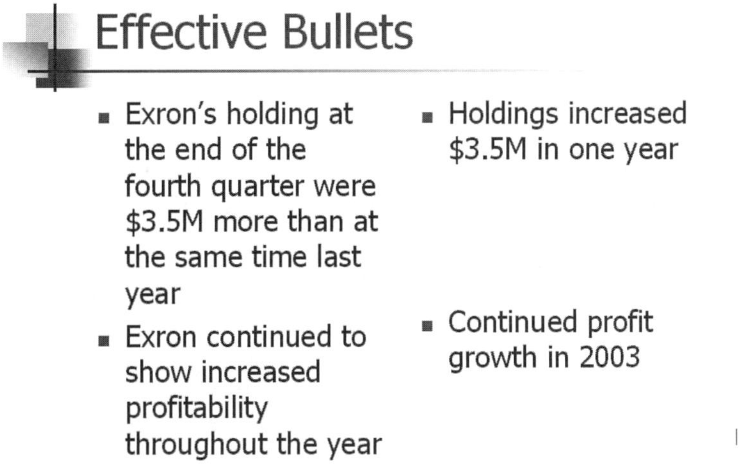

 # Effective Bullets

- Exron's holding at the end of the fourth quarter were $3.5M more than at the same time last year
- Exron continued to show increased profitability throughout the year

- Holdings increased $3.5M in one year

- Continued profit growth in 2003

Some situations call for large chunks of text (for example, a quote). Even then, however, just how much of the quote needs to appear on the slide? Can you use an ellipsis (…) with only the salient parts of the quote on the slide, while verbally presenting the entire quote (see Figure 4.2)?

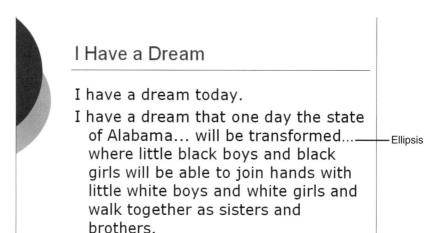

FIGURE 4.2
Even when you're using a large chunk of text, you can look for ways to reduce its size.

> # I Have a Dream
>
> I have a dream today.
> I have a dream that one day the state of Alabama… will be transformed… where little black boys and black girls will be able to join hands with little white boys and white girls and walk together as sisters and brothers.

Ellipsis

In short, with PowerPoint you should use words more as symbolic representations than as fully expanded narratives.

Using Appropriate Visual Material

Graphic material, used appropriately, can be even more effective than words in communicating information that people can remember. For example, corporations spend millions of dollars developing simple graphical logos to help your mind remember their products.

Unfortunately, many PowerPoint presenters view graphics merely as window dressing, often using clip art images gratuitously. As you contemplate these presenters' slides, you find yourself trying to figure out why a particular graphic image was used. In the meantime, you miss the point of the slide or what the speaker is saying to you.

Students, especially younger ones, expect graphic material, and the liberal use of clip art can help hold their attention as well as enhance comprehension. However, you have to be more careful with older audiences. If you're going to use visual material, it better be good and have a purpose. A poorly conceived data chart, for example, will only confuse and distract. A well-designed chart, on the other hand, can reduce the time you spend explaining because audience members can use the chart to easily make connections between facts and concepts.

Holding the Audience's Attention

For any successful presentation, you need to present information that is relevant, timely, and interesting. You can entertain all you want, but if the audience members walk away saying "So what?" you've probably failed.

You also need to remember that not everyone learns the same way. Some people learn best by reading words. Others do better with visual images. Some respond to auditory information.

One key, then, to holding the audience's attention is to vary the way you present your information. You should change from bullets, to graphs, to sound clips, to illustrations, and so on. Too much of any one thing can bore an audience.

I've also found that a periodic unexpected change of pace can wake up an audience. For example, say you're plodding through your presentation, displaying one bullet at a time. But suddenly as you finish a bullet point that summarizes a drop in the market, you use a sound effect or motion image to simulate falling. Even the most jaded or stuffy audiences will respond to a periodic, well-chosen, audio-visual effect.

Ultimately, once again, you need to know your audience. An engaging presenter can hold most audiences spellbound without using anything more than voice and gestures. For the rest of us, using PowerPoint appropriately can help us hold the audience members' attention while increasing their comprehension and ability to remember what we tell them.

Creating Content by Outlining

You know what you want to tell the audience, and you're now ready to organize your presentation. You could, like most people do, simply jump in and start creating slides. If you do that, you'll soon discover, however, that it's easy to lose sight of what you're trying to accomplish because you get bogged down in details or distracted by bells and whistles that just beg to be used.

In my own experience, confirmed by many presenters and teachers I've worked with, good presentations using PowerPoint require even greater organization and preparation than typical, off-the-cuff boardroom or classroom discussions.

This section explores the use of PowerPoint's outline feature, which helps you create the structure of a presentation before you fill in the details or get lured away from your objectives by the siren call of graphics, animations, and other fancy PowerPoint features.

Organizing Textual Material in Outline Form

PowerPoint's outline feature automates the process of organizing the textual components of a presentation. Consider the following text outline:

I.   Plant Safety Discussion

II. Areas of Concern

    A. Production Line

    B. Loading Dock

III. Measuring Results

In a PowerPoint presentation, the main topics listed with Roman numerals in this outline become slide titles. On the second slide you also find two bullet topics, for the A and B points in the outline.

Further, if you add or delete topics, PowerPoint automatically adds or deletes slides or bullets to match your outline. For example, if you need to establish a working committee before measuring the results, you insert a new Point III (Slide 3), and Point III automatically becomes Point IV (Slide 4).

Some slides contain little or no text when you use this method. But creating a text-based outline first, with at least a title for each intended slide, helps you remember where to place all your slides, both textual and visual.

To begin a new slide show using the outline feature, follow these steps:

1. Start PowerPoint.

2. Select the Outline tab at the left of the PowerPoint screen. PowerPoint displays the first slide icon and provides an area where you can type outline text (see Figure 4.3, which shows text already added).

3. Click just to the right of the first slide icon. PowerPoint displays a blinking insertion point.

4. Type the text of the title of your first slide (for example, `Plant Safety Discussion`). Note that the text you type appears both in the outline and in the title placeholder on the slide editing screen (refer to Figure 4.3).

You've now created the first major topic in your outline, which also happens to be the title of the title slide in your slide show. You'll enter the subtitle for the first slide in a moment.

Adding New Slides

As you create an outline in PowerPoint, you use certain basic keystrokes to quickly enter and arrange the outline. For example, each time you press the Enter key, PowerPoint adds a new outline item, of the same type as the one you were just working on.

FIGURE 4.3

The outline area helps you focus on the content of a presentation without worrying about what it looks like.

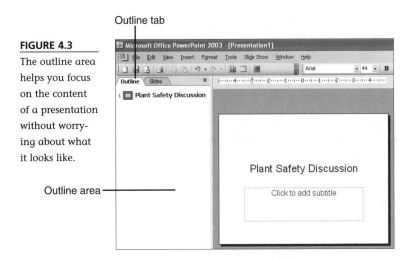

The example shown in Figure 4.3 shows the title of a slide, equivalent to a main outline topic. To insert a new slide (that is, a main topic), you simply press Enter. PowerPoint automatically inserts a new slide, at which point you can type the second main topic—the second slide's title (see Figure 4.4).

FIGURE 4.4

You can press Enter to add a new outline element.

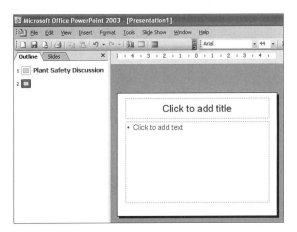

Adding Bullets

At this point in creating a slide show by using the outline feature, you could continue through the entire outline, adding all the major points first, and then return to add the subtopics. Or, you could add subtopics while they're fresh in your mind.

Subtopics in a PowerPoint outline become a slide's bullet points. To add bullet points to a slide, such as Slide 2, follow these steps:

1. Position the insertion point at the end of the title line.

2. Press Enter. PowerPoint adds another slide.

3.  Press the Tab key. PowerPoint moves the insertion point to the right, changing Slide 3 to the first bullet for Slide 2 (see Figure 4.5). You can also cause this to happen by clicking the Increase Indent button on the toolbar, but I think you'll soon learn that using the Tab key is much quicker.

FIGURE 4.5

You can use the Tab key to move an outline element to the right and convert it to a bullet or subbullet.

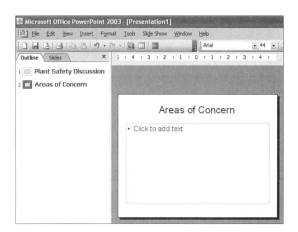

4. Type the first subtopic, which becomes the text of the first bullet.

The next time you press Enter, PowerPoint gives you another bullet. You can continue to add bullets until the list is complete.

Bullets on a title slide (usually your first slide) are the equivalent to the subtitle. If you position the insertion point at the end of the title text and then press Enter and then Tab, you can type the subtitle information. You can then press Enter and then Shift+Tab to create the second slide, typically a bullet slide.

Changing Outline Levels

You can quickly and easily change outline levels from titles, to bullets, or to subbullets, and back again. For example, earlier in this chapter you

caution

It's tempting to cram as many bullet points as possible onto each slide. It's also easy to get too wordy. To keep your slides visually attractive and easy to remember, limit yourself to only a few, carefully worded bullets.

changed a title to a bullet by simply pressing the Tab key. When you press Enter, you add another bullet.

If you want to start adding slide titles again, follow these steps:

1. After your last slide bullet, press Enter to get a blank bullet.

2. Press Shift+Tab. PowerPoint shifts the bullet to the left and changes it to a slide. You can also accomplish this by clicking the Decrease Indent button on the toolbar, but using Shift+Tab is usually much quicker.

3. Type the slide title and then press Enter to get a new slide, or press Enter and then Tab to get a new bullet.

Editing Outline Material

You edit outline material much as you do any word processing text. You can do things like select, delete, cut and paste, and add or change text attributes such as font, color, or size. You see changes in text content in the outline, but you see changes in formatting only on the slide itself.

Although editing involves making changes to the text, quite often it also involves rearranging and organizing the textual material. For example, suppose you need to add a slide in the middle of the presentation. To insert outline material, you follow these steps:

1. Position the insertion point at the end of the line preceding where you want to insert a new item.

2. Press Enter. PowerPoint inserts the next item, which is the same type (slide or bullet) as the item that precedes it.

3. Press Tab or Shift+Tab to move the item right or left, until it becomes the bullet, subbullet, or slide level you want.

4. Type the text of the inserted item.

You can also quickly rearrange the items in an outline. Consider, for example, Figure 4.6. The Implementation Committee slide lists the committee's various members, but it might be politically wise to place the management member last, to emphasize the importance of worker involvement. To move an outline item, follow these steps:

1. Move the mouse pointer to the icon of the item you want to move (for example, the bullet preceding "One Management Team Member"). The pointer turns to a four-way arrow (refer to Figure 4.6).

FIGURE 4.6

Reorganizing an outline is easy when you use drag and drop.

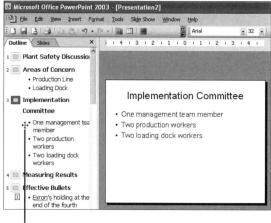

Mouse pointer (four-way arrow)

2. Click and drag the icon to its new location. PowerPoint displays a horizontal line to indicate where the item will be placed when you release the mouse button (see Figure 4.7).

FIGURE 4.7

A horizontal line shows where to drop the outline element you're moving.

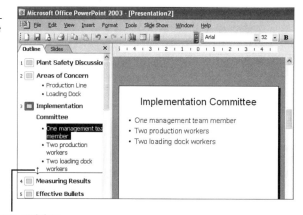

Drag to here and drop

3. Release the mouse button to drop the item in its new location.

You could, of course, select and cut an outline item and then paste it in its new location. Depending on your keyboard skills and speed, either method may be equally efficient.

You can also rearrange outline levels. For example, if you want to change a bullet to a slide level title, follow these steps:

1. Move the mouse pointer to the icon of the item you want to change. The pointer turns to a four-way arrow.

2. Click and drag the icon left. PowerPoint displays a vertical line to indicate the level the item will become when you release the mouse button (see Figure 4.8).

Drag to here and drop

FIGURE 4.8

The vertical line shows what level you're at while you're dragging an outline element.

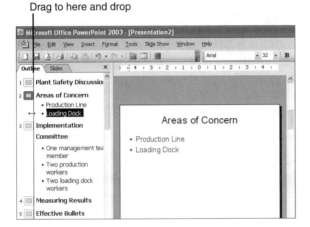

3. Release the mouse button to drop the item at its new level.

And you thought this was going to be hard!

If you want to use the keyboard to change outline levels of existing text, you simply position the insertion point anywhere on the outline item. Then you press Tab or Shift+Tab to move right or left.

Table 4.1 shows a handy summary of ways to manage outline levels and items in PowerPoint's outline screen.

TABLE 4.1   Managing Outline Levels

Procedure	Options
Add an item	■ Press Enter to add slides or bullets. ■ Click New Slide to add a new slide (not bullets).
Change a slide title to a bullet	■ Press Tab. ■ Click Increase Indent. ■ Drag the icon to the right.

Table 4.1 (continued)

Procedure	Options
Change a bullet to a slide title	■ Press Shift+Tab. ■ Click Decrease Indent. ■ Drag the icon to the left.
Rearrange the sequence of an outline item	■ Drag an icon up or down. ■ Cut and paste the outline item.

By now you've become an expert at organizing presentations by using PowerPoint's outline feature. A well-conceived outline is the foundation for a successful presentation. I like to create an outline, let it sit for a while, and then come back to it to see if my fresh eyes see things that need to be changed. Building a presentation is much easier when you have a solid outline.

Making Slides Readable

Text can be an important part of PowerPoint slides, but it's not the only part. If that were the case, you could simply prepare a nice detailed outline, print it, and pass it out to audience members. That certainly would be less costly than a laptop computer and data projector!

To make text on slides as effective as possible, you should consider the following:

- Reduce the amount of text for titles and bullets to the bare essentials. You can fill in the details verbally during your presentation.

- Stick with fonts that are easy to read. Funky fonts may seem cool, but they often require extra effort to read.

- Use colors that provide high contrast between the text and the background. Try out a color scheme, and see what it will look like before you subject your audience to something that might be difficult to read. For example, red text on a dark blue background might seem like a good idea until you actually try it. However, although white backgrounds with dark text provide the highest contrast, audience members' eyes tire quickly when they have to look at a white background. Try choosing darker backgrounds with appropriately contrasting text.

- Make the font size appropriate to the size of the screen and the distance of the audience from the screen. You might get away with smaller fonts (and more text) in a small meeting room, but large fonts with minimal text are called for in a large lecture hall. If you're not sure the size you're using will work, try it out yourself in the room you'll be using.

By default, PowerPoint uses its AutoFit feature to make text fit within its placeholders. Thus, if you continue to add bullets, PowerPoint begins reducing the size of the font to accommodate the extra text. Generally, this is not a good thing for two reasons: The font gets smaller and harder to read, and the size of the fonts from one slide to another becomes inconsistent.

Fortunately, you have several alternatives to letting AutoFit shrink your text. As soon as your text exceeds the capacity of the placeholder, PowerPoint shrinks the text and displays the AutoFit Options icon (see Figure 4.9, which has the AutoFit Options menu already showing).

FIGURE 4.9

PowerPoint's AutoFit feature shrinks text size if you try to insert too much text.

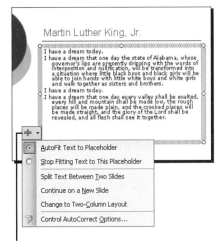

AutoFit Options button

Move the mouse pointer to the AutoFit Options button and then click its drop-down menu to display the following choices (refer to Figure 4.9):

- ■ **S**top Fitting Text to This Placeholder—When you select this option, the font does not change, and extra text disappears off the edge of the placeholder.

- ■ Split Text Between **T**wo Slides—When you select this option, extra text is moved to a new slide.

- ■ Change to a Two-**C**olumn Layout—When you select this option, the items are presented in two columns. Bullet items with minimal text often work well arranged in two columns instead of on two separate slides.

If you try an AutoFit option and don't like it, you can click Undo to restore the original slide and then try something else.

Importing Outline Material from Word

You can use outline text from Word to create outlines in PowerPoint. There are two concerns with doing this, however:

■ Word text must be properly formatted before it imports cleanly to the PowerPoint outline format. This is difficult, at best.

■ Word outlines typically tend to be wordy, if you'll pardon the pun. You'll probably have to trim the Word text to make it work as PowerPoint text.

If you already have text in Word format that you'd like to use in a PowerPoint slide, it's probably easiest to simply copy from Word and paste into PowerPoint's outline area. You then can edit titles and bullets as necessary. However, I prefer to create entirely new title and bullet text, very much condensed from my original Word material.

Using Slides from Another Slide Show

If you make a lot of presentations, you might find that you can use certain slides over again, sometimes with only minor modifications. Learning to import slides from other slide shows can save you time in the long run.

To import slides from another slide show, follow these steps:

1. Position the insertion point in the outline where you want to insert the new slides.

2. Choose **I**nsert, Slides from **F**iles. PowerPoint displays the Slide Finder dialog box (see Figure 4.10, which already shows slides from a selected slide show).

FIGURE 4.10

You can use the Slide Finder dialog box to find slides in other PowerPoint presentations and insert them into the one you're working on.

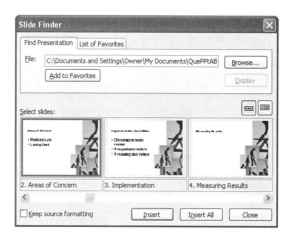

3. Type the name of the PowerPoint slide show you want to use or click the **B**rowse button to look for the slide show. After you type or find the name, click **D**isplay to see thumbnails of the slides in that show (refer to Figure 4.10).

4. Scroll through the gallery of slides until you find the one you want. Click it once to select it. You can continue to look for and select other slides and insert them all at once.

5. Choose the **K**eep Source Formatting option on the Slide Finder dialog box if you want to import the slide's design and other formatting. Otherwise, PowerPoint imports only the slide's text.

6. Choose **I**nsert to insert the selected slides or choose In**s**ert All to insert all of the slide show's slides. PowerPoint inserts them into the presentation you're working on.

At this point you might have to edit the text or rearrange the slides, but in the meantime, you've saved yourself considerable time and effort.

THE ABSOLUTE MINIMUM

In this chapter, you have learned that it's a good idea to do a little planning and organizing before setting out to create slide show slides. In particular, you did the following:

- You learned how important it is to size up the target audience before you prepare a presentation.
- You explored PowerPoint's outline feature, which helps you organize the content of a presentation.
- You learned that it's possible to use in your PowerPoint slide show preexisting text from Word documents or slides from other PowerPoint presentations.

In Chapter 5, "Working with Text Objects," you'll learn how to add and manipulate text objects, in addition to the text placeholders you're already familiar with.

IN THIS CHAPTER

- Become an expert at creating and modifying title boxes
- Learn more about bullets and how to make them appear one by one
- Learn to use the spelling and style checkers
- Discover how to create, move, copy, and rotate text boxes
- Learn how to add color, lines, and fills to any text box

5

WORKING WITH TEXT OBJECTS

Unlike typical word processing documents that consist of linear streams of text, PowerPoint documents are built with objects—brushstrokes of text or images arranged on the artistic canvas of a slide in accordance with the creative desires of the presenter.

In this chapter you'll learn how to add and modify all manner of text objects. Much of what you'll learn about text objects also applies to other object boxes.

Understanding PowerPoint Slide Layers and Objects

PowerPoint slides consist of three major elements (see Figure 5.1):

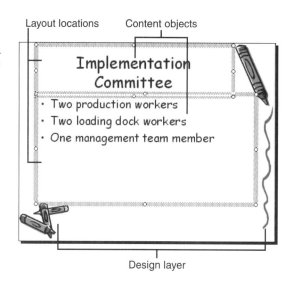

FIGURE 5.1

PowerPoint slides consist of objects placed in a layout on a design background.

- *Design layer*—This layer is either blank or a background design, along with coordinated text and drawing sizes and colors. PowerPoint's design templates include a design layer, or you can create your own design layer.
- *Layout layer*—This layer helps determine the standard placement of certain text and other content placeholders.
- *Content layer*—This layer includes the actual content of placeholders as well as other objects, such as clip art or drawing images.

Creating Title Boxes

Nearly every slide has at least a title box, whose position and size are determined largely by the design and layout layers. Title boxes are nearly identical to regular text boxes, except that they appear automatically and are called *placeholders* to denote their purpose. Empty title box placeholders always remain while you're editing a slide, but the placeholder box does not appear when you play a slide show.

Adding, Editing, and Formatting Text

In Chapter 2, "PowerPoint Quickstart," you gained some experience adding and modifying text within a title box. For example, you learned the following:

■ You can click a title placeholder to begin adding or editing text. A title box appears with hash marks (///) all the way around it and with eight small circles called *sizing handles* (you'll learn more about this in a moment). The hash marks indicate that you are in the text edit mode and that you can make changes to individual parts of the title box text (see Figure 5.2).

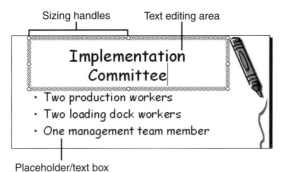

Sizing handles   Text editing area

FIGURE 5.2

A text box is
surrounded by
hash marks and
sizing handles
when you're
adding text to it.

Implementation
Committee
· Two production workers
· Two loading dock workers
· One management team member

Placeholder/text box

■ Within the title box, you can type, delete, select, and cut or copy and paste.

■ You can add text formatting and attributes—such as bold, italic, font style, or text color—to title box text.

I don't want to assume too much here, but I also don't want to bore you with stuff you already know. Let's review just a bit. Suppose you want to edit a title and change the font of one of its words. These are the steps:

1. Click the title. PowerPoint displays the title placeholder box along with the blinking insertion point.

2. Move the right or left arrow keys to get the insertion point to the word you want to change, press Delete or Backspace to remove characters, and type any needed additional characters.

3. With the mouse, click at the beginning of a word and drag to the end of the word to highlight it.

4. **B** **S** Click any of the buttons on the Formatting toolbar, such as Bold or Shadow, or use the Formatting toolbar to select a different font or font size.

5. Click outside the title box area to close the box.

Moving and Sizing Title Boxes

You can work with a title box that surrounds the text of a title. Among other things, you can do the following:

- Move the title box
- Change the shape or size of the title box
- Select the title box as a complete object and apply attributes to its entire contents

Suppose you find that the automatic placement of the title box placeholder isn't quite right for your needs. You can follow these steps to move a title box placeholder:

1. Click the text of the title box to display the box that surrounds it.

2. Move the mouse pointer toward the edge of the box itself. When the mouse pointer turns to a four-way arrow, click and drag the box.

3. Release the mouse button to drop the box in its new location. Note that the hash marks change to a dotted pattern, indicating that you're working with the entire box (see Figure 5.3).

FIGURE 5.3

When the text box becomes a dotted pattern, you have successfully selected the entire box.

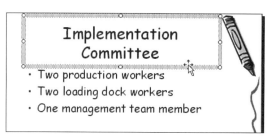

4. Repeat these steps until the box is positioned exactly where you want it.

If you move the box slowly, you might see it "jump" instead of glide smoothly across the screen. This happens because PowerPoint automatically makes all objects, title boxes included, *snap to grid*. The screen area is invisibly divided into a grid of vertical and horizontal lines, spaced 1/12 inch apart. By snapping objects to this grid, PowerPoint helps you more easily align objects.

➪   For information on changing the Snap to Grid option, see **p. 106**.

You can also change the size and shape of a title box by using the box's sizing handles. To do so, follow these steps:

1. Click the text of the title box to display the box.

2. Move the mouse pointer toward a sizing handle until it turns into a two-way arrow.

3. Click and drag the sizing handle to change the shape of the box. Note that as you drag, the mouse pointer changes to a crosshairs shape (see Figure 5.4).

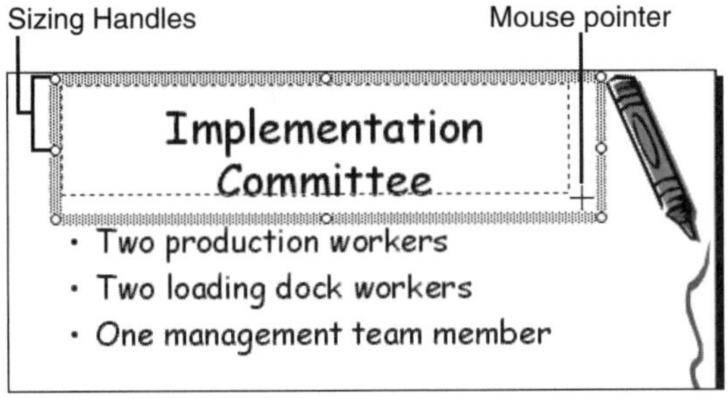

FIGURE 5.4

You can use the sizing handles to change the size or shape of an object box.

Dragging a box's sizing handles produces the following results:

- Dragging a top or bottom sizing handle changes only the height of the box.
- Dragging a side sizing handle changes only the width of the box. Making a box more narrow may cause the text within it to wrap. Widening the box may allow text to fit on one line or on fewer lines.
- Dragging a corner sizing handle changes both the width and height, but only from two sides.
- Changing the size of a title box does not necessarily change the font size of the text. The AutoFit feature may allow the text to shrink a bit, but only to a minimum size that is large enough for a slide title.

Working with Bullet Boxes

Bullet box placeholders are much like title box placeholders (see Figure 5.5). You can edit and format text within them, and you can move and size them just as you do title box placeholders. But they're also a bit more interesting because you can customize bullets, turn bullets off altogether, or animate bullets so that they display onscreen one at a time.

Another important difference between title boxes and bullet boxes is the way changes apply to the items within the boxes. Because there's only one title in a title box, format changes apply to the entire title.

FIGURE 5.5

Bullet box place-holders look like title boxes, except for the content.

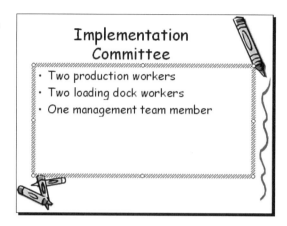

In a bullet box, if you are in edit mode (in which the box consists of hash marks), changes apply only to the currently selected bullet. If you want to apply changes equally to all bullets in the box, you must first select the bullet box placeholder by moving the mouse pointer to the edge of the box (the pointer turns to a four-way arrow) and clicking to select the box. You shouldn't worry if you forget this little tip. Each time you forget, you are reminded when you see that you applied your changes to only one bullet.

Customizing Bullets

Bullets, in the traditional sense, are simple, small dots that look like bullet holes. In PowerPoint, however, bullets can also be special characters or graphic buttons. The default bullet style for a slide show depends on the design layer. For example, the default no-design style gives you small black dots. The Competition design gives you three-dimensional diamond-shaped bullets (see Figure 5.6).

Graphic bullet

FIGURE 5.6

Each design layer uses a bullet style that looks good with it.

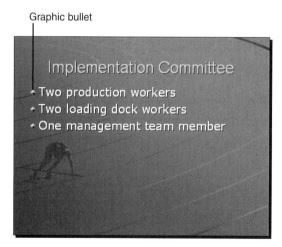

Sometimes the default bullet style just doesn't suit your tastes. It might be too snazzy or too boring. Or its color might not offer enough contrast to make your bullet points stand out.

To customize the bullet style for all the bullets in a single slide, follow these steps:

1. Click the bullet placeholder.

2. Move the mouse pointer to the edge of the placeholder box (at which point the mouse pointer turns to a four-way arrow) and click to select the entire placeholder box. If you miss this step, changes you make apply only to one bullet in the box, not to all of them.

3. Choose F**o**rmat, **B**ullets and Numbering. PowerPoint displays the Bullets and Numbering dialog box (see Figure 5.7).

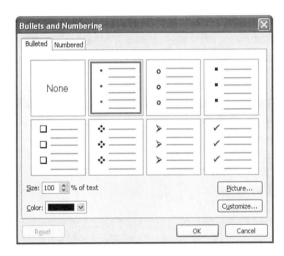

4. If a style you like appears, select it. Otherwise, choose one of the following options:

■ *Size*—If a bullet is simply too small, you can use this option to increase the bullet's size to a percentage of the size of the text.

■ *Color*—You can click the drop-down list box to choose a different, perhaps more dramatic, color.

■ *Picture*—If you click this button, PowerPoint displays the Picture Bullet gallery (see Figure 5.8) from which you can choose a variety of graphical bullet styles.

FIGURE 5.8

PowerPoint provides several graphical bullet styles in the Picture Bullet gallery.

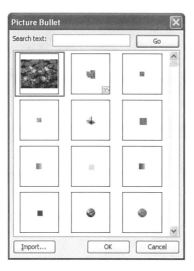

■ *Customize*—If you click this button, PowerPoint displays a palette of symbols from several different graphical font styles (see Figure 5.9).

FIGURE 5.9

Using typographical symbols is an easy way to come up with a bullet that matches the mood or content of your bullets.

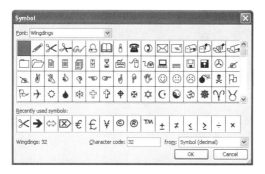

5. After you customize your bullet type, click OK twice to apply the new style to the bullets in the placeholder.

Unfortunately, the changes you make to a bullet placeholder apply only to the current slide. If you want the same kind of bullets throughout a slide show, you have to repeat these steps for each slide that contains bullets or customize the master slide for the design you're using.

➪ For information on changing the design layer, including changing the bullet style for all bullet boxes in a slide show, see **p. 358**.

Turning Off Bullets

What we call bullet placeholders in reality are text boxes with the bullet feature turned on. If you want text, such as a quote, to appear as a chunk of text rather than as a list of bullet points (see Figure 5.10), you use the Title and Text layout, but you turn off the bullets.

FIGURE 5.10

If you want unbulleted text, you can use a bullet box but turn off the bullets.

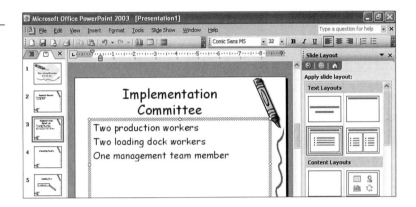

To turn off bullets in a text/bullet placeholder, you follow these steps:

1. Select the text box. Be sure to click its edge so your changes apply to the entire box.

2. Click the Bullets button on the Formatting toolbar. PowerPoint turns off the bullets.

If you turn off the bullet for just one item in a text box, it means you forgot to select the entire box. To turn off the bullets for all the items in the text box, you just repeat the preceding steps.

Animating Bullets with Preset Animations

One very basic but powerful PowerPoint feature is the capability to *animate* bullet points. *Animation* simply means that something on the screen moves. For example, with bullets and their associated text, you can use animation to make them appear one at a time.

Animating bullets is more than just pizzazz. It helps keep your audience members focused by not allowing them to read ahead. It also helps them take notes so they know when you've moved to the next topic. You can also use animated bullets to create surprise effects—for example, to reveal the names of the winners of an employee contest or to do a "top 10" countdown.

To animate bullets by using a preset animation, follow these steps:

1. Choose Slide Show, Animation Schemes. PowerPoint displays the Slide Design - Animation Schemes task pane (see Figure 5.11).

FIGURE 5.11

You can make bullets move by choosing an appropriate bullet animation from the Animation Schemes task pane.

2. Choose an animation style from among these option categories:

   ■ *Recently Used*—Listed first are styles you've used recently, which PowerPoint thinks might be likely choices.

   ■ *No Animation*—By default, PowerPoint bullets are not animated.

   ■ *Subtle*—This group offers various styles that appear gently, without a lot of fanfare. For most presentations, these are the ones you'll probably use.

   ■ *Moderate*—These animations are a little bolder than those in the Subtle group, and they offer a nice change of pace.

   ■ *Exciting*—These are the animations you'll save for wake-up slides or perhaps to capture the attention of a younger crowd.

3. When you choose an animation style, PowerPoint previews it for you. If you miss the preview or want to see the animation again, click the Play button. If you want to see how the animation style looks in the actual slide show, click the Slide Show button. Press the Esc key to return to the Normal view.

4. By default, a selected animation style applies only to the currently selected slide. If you want to make it the standard animation scheme through the slide show, click the Apply to All Slides button.

Using animated bullets can be fun, but you should also have a purpose in using them. Consider the following:

- A gentle movement with each bullet slide can create the subtle impression that something is happening, that progress is being made.
- Wild movements all the time can give the impression that you're trying to show off or that entertaining is more important that communicating.
- Using animated bullets requires you to advance each bullet. This works well if you plan to spend some time on each bullet item. However, if you have lots of information to cover and you might give only cursory attention to a slide of bullets, you should probably not use bullet animation.
- You should avoid the temptation to use different animation schemes for each bullet slide. Instead, you should select a scheme you're comfortable with and apply it to all slides. Otherwise, your audience will try to guess what bullet animation you'll use next instead of focus on what you're trying to communicate.

⇨ For information on custom animations, see **p. 203**.

Using the Spelling Checker

Thus far in the book I've tried to get you to abandon your word processing ways of thinking, but the spelling checker is one tool that you're likely to be familiar with from other programs that can also be useful in PowerPoint.

To check the spelling in slides, follow these steps:

1. Choose **T**ools, **S**pelling or press F7.
2. PowerPoint displays the Spelling dialog box and begins checking the slide show for spelling errors (see Figure 5.12).
3. When the spelling check pauses to point out an error, choose the appropriate options (for example, **I**gnore or **C**hange).
4. When PowerPoint tells you the spelling check is complete, click OK.

FIGURE 5.12

You can use the spelling check feature to find and correct spelling errors in PowerPoint text.

PowerPoint also prompts you to correct misspelled words as you create your text: It displays a squiggly red underline beneath words that don't match its spelling dictionary. You have several options, besides just ignoring the prompt:

■ You can correct the word as you go, thus removing the red line.

■ You can right-click the misspelled word to display a context menu that displays possible correction choices (see Figure 5.13) and then select a correct choice.

FIGURE 5.13

You can right-click a misspelled word and choose the correct one from the context menu, without having to run the spelling checker.

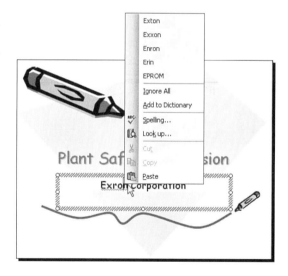

■ From the context menu, you can perform spelling checker options, such as ignoring, adding to the dictionary, or running the spelling checker.

■ Choose Loo**k** Up from the context menu to look up the word in the dictionary or thesaurus. PowerPoint displays various options in the Research task pane.

⇨ If you don't like the automatic spelling checker red line prompt, you can learn how to turn it off on **p. 364**.

Using the Style Checker

You might be quite good at using appropriate text styles in a typical word processing document. But style rules for a presentation often are a bit different than those for documents. PowerPoint provides a style checker that prompts you when it sees something amiss.

When you see a yellow lightbulb appear on a slide, click it to see what the style checker thinks is wrong. The Office Assistant appears, with suggestions for possible changes. Click the option that makes the most sense or click OK to dismiss the Assistant.

⇨   To learn how you can change PowerPoint's default style rules, see **p. 368**.

Inserting Text Boxes

Title, subtitle, and bullet placeholders are really just text boxes with predetermined locations and sizes. However, you're certainly not limited to these placeholders for text that you want to appear on slides. Indeed, you can add as many text boxes as you want. In most respects, they're very similar to placeholders, but you can add, delete, move, and manipulate them more freely than you can placeholders.

Creating and Positioning Text Boxes

You can create two basic types of text boxes: A single-line box expands horizontally as you type, and a multiline box expands vertically as you add text. To insert a typical text box into a slide, you follow these steps:

1. Choose **I**nsert, Te**x**t Box, or click the Text Box button on the Drawing toolbar. PowerPoint seems to do nothing, but it's really waiting for you to take the next step.

2. Move the mouse pointer to the slide area and note that the point looks like an inverted cross.

3. To create a single-line text box, click where you want the text of the text box to begin. PowerPoint creates a small text box, with a blinking insertion point (see Figure 5.14, which shows text already added).

4. Type the text box text, and PowerPoint expands the text box horizontally to make room for it. Note that the text does not wrap, although you can press Enter to type a second line.

5. Click anywhere outside the box to deselect the box.

FIGURE 5.14
You can add as many text boxes as you need for labels, quotes, or descriptions.

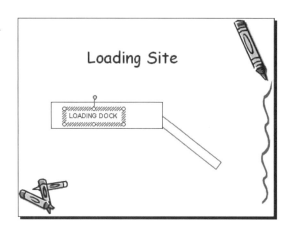

To create a multiline text box that expands vertically instead of horizontally, follow these steps but click and drag to define a width for the box. Then, as you type text, the box expands vertically as text wraps at the margins you specified.

After you create text boxes, you can position and size them as you need. For example, you can click a text box to display the box and its sizing handles, along with a rotation handle (refer to Figure 5.14). You can drag a corner or side sizing handle toward the center of the box to force the text to wrap vertically. You'll soon discover that when you change the text in a text box, you automatically change the size of the text box. As you add or remove text or as you change the font size within the text box, the box size increases or decreases. In other words, text boxes are only as large as the text they contain.

You can easily position a box exactly where you want it by clicking the box itself (the pointer becomes a four-way arrow) and dragging the box to a new location.

Rotating Text

One of the really nifty things you can do with text boxes is rotate them. This is particularly handy if you're creating a label to identify something onscreen and it makes sense to rotate the label (for example, on a map).

To rotate a text box, simply move the mouse pointer to the green rotation handle and drag the handle clockwise or counter-clockwise (see Figure 5.15). Note that while you drag the rotation handle, both the original and the new positions display onscreen.

tip

To rotate a text box in 15-degree increments, you hold down the Shift key while dragging the rotation handle. This makes it easier to perfectly align the rotation.

You can use this trick when you're rotating any PowerPoint object—not just text boxes.

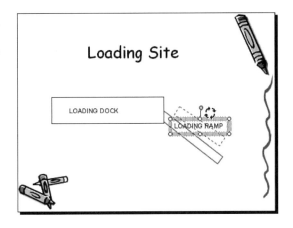

Placeholders, by default, do not display rotation handles. That's because
typically you don't need or want to rotate titles or bulleted lists.
Nevertheless, placeholders, too, can be rotated. To rotate a placeholder, click it to display the placeholder box, and then choose D**r**aw, Rotate or Fli**p**, Free Ro**t**ate from
the Drawing toolbar. PowerPoint displays green rotation handles at the four corners
of the placeholder (see Figure 5.16). Drag any of the rotation handles to rotate the
placeholder.

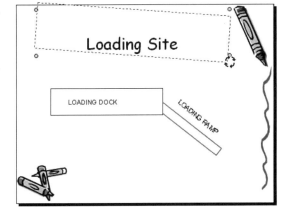

Copying Text Boxes

Sometimes you need to duplicate a text box—for example, a label that you use more
than once—either on the same slide or on more than one slide. To copy a text box,
click the box and then click the edge of the box to select the entire box. Next, choose
Edit, **C**opy to copy the box, or use your favorite method for copying. PowerPoint displays the copied text on the Clipboard task pane (see Figure 5.17).

Copied clip

FIGURE 5.17

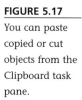

You can paste copied or cut objects from the Clipboard task pane.

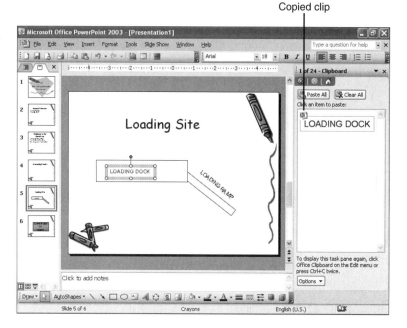

If you want the copied text pasted in the current slide, you simply click the Clipboard item or use another method for pasting. If you want to paste it on another slide, go to that slide and click the Clipboard item or paste it using another method.

Note that the copied text is placed in exactly the same location as the original. This can be handy if you're trying to replicate a text box at the same location on several different slides. When you play the slide show, the text box appears to be stationary, while other information on the slides comes and goes.

When you copy to the same slide, however, sometimes you don't even realize you've pasted text because the copied text covers the original. In this case, you can just click the edge of the copied text and drag the box to its new location.

An easy way to avoid this problem altogether—and an even simpler way to copy an object on the same slide—is to hold down the Ctrl key while dragging the text box (see Figure 5.18). You release the mouse button to place a copy of that text box in a different location.

FIGURE 5.18
While holding down the Ctrl key, you can drag an object with the mouse to copy it.

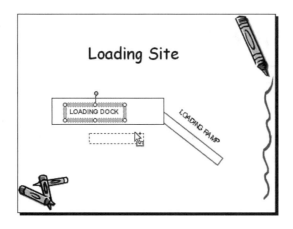

Changing Text Box Attributes

Besides working with its content, you can also change the characteristics of a text box itself. By default, text boxes are invisible. However, you can make a text box stand out by putting a line around it, filling it in with color, or changing the attributes of any text you have or will yet put in the box (see Figure 5.19).

FIGURE 5.19
You can add a professional flair by using gradient shading to fill a text box.

Fills and lines apply to all types of PowerPoint objects, not just text boxes. For more information, see **p. 130**.

The Absolute Minimum

Textual information constitutes the most basic elements of a slide presentation. Even largely visual presentations can benefit from well chosen and placed text objects. In this chapter, you did the following:

- You learned how to add and edit text in titles, bullet boxes, and text boxes.
- You explored how to move, rotate, and copy text boxes.
- You discovered that you can make text boxes both functional and attractive by adding lines and fills to them.

In Chapter 6, "Working with Graphic Objects," you're finally going to get to do what you've been wanting to do all along: add graphic images and learn how to make them work for you.

IN THIS CHAPTER

- Find out why it's easy, fun, and useful to add graphic images to a slide show
- Learn how to find, insert, and manipulate clip art images
- Discover how to acquire images from scanners, digital cameras, or the Internet
- Learn how to combine, modify, and save PowerPoint images

6

WORKING WITH GRAPHIC OBJECTS

PowerPoint is a visual medium, and therefore, creating slide shows in PowerPoint is akin to an artistic experience. Adding titles, bullets, and other text is a start, but graphic images and drawing objects add the *art* to your slides. Certainly you can create beautiful slides that impress but don't communicate. But used properly, graphic elements can get across ideas that words alone might not be able to. Consider, for example, the poor, lonely polar bear in Figure 6.1. Doesn't that bring the concept of global warming a little closer?

This chapter explores the use of images that you'll likely have access to, such as PowerPoint's own clip art images, bitmap images you create by using a scanner, and images you obtain from sources such as the Internet.

FIGURE 6.1
The right combi-
nation of words
and graphic
images can
make a signifi-
cant impact on
an audience.

Inserting Clip Art

The most easily accessible art you have comes with PowerPoint in the form of clip
art images. These are images created by an artist in such a way that they can be
enlarged, shrunk, or even distorted. Further, they're often combinations of images
that can be separated. You can also modify them by changing colors or adding
drawings of your own.

To insert a clip art image, follow these steps:

1. Choose **I**nsert, **P**icture, **C**lip Art. Or click the Insert Clip Art button on
   the Drawing toolbar. PowerPoint displays the Clip Art task pane. For
   now, don't worry about looking for anything specific. You'll do that later.

2. Click the Go button in the task pane. PowerPoint uses the Results area to display all the clips found in the specified search (see Figure 6.2). If you don't
   specify anything to search for, PowerPoint finds only a relatively small number of standard clip art and other media images.

3. Scroll through the results until you find an image you'd like to insert and
   click the image to place it on the slide.

FIGURE 6.2

The Clip Art search functions help you find the images you need.

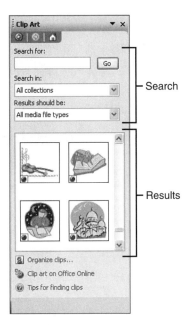

Finding Images by Using the Clip Organizer

Inserting an image from the Clip Art task pane is easy. Finding exactly the right image can be more difficult, but PowerPoint makes it easy to search for and find clip art images.

Let's poke around a bit to see how the Clip Art task pane works. First, click the Search In drop-down list box to see which collections are active and to select or deselect collections (see Figure 6.3).

Collections are organized hierarchically, with main groups of folders and several subfolders. As you search a hierarchy, you'll find the following:

- A plus sign to the left of a folder means there are subfolders that you don't see. Click the plus to expand the selection.

- A minus sign to the left of a folder means it's already expanded. Click the minus to collapse the folder and hide the subfolders.

- A check mark in a single check box beside a collection means that the collection is selected but some of its subfolders are not.

- A check mark in a stack of check boxes means that the collection and all its subfolders are selected.

FIGURE 6.3

You can limit a
search to specific
collections or
add collections,
such as the clip
art collection
found at the
Microsoft Web
site.

Practice selecting and deselecting various collections and folders. When you're ready
to select a specific collection, you'll find these options:

- *My Collections*—This group includes all folders on your local hard drive that
  contain usable clip art images. Unfortunately, most of the images aren't
  really usable, but Windows thinks they are. The only real usable images are
  in locations that you've used to store photos or downloaded images. You
  probably want to deselect locations such as Windows or other system folders.

- *Office Collections*—This group contains the images that come with Office
  2003. This group also contains quite an array of specialized categories, such
  as Animals, Emotions, and Leisure. You'll soon find, however, that most of
  the categories are empty promises, containing only one or two images.

- *Web Collections*—Initially, at least, the only collection in this group is
  Microsoft's Clip Art on Office Online. The good news is that this collection is
  extensive, and the many subfolders contain dozens of very useful images.
  The bad news is that you have to be online through a modem or network to
  see or access these images. The rest of the good news is that you don't have to
  memorize a Web address because PowerPoint automatically goes to the location where these images are found.

After you select the collections you want to use, click the Results Should Be drop-
down list box to select the media types you want to search for (see Figure 6.4).

FIGURE 6.4

Besides clip art, you can search for all sorts of media, including photographs, movies, and sounds.

You can also browse and select specific media formats. Unless you're an expert, most of these different media formats won't mean much to you. Nor does it really matter. Just select the broad categories you want, such as Clip Art or Photographs. At this point, let's not complicate things with the categories Movies and Sounds.

The final step is to search the selected collections. If you click the Go button, PowerPoint finds and displays all the images in the selected collections.

However, you can further narrow your search by typing one or more keywords, such as **dog**. Then when you click the Go button, PowerPoint finds only images that include "dog" or "dogs" in their keywords, and it displays the results in the Results area. If you search only the local Office collections, you'll find only one such image, but if you include the Clip Art on Office Online collection, you'll find dozens of dogs, of all breeds and colors, and in both cartoon and realistic renditions (see Figure 6.5, which also shows an expanded Results area). The small globe at the lower-left corner of an image means that it's a Web-based image.

You can expand the Results area, as shown in Figure 6.5, by clicking the Expand Results button at the upper left of the Results area. This enables you to see more images at once.

FIGURE 6.5

Local searches may result in few matches; if you go to the Internet (Web Collections), you're more likely to find what you're looking for.

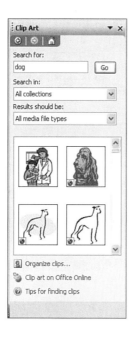

Using Images from the Clip Organizer

After you find the image you want, you can insert it into a slide by clicking it. However, with an image you think you'd like to use a lot or find more quickly, you can copy the image to a specific collection, such as a folder on your computer's hard drive. Even better, if it's an online image, you can download it to a local collection. To move an image to an easy-to-find collection, follow these steps:

1. In the Results area, move the mouse pointer to the right side of the image and click the drop-down menu.

2. If the image is already in your local Clip Art collection, choose Cop**y** to Collection. If the image is online, the menu changes. Choose Make **A**vailable Offline. PowerPoint displays the Copy to Collection dialog box (see Figure 6.6).

3. At the top of the My Collections folder are Favorites and Unclassified Clips. You can click either of these because the image actually goes to the same real location. You can also click **N**ew to create a new folder.

4. Click OK to copy the image to the specified collection folder.

FIGURE 6.6

FIGURE 6.6

You can copy images from the Web Collection to your hard drive so you have local access to the images.

You now can insert these images in two different ways:

- *From the Clip Organizer*—When you insert clip art from the task pane, you can search for and select images from your My Collections folders.

- *From file*—When you choose **I**nsert, **P**icture, **F**rom File, PowerPoint displays the Insert Picture dialog box and by default shows the images and folders of images stored in My Pictures.

Does all this sound a little confusing? Don't worry. Just remember that you can quickly get to your personalized collection by choosing **I**nsert, **P**icture, **F**rom File.

Modifying Clip Art

You've just learned the most difficult part about using clip art images. Now comes the fun part: changing clip art images so they work for you exactly the way you need them to.

Moving and Sizing Graphic Objects

The most common changes you make to an image are to its size and location. To change the size of an image, first click the image to display the sizing and rotation handles (see Figure 6.7). Then size the image by using these options:

- Click and drag any corner sizing handle to enlarge or reduce the image *proportionally*.

- Click and drag a side sizing handle to *distort* the image horizontally.

- Click and drag a top or bottom sizing handle to distort the image vertically.

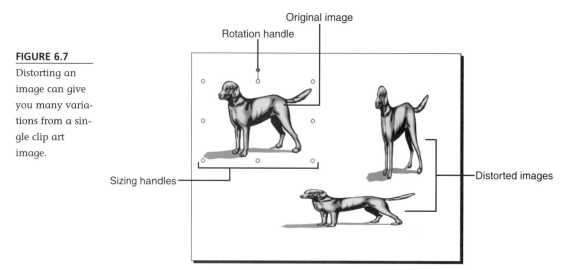

FIGURE 6.7

Distorting an image can give you many variations from a single clip art image.

You can come up with some pretty interesting variations such as small, short, and skinny dogs, or large, tall, and fat ones, all from the same image (refer to Figure 6.7).

To move an image, simply position the mouse pointer over the image and when the pointer turns to a four-way arrow, click and drag the image to the desired location. You might need to make several attempts before you get the image in just the right location and at the right size.

Using Snap to Grid

PowerPoint's *Snap to Grid* feature sometimes helps and sometimes gets in the way of positioning an image exactly where you want it. By default, the screen is invisibly divided into 1/12-inch segments. Thanks to the Snap to Grid feature, when you drop an image, it automatically jumps to the closest grid marker. This can be helpful when you're trying to align several objects at the same horizontal or vertical location. But if you need to nudge an image somewhere between the grids you have two options:

- Turn off the Snap to Grid feature by choosing **V**iew, Gr**i**d and Guides and from the dialog box that appears, deselect Snap Object to **G**rid.

- Temporarily override the Snap to Grid feature by holding down the Ctrl key and using the arrow keys to move the selected image right, left, up, or down in very tiny increments.

Don't forget that although you normally, and more easily, move images by using the mouse, you can use the keyboard, too.

Rotating an Image

Sometimes the orientation of an image isn't quite right. For example, the dog might be facing the wrong way or might need to be heading up hill.

To rotate an image, click it once to display the sizing and rotation handles (refer to Figure 6.7). Then, drag the rotation handle right or left as desired.

To turn the image completely around, *flip* the image by following these steps:

1. Click the image to select it.

2. <kbd>Dr̲aw ▾</kbd> Click the **Dr**aw button on the Drawing toolbar. PowerPoint displays a menu of options.

3. Choose Rotate or Fli**p**, Flip **H**orizontal. PowerPoint flips the image so it's heading in the opposite direction.

You can also flip an image vertically—for example, if you want your dog to lie on its back!

Formatting Graphic Objects

PowerPoint provides literally thousands of clip art images, but sometimes it's hard to find exactly the image you want. For example, you might find the perfect breed of dog, but it's the wrong color.

PowerPoint enables you to *format* images in a variety of ways, some of which don't really apply here. But let's take a look at a few ways that formatting a picture might be of value to you.

Double-click an image to open the Format Picture dialog box. You can also click the image you want to change and choose F**o**rmat, **Pi**cture or you can right-click the image and choose Format Pi**c**ture to open the Format Picture dialog box. Although typically the Picture tab displays automatically, let's start with the Colors and Lines tab (see Figure 6.8), which will help us as we talk about other ways of formatting a picture.

Each image is actually contained inside an invisible box. The Colors and Lines tab enables you to add color or lines to that box. For example, if you add a solid fill color and a line, you essentially frame the image (see Figure 6.9).

- The Size tab (see Figure 6.10) lets you specify the exact size, dimensions, and rotation of an image. You can also choose Lock **A**spect Ratio so that changing an image's height, width, or scale automatically changes both height and width proportionally. Nevertheless, with this check box selected, you can still distort an image by dragging a side, top, or bottom sizing handle.

FIGURE 6.8

The Format
Picture dialog
box is a power-
ful tool for mod-
ifying images
and the image
boxes that con-
tain them.

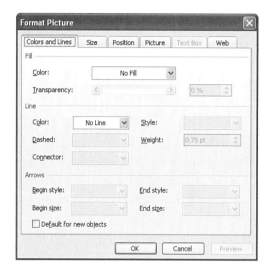

FIGURE 6.9

You can use
lines and fills to
frame an image.

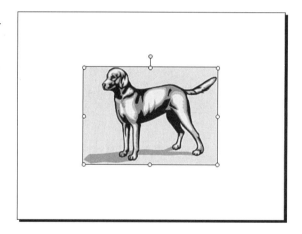

■ The Position tab enables you to specify the exact location of the image, relative to the top-left corner of the slide or to the center.

■ The Picture tab, which appears first when you are formatting a picture, provides some interesting formatting options (see Figure 6.11). For example, you
can use this tab to do the following:

■ Crop an image. If you reduce the size of the image's box, you crop or trim the
edges of the image. For example, if you crop the bottom by .5" you trim that
much off the bottom of the image. This can be useful if there's a part of an
image that you really don't want to include in the slide. If you use a negative
number, such as –0.5", you actually *add* that much to the box. This gives you
more space between the image and the edge of the box.

FIGURE 6.10

Use the Format Picture dialog box to precisely change an image's size or shape.

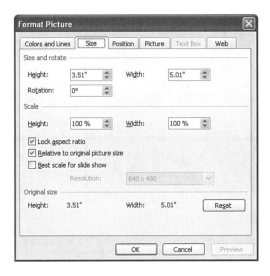

FIGURE 6.11

The Picture tab of the Format Picture dialog box lets you crop an image, make it brighter or darker, or even change its colors.

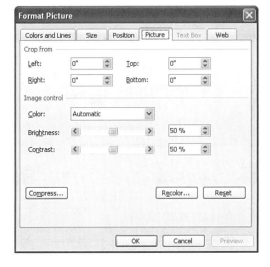

▪ Change the color of the image to grayscale, black and white, or a washout (faded) effect. Washout is simply a preset of the Brightness and Contrast controls.

▪ Click Recolor to display the Recolor Picture dialog box, which enables you to switch certain colors for others (see Figure 6.12). Simply click the color you want to change and then from the **N**ew drop-down menus, select the new color. Note that you might have to scroll through a lengthy list of colors to find the one you want to change.

FIGURE 6.12

FIGURE 6.12

If you don't like the color of a clip art image, just change it!

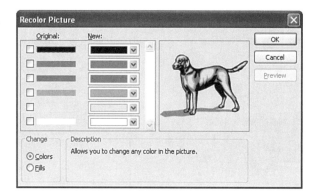

■ Use the Reset button to change cropping and image control settings back to the original, but leave recolor changes alone. You can change those back by going to the Recolor Picture dialog box and unchecking the color changes.

Spend some time playing with the picture formatting options. Many of these options are used with other graphic objects as well.

tip

When fiddling with colors or other image changes, if you have the opportunity to preview the changes, take it! It's easier to change your mind before exiting a dialog box than it is to fix the changes later.

If the dialog box covers the image you're trying to preview, just click the title bar on the dialog box and drag it to the side.

And don't forget Undo if you make a mistake or want to try something again!

Combining Clip Art and Other Objects

The more objects you add to a screen, the more you have to consider how they relate to each other in terms of size, location, rotation, and so on. Fortunately, PowerPoint enables you to fine-tune these relationships, helping you create a virtual work of art.

Changing the Visual Order of Objects

Each time you add an object to a slide, it's as if you're laying the object on a table. The first object is on the bottom, and the last object is on top. In PowerPoint, objects are said to be to the back (first) or to the front (last). Fortunately, PowerPoint enables you to change the order of your objects.

Suppose you add an image of a cat and then add an image of a dog. Because of the order in which you add them, the dog appears in front of the cat. Because the cat is small, you want it to appear in front of the dog. To change the order of an object, follow these steps:

1. Select the image you want to change (for example, the cat).

2.  Click the D**r**aw button on the Drawing toolbar and choose O**r**der. You can also right-click the object and choose O**r**der.

3. Choose the direction you want the object to move: Bring to Fron**t** (all the way to the front or to the top of the pile), Send to Bac**k** (all the way to the back), or Bring **F**orward or Send **B**ackward (just one layer forward or backward).

You can repeat these steps with other objects until you have just the right order (see Figure 6.13). Don't forget that you can change the order of any object: image, text box, placeholder, graph, and so on.

FIGURE 6.13

You can adjust the order of onscreen images to create a three-dimensional look.

Grouping and Ungrouping Objects

After you painstakingly position two or three objects, you might find that as a group, they're out of alignment with the slide's text or with some other critical part of the slide. To move the group of objects all at the same time, you have two options: select them all and move them or group them to make them one object.

To select multiple objects to move (or to copy or delete), follow these steps:

1. Click the first object to select it. Sizing handles appear to let you know what you've selected.

2. Hold down the Ctrl key (or the Shift key) and click the second object. Sizing handles now appear on both objects.

3. Continue with the Ctrl key (or the Shift key) pressed and click other objects. If you accidentally select a wrong object, click it again to deselect it.

4. Release the Ctrl (or Shift) key.

You can now drag the group of objects to a new location, or otherwise manipulate them the same way you do with just one object.

Draw ▾ To keep the group of objects together so you don't have to reselect them each time, follow the steps above to select the objects and then click the Draw button on the Drawing toolbar and choose **G**roup. You can also right-click the group and choose **G**rouping, **G**roup. PowerPoint then displays only one set of sizing and rotation handles for the entire group.

If you want to move or delete a single part of a combined group of objects, you have to ungroup them first. Simply right-click the group and choose **G**rouping, **U**ngroup. You can also choose the **U**ngroup option from the **D**raw button on the Drawing toolbar.

You probably didn't realize this, but nearly all clip art images consist of groups of drawing images. You can ungroup such images and remove or change parts you don't like. The process is a bit more complex than what I just described, but not terribly so. For example, say you've found the perfect lamp to illustrate your point, but you don't want the fan that comes with it. Just follow these steps to ungroup and modify a clip art image:

1. Insert the image into a slide.

2. Select the image.

3. Draw ▾ Click the **D**raw button on the Drawing toolbar and choose **U**ngroup. PowerPoint gives you a warning that this is an imported picture, not a group, and asks if you want to convert it to a drawing object.

4. Click Yes and then choose **D**raw, **U**ngroup again. PowerPoint displays a gazillion objects, each with its own set of sizing handles (see Figure 6.14).

5. Click each object you want to remove and press Delete (for example, the objects that comprise the fan), until only the image you want remains.

The problem now is that you have half a gazillion objects, and trying to select each to move or size it would be nearly impossible. But here's an easy way to select them all:

1. Imagine the entire image as if it were sitting in a frame. Click at one corner of the imaginary frame and drag to the opposite corner (see Figure 6.15). Note that you must include all of an object in the frame you drag, or it is not included in the selection.

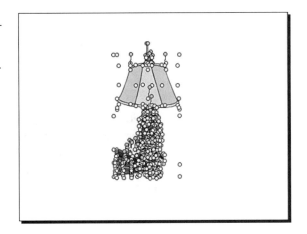

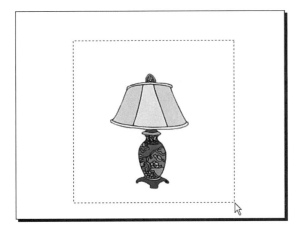

2. Release the mouse button, and sizing handles appear on all the components of the image.

3. Click the **D**raw button on the Drawing toolbar, and choose **G**roup. Voilá. You now have just the image you want, and you can move, size, rotate, or format it to your heart's content.

Inserting Bitmap Images

Bitmap images are a type of graphic object you can use to enhance the visual power of slides. The procedures for obtaining and manipulating these images are some-times a bit different than those for clip art.

Understanding Bitmap Images

Clip art images, like those described earlier in this chapter, are called *vector graphics* or *vector images*. For example, a straight line in a vector image consists of two points, or vectors. The computer generates the line between these two points, so regardless how you change the points, the line is always smooth and complete.

Bitmap images, on the other hand, require a *bit*, or dot, at each point along the way. It's as if the line were painted, and if you make it longer, the paint pulls apart. If you stretch a bitmap image, the image distorts because the computer doesn't know how to fill in the missing information. Such distortions are sometimes referred to as the "jaggies" because the image has jagged edges (see Figure 6.16).

FIGURE 6.16

Distorted (enlarged) bitmap images often have jagged edges.

Bitmap images (such as photographs or scanned images from books or other sources) usually appear more complete and more realistic that clip art images. Bitmap images are also much larger than vector images when saved to disk. Having many of them in a slide show can slow down the presentation. But the drawbacks of these larger images are usually outweighed by the detail and realism they provide.

Inserting Images from Files

Bitmap images are typically separate files you save on your hard drive. It helps to remember their filenames and where you saved them. You then can follow these steps to insert a bitmap image:

1. Choose **I**nsert, **P**icture, **F**rom File. You can also click the Insert Picture button on the Drawing toolbar. PowerPoint displays the Insert Picture dialog box (see Figure 6.17), which is similar to the Open, Save, and other file management dialog boxes. When you're inserting an image, by default it starts in the My Pictures folder under My Documents.

FIGURE 6.17

Insert bitmap images by inserting pictures from file.

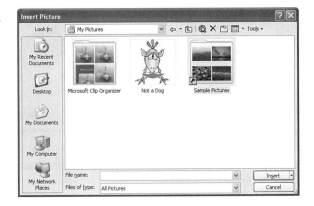

2. Find the picture you want—either in the selected folder or by browsing to the location where you saved the bitmap image.

3. Select the image and click Insert to place the image on the slide (see Figure 6.18).

FIGURE 6.18

Bitmap images can be sized and rotated by using the sizing and rotation handles.

Note that the image appears with sizing and rotation handles, just like other images and text objects. You can move, size, or rotate the bitmap image.

Acquiring Images

PowerPoint provides hundreds of clip art images but only a handful of bitmap images. However, for effective presentations, much of what you need will be in the form of bitmap images you acquire through other sources, such as by using a scanner, digital camera, the Internet, or screen shots.

Using a Scanner

A common source for bitmap images is a scanner. If you don't have ready access to a scanner, you might want to consider purchasing one. Even very inexpensive scanners are quite adequate for the kind of images you use in PowerPoint.

You can scan images separately, save them, and later insert them into PowerPoint, or you can scan images directly into PowerPoint. To scan an image directly into PowerPoint, follow these steps:

1. Choose **I**nsert, **P**icture, From **S**canner or Camera. PowerPoint displays the Insert Picture from Scanner or Camera dialog box (see Figure 6.19).

FIGURE 6.19

You can use devices you have set up on your computer, such as scanners or cameras, to capture images directly into PowerPoint.

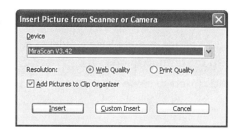

2. Select your scanner in the **D**evice drop-down list box.

3. Choose the resolution quality you want. W**e**b Quality is all that's required for PowerPoint presentations because both PowerPoint and Web sites seen in browsers use a computer's screen resolution, usually only about 72 dots per inch (dpi). **P**rint Quality does not make images any better in PowerPoint, but it does increase the saved file size of a scanned image significantly.

4. To customize what gets scanned and inserted, click **C**ustom Insert. If you just choose **I**nsert, you get a default scan size and location that might not match exactly what you are trying to scan.

5. Windows starts your scanner software, which varies depending on your scanner and your computer setup. Even the most elementary programs, however, give you several options that might be valuable (see Figure 6.20, which shows a simple scanning program):

   ■ *Color*—Usually you can choose whether to scan in color or grayscale (usually best for photos), or pure black and white (usually best for line art drawings).

   ■ *Quality*—You might have to try various settings to determine which will give you the optimal crispness you want.

FIGURE 6.20

This scanning program lets you customize the size and other qualities of a scan before inserting it into PowerPoint.

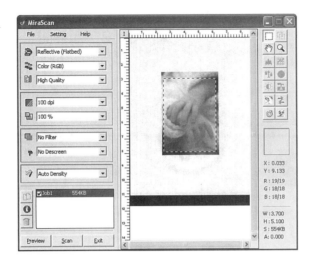

■ *dpi*—dpi stands for dots-per-inch and refers to the number of dots you see onscreen. 72–100 dpi is entirely adequate for most screen presentations, whereas 300 dpi or better gives better print quality. Keep the dpi relatively low for screen or Web presentations.

■ *Size*—This is one area that you really can use to your advantage. Because bitmap images tend to distort and have jagged edges when you enlarge them in PowerPoint, it's best to scan them at roughly the same size at which you want them to appear in a slide show. For example, if you scan a 1-inch by 1-inch photo and enlarge it to 4 inches by 4 inches in PowerPoint, it will look quite grainy and rough. If you scan it at 400% from your scanning software, the result will likely be much smoother.

■ *Brightness/contrast*—Some software enables you to change brightness and contrast settings before you scan to give you a richer, clearer picture.

6. Choose Scan or whatever button finalizes a scan in your scanning software. The scanner does its work, and returns you to PowerPoint, inserting the resulting scanned image (see Figure 6.21).

Note that although you can fiddle with scanning and touch-up options when you acquire an image, you'll always get the best results when the original is of high quality.

FIGURE 6.21

A scanned image can add realism and visual impact to a slide.

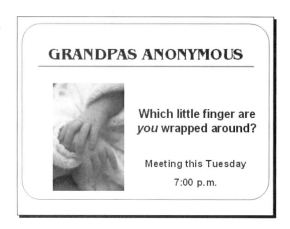

Using Images from a Digital Camera

Digital cameras are readily available and make it easy to acquire timely, relevant photos for up-to-the-minute slide shows. You can capture product images, photos of building progress, pictures of company staff, and more (see Figure 6.22).

FIGURE 6.22

Photos captured by a digital camera make it possible to pre-pare up-to-the-minute presentations.

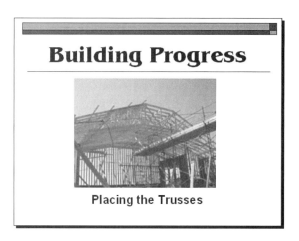

Digital cameras typically come with software that enables you to save images directly to your computer's hard drive. After doing so, you follow the steps for insert-ing a picture from file, as noted in the "Inserting Images from Files" section, earlier in this chapter.

However, you can also insert images directly from your camera if you have the proper connections between your camera and your computer, as well as the software that enables you to do so. If this is set up properly, choose **I**nsert, **P**icture, From

Scanner or Camera and in the resulting dialog box (refer to Figure 6.19), simply choose your camera from the **D**evice drop-down list box. Then choose **C**ustom Insert to select the picture you want.

Using Images from the Internet

Another rich resource for bitmap images is the World Wide Web. Although you have to take care to comply with copyright laws, you can find many Web sites that offer free images, including photos, clip art, and decorative lines, borders, and buttons.

To insert an image into a slide show from an Internet Web site, follow these steps:

1. Switch to your Internet browser and right-click the image you want to download.

2. From the context menu, in Netscape choose Save **I**mage As, or in Internet Explorer choose **S**ave Picture As.

3. Provide a name and location on your hard drive (for example, `c:\My Pictures\webimage.jpg`). Use the same filename extension as used on the Web site (for example, `.gif` or `.jpg`).

4. Click OK to save the image.

5. Switch back to PowerPoint and choose **I**nsert, **P**icture, **F**rom File.

6. Browse to the location where you saved the image, select the image, and choose In**s**ert.

> **caution**
>
> Just because images can be downloaded from the Internet does not mean they are free. Copyright laws and restrictions apply to Internet graphics as they do to print graphics. If you aren't sure whether you can use a graphic image, you should ask the owner of the Web site that contains the image.

After PowerPoint inserts the image, you can select the image and move, size, or rotate it as you would any other PowerPoint object.

If you don't want to keep the image as a separate file, you can simply right-click the image in your browser, choose Copy from the context menu, and then switch back to PowerPoint and paste the image on a slide.

Capturing and Inserting Screen Shots

You'll find, sometimes, that you'd like to show images from your computer in a slide show. For example, if you're training others in a certain software program, you might want to display dialog boxes or other screen activity. Or if you're teaching students about a Web site but don't have an Internet connection (or have a very slow one), you might want to capture Web site screens as viewed in a browser.

To capture an entire screen and insert the screen shot in your slide show, follow these steps:

1. Get to the screen you want to capture (for example, a Web site in your browser).

2. Press the PrtSc (Print Screen) key on your keyboard. Windows copies an image of the entire screen to the Windows Clipboard.

3. Switch to the appropriate slide in your slide show and choose **E**dit, **P**aste to copy the screen shot to the slide (see Figure 6.23).

FIGURE 6.23

Screen shots are easy-to-capture bitmap images.

4. Size the image so that it fills the entire screen.

When you play the slide show, it appears that you are showing the actual Web site. In fact, it's so realistic that you might find yourself trying to click buttons on the screen shot of your browser!

If you want to copy less than a full screen, you can copy only the active window (for example, a dialog box) by holding down the Alt key and pressing PrtSc.

Using the Picture Toolbar to Modify Bitmap Images

Earlier in this chapter, you learned how to use the Format Picture dialog box to modify clip art images. You can use the same methods to modify bitmap images as well.

However, you can also use the Picture toolbar to modify either clip art or bitmap images. To activate the Picture toolbar, simply right-click an image and from the context menu choose Show Picture Toolbar. You can also choose **V**iew, **T**oolbars and select the Picture Toolbar. PowerPoint displays the Picture toolbar (see Figure 6.24).

From the toolbar, you can quickly access the same features you find in the Format Picture dialog box, but in some cases, the features are even easier to use. For example, cropping an image by using the Picture toolbar icon enables you to see what you're cropping. Hover the mouse pointer over each button to see what it's used for.

To close the Picture toolbar, simply click its Close button or right-click an image and from the context menu choose Hide Picture Toolbar.

Saving Images Created in PowerPoint

You might not think you're an artist, but you'll probably surprise yourself. At some point, you'll step back and say to yourself, "Hey, that's pretty good!" In fact, you might even want to save an image you've created or modified for use in other

note

PowerPoint has several useful tools for making basic modifications to both clip art and bitmap images. However, if you're serious about fine-tuning bitmap images, especially photographs, you'll probably want to investigate using other programs outside of PowerPoint, such as Photoshop.

slide shows or even in Word documents or on Web pages. You can save single images, grouped images, or combinations of images, clip art, and text.

To save an object separately from your PowerPoint slide show, follow these steps:

1. Select the object or objects you want to save. You might want to group them first into a single object.

2. Right-click the image and choose **S**ave as Picture. PowerPoint displays the Save as Picture dialog box.

3. Choose a location and a filename.

4. From the *Save as* **T**ype drop-down list box, select a graphics format for the image. By default, PowerPoint saves images in the EMF (Enhanced Windows Metafile) format. But you can also save images in the JPG, PNG, or TIFF formats, or in a generic bitmap format. JPG (pronounced "jay-peg") and PNG formats are commonly used on Web pages.

5. Choose **S**ave to save the selected image as a separate file.

If you later want to use the image, simply insert it by selecting **I**nsert, **P**icture, **F**rom File.

THE ABSOLUTE MINIMUM

PowerPoint is a visual medium. Therefore, graphic images, such as clip art or scanned photos, can add immense value to a slide show. In this chapter, you did the following:

- You learned how to find and insert clip art images.

- You found out how to move, size, distort, rotate, copy, and delete graphic images.

- You learned how to change the layer order of images and how to group and ungroup images.

- You explored the difference between vector (clip art) and bitmap images.

- You discovered how to acquire bitmap images from a scanner, from a digital camera, or from Internet Web sites.

In Chapter 7, "Creating Drawing Objects," you'll explore the Draw program and learn to create graphic images of your own.

7

CREATING DRAWING OBJECTS

Sometimes less is more. In Chapter 6, "Working with Graphic Objects," you learned how to insert clip art and bitmap images. But sometimes all you really need is a simple graphic element to highlight, emphasize, or point to something you're trying to show onscreen. You don't need complex images to do it. All you need is a box, an arrow, or a line.

This chapter explores the use of the Draw feature, which also happens to be available in other Office 2003 applications, such as Word and Excel.

Using the Drawing Toolbar

The *Draw program* is a collection of tools that enable you to create shapes and lines and to format them according to your needs. Although most of the program's options can be found in PowerPoint's menus, the ones you use most are conveniently located on PowerPoint's Drawing toolbar (see Figure 7.1). (Throughout this chapter, I focus on the use of this toolbar and only rarely mention menu alternatives.)

FIGURE 7.1

Using the Drawing toolbar is the most convenient way to access PowerPoint's drawing features.

This toolbar appears when you first use PowerPoint, and unless you turn it off, it is always available while you're creating and editing slides. Most of the toolbar's buttons are typical in that you simply click them to begin using a feature. However, some of them are used a bit differently. Among the types of Drawing toolbar buttons are the following:

- Buttons that activate a dialog box, such as the Insert WordArt, Diagram, Clip Art, and Picture buttons.

- Buttons that display menus, such as the D**r**aw and A**u**toShapes buttons.

- Buttons that display palettes to choose from, such as the Line, Dash, Arrow, Shadow, and 3-D Style buttons.

- Buttons that change semi-permanently when you choose one of their options. For example, if you click the drop-down arrow next to the Fill, Line, or Text Color boxes and choose a new color, that color then becomes the default the next time you just click the button.

- Buttons that activate a feature but then wait for you to do something. For example, if you click the Rectangle button, nothing seems to happen until you move the pointer to the slide and drag to create a rectangle.

You'll get used to these differences in buttons eventually. At first, however, you'll sometimes find yourself getting the wrong results because you've clicked the wrong button. If this happens, just choose **E**dit, **U**ndo or press Ctrl+Z to undo your unintentional mistake.

By default, the Drawing toolbar appears across the bottom of the screen, but as with any toolbar, you can drag it to any side of the screen or out to the middle as a floating toolbar.

If you can't find the toolbar at all, it's probably turned off. To fix this, choose **V**iew, **T**oolbars and click the Drawing toolbar. Then drag it to the location you want.

➪ For more information on repositioning toolbars, see **p. 371**.

Adding Lines, Closed Shapes, and AutoShapes

On with the show. What you really came here for was to learn how to add your own graphic creations. The Draw program helps you create two basic types of images:

- *Lines*—These include straight lines, multisegment lines, and lines with arrowheads.
- *Closed shapes*—The rectangle and circle shapes are the two most commonly used closed shapes, and PowerPoint also provides a bevy of preformatted shapes, such as buttons, banners, flowchart symbols, and more.

Let's start by experimenting with closed shapes.

Adding Rectangles and Ovals

To create a closed shape, such as a rectangle, follow these steps:

1. Click the Rectangle button. PowerPoint seems to do nothing, but it's really waiting for you to take the next step.

2. Move the mouse pointer to the slide area. The pointer appears as a crosshairs.

3. Position the pointer at one corner of the rectangle you are about to create (for example, the upper-left corner).

4. Click and drag the pointer to the opposite corner (for example, the lower-right corner).

5. Release the mouse button. PowerPoint inserts a rectangle, complete with a thin-line border and filled with a color that automatically matches the design template you're using (see Figure 7.2).

Note that the image displays sizing and rotation handles, just like other PowerPoint objects.

 You can add ovals by using the same steps. Just click the Oval button and then drag the oval or circle shape on the slide.

FIGURE 7.2

Click and drag to create closed shapes.

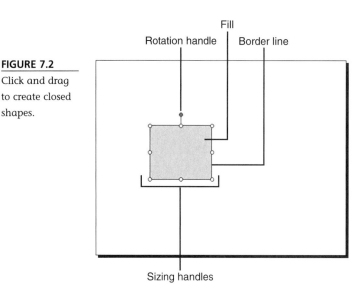

The following tricks work with most closed drawing objects:

- If you want to draw a perfectly proportioned object (for example, a square or circle), hold down the Shift key while dragging the shape. PowerPoint forces the shape to an equally proportioned height and width.

- If you want to start at the center of the shape and expand it outward, press Ctrl as you draw. PowerPoint expands the shape from the center point as you drag away from that center point.

- To start from the center *and* make the shape perfectly proportional, press *both* Ctrl and Shift while dragging the shape.

Cool, eh? Now you can impress your geometrically challenged friends with your perfect squares and circles!

Adding Lines and Arrows

Adding lines and line-type arrows is as simple as adding closed shapes. Follow these steps:

1. Click the Line button.

2. Move to the slide and drag from one end of the line to the other.

3. Release the mouse button to insert the line (refer to Figure 7.2).

Notice that the line object displays sizing handles, but no rotation handle. You can adjust the length and orientation of a line by dragging a sizing handle. You can also essentially rotate the line by using the opposite end of the line as the rotation axis.

If you want to rotate a line on its center axis, choose D**r**aw, Rotate or Fli**p**, Free Ro**t**ate. PowerPoint changes the sizing handles to green rotation handles. Drag the rotation handles to rotate the line.

Adding line-type arrows is similar to adding lines, but you have to remember which direction the arrow points when you drag the arrow. Follow these steps:

1. Click the Arrow button.

2. Move to the slide and drag from one end to the arrowhead end.

3. Adjust or rotate the arrow the same way you do a line.

To select a line or an arrow, just move the pointer to the line until the pointer turns to a four-way arrow. Click once to select the line or drag to move it.

Adding AutoShapes

AutoShapes are fancier, predesigned closed or line shapes. To get an idea of what AutoShapes are available to you, click the A**u**toShapes button. PowerPoint displays the AutoShapes menu, and as you hover the mouse pointer over each menu item, PowerPoint displays palettes of AutoShape choices (see Figure 7.3).

FIGURE 7.3

AutoShapes are predesigned lines and closed shapes that save you the trouble of creating your own shapes.

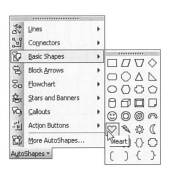

Let's try a few different shapes to learn how AutoShapes work, which sometimes is different from the rectangles or lines you're already familiar with.

To create and modify a smiley face, for example, follow these steps:

1. Choose A**u**toShapes, **B**asic Shapes and click the smiley face icon.

2. Move to the slide and drag the size face you want. Don't forget to press Shift if you want a perfect circle.

3. Release the mouse button to draw the face. PowerPoint displays the object with sizing and rotation handles, as well as a yellow diamond-shaped *glyph*, which is used to change the shape or size of only a part of the object (refer to Figure 7.2).

4. Drag the glyph as desired. For example, you could drag the smile upward, turning it into a frown.

Try several other closed shapes, dragging glyphs when present, and also sizing, rotating, and moving the objects. You'll soon find just how powerful AutoShapes can be. With relatively little artistic talent, you can create shapes that look and *do* what you want them to.

Other types of AutoShapes are lines and connectors. To create a multisegment line, for example, follow these steps:

1. Choose A**u**toShapes, **L**ines and click the Freeform line icon.

2. Move to the slide and click (but don't drag) at the point where you want the line to start.

3. Move the mouse pointer to where you want the line to stop and turn in a different direction and then click again.

4. Continue clicking at each turn until you arrive at the end of the line.

5. To complete the line, double-click. PowerPoint inserts a multisegment line (refer to Figure 7.2).

If you join the beginning and the end of the line, when you double-click, PowerPoint creates a closed object and adds a colored fill (refer to Figure 7.2).

The sizing and rotation handles shown in Figure 7.3 don't allow you to edit the shapes of the individual lines. Instead, you must right-click the object and select **E**dit Points. PowerPoint displays the object with edit points (see Figure 7.4). Drag the edit points to create exactly the shape you need.

Other line options include double-ended arrows, scribble (like drawing with a pencil), and curve, which is similar to a multisegment line, but as you turn the corner, instead of taking a sharp angle, the line curves gently. This option is particularly useful when you're drawing maps.

Connector lines are semi-automatic multisegment lines. You can draw connector lines by themselves, but as their name implies, they're really designed to help you draw perfect lines or arrows between two objects.

FIGURE 7.4

By using edit points, you can change individual parts of a multisegment drawing.

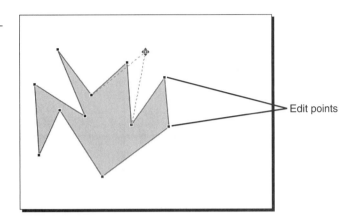

Edit points

Adding Text to AutoShapes

Certain AutoShapes automatically prompt you to add text to them (for example, *callout* shapes). Callouts are the speech or thought bubbles you often see in cartoons. To add a callout to a slide, follow these steps:

1. Choose A**u**toShapes, **C**allouts and select a callout shape.

2. Move to the slide and click and drag the approximate size of the callout, just as you do when you create a rectangle or an oval.

3. When you release the mouse button, PowerPoint displays the callout and also a text box and a blinking insertion point.

4. Type the text of the callout. You can also format the text just as you do with any text box.

5. Click the edge of the callout box to select it and to display the callout pointer glyph.

6. Drag the pointer glyph so that it points to the object doing the speaking (see Figure 7.5).

You can also add text to any other closed object. Simply right-click the object, and from the context menu choose Add Te**x**t. PowerPoint displays a text box and an insertion point.

Adding Action Buttons

One type of AutoShape that has a specific purpose is the action button. You create action buttons the same way you do any closed object, but when you release the mouse button to create the button, PowerPoint displays the Action Settings dialog box. We'll talk about linking objects later; for now, just click Cancel. Adjust the button size and shape and then drag the glyph to change the three-dimensional height of the button (see Figure 7.6).

Modifying and Formatting Shapes

Besides changing the size, shape, or rotation of a drawing object and besides adding text to a drawing object, you can also modify an object's characteristics, such as fill and line styles or colors, and you can add shading or three-dimensionality.

Using Basic Shape Formatting

Line shape drawing objects, by default, are thin (about 1/100 inch), solid, and black.

To format lines, follow these steps:

1. Select the object by clicking it once. If you don't select the object first, PowerPoint doesn't know what to change.

2. ▤ Click the Line Style button. PowerPoint displays a palette of line styles and thicknesses.

3. Click a line style to apply it to the selected object. If you change a line's thickness, you also automatically change the size of its arrowhead, if it has one.

4. ▤ If you want a dashed, rather than solid, line, click the Dash Style button and from the palette choose a dash style.

5. ▨ To change a line color, click the Line Color button to apply the last line color you used. But if you want a different color, click the drop-down menu at the right of the Line Color button. PowerPoint displays a palette of line color choices, including the following:

   ■ *No Line*—This turns off the line altogether. Although this option doesn't make much sense here, it does make sense when you're modifying the border line of a closed object.

   ■ *Automatic*—The colors displayed beneath the Automatic bar are those that likely go best with the color scheme used in the current design layer.

   ■ *More Line Colors*—Although a color from beneath the Automatic bar is likely to coordinate with other colors on your slide, you might want something that stands out a little more or matches a particular image you have in mind. Choosing this option displays a more extensive palette of colors to choose from.

   ■ *Patterned Lines*—You can choose a solid or patterned line, such as hash marks or a checkerboard pattern.

⇄ If your lines have arrowheads that you want to modify, or if you want to add arrowheads to lines, click the Arrow Style button. From the palette that appears, select an arrow style. Note that some arrowheads may not be visible until you deselect the line because the sizing handles cover them up. Click **M**ore Arrows or double-click the line or arrow to go to the Format AutoShape dialog box, which offers more style and size options.

Line formatting options apply also to the border lines of closed objects. In addition, you can change a closed object's fill color and pattern.

To change an object's fill, follow these steps:

1. Select the object.

2. ▨ Click the drop-down list box to the right of the Fill Color button. PowerPoint displays several options, some of which are similar to those found on the Line Color button.

3. To select a custom color, choose **M**ore Fill Colors. Then, instead of using the Standard palette colors, click the Custom tab and go wild with the Custom palette (see Figure 7.7). You can choose any color or many shades of that color, and you can specify how transparent you want it to be (that is, how much you want objects behind the fill to show through).

FIGURE 7.7

The Custom palette lets you choose from thousands of colors.

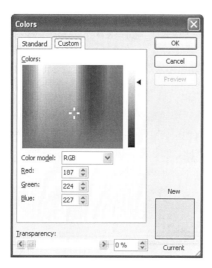

After you select a new color, note that the paint bucket on the Fill Colors button changes to the color you just selected. That's the color you'll get the next time you change a fill if you just click the button.

Using Gradient Shading

One really useful fill option that's also found on the Fill Color button is the gradient shading effect. *Gradient shades* change gradually from the fill color to black or from one color to another. Let's take some time to explore this option.

Select a filled object and then click the Fill Color button drop-down list. Choose **F**ill Effects to display the Fill Effects dialog box (see Figure 7.8).

You need to select a Colors option from among these choices:

- *O***ne** *Color*—By default, PowerPoint uses your chosen color and blends it with black (refer to Figure 7.8). Click O**n**e Color to display your color (under Color **1**). You can also change the contrast color's darkness or lightness by using the Dar**k** to Light slider.

- *T*wo *Colors*—This option changes the contrast color to white, and it also displays color boxes for both Color **1** and Color **2** (see Figure 7.9). You can change either or both colors to get just the right blend of colors.

FIGURE 7.8

Fill effects include gradient shading, textures, patterns, and pictures.

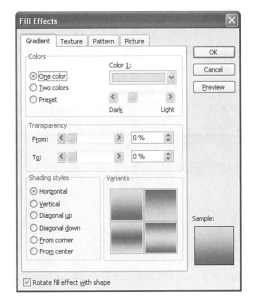

FIGURE 7.9

You can specify two colors to blend.

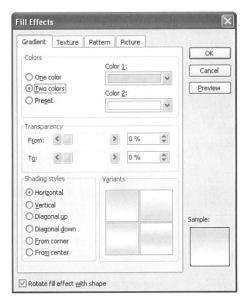

■ *Preset*—This option lists gradients of three or more colors that have descriptive names. For example, Horizon changes from white to a reddish brown foreground to white to sky blue and back to white. Play with these and see what's available. You just might find something you can use later.

With the One Color or Two Colors options, you can also set the degree of transparency of either or both colors, although this isn't a setting you'll use very often. More useful are the shading styles, which consist of horizontal, vertical, angled, or radial gradients, with four variants for each. To select a style, choose the style from the left side and then click a variant (refer to Figure 7.9).

Finally, by default if you rotate a filled object, the gradient style rotates along with it. The results of your changes appear in the Sample box, but you can also click **P**review to preview your selection before clicking OK to apply it.

Other fill backgrounds, found on the other tabs of the Fill Effects dialog box, include the following:

- *Texture*—This is a collection of stone, wood, fabric, and other textures. Click a texture and then click OK to apply it.

- *Pattern*—Besides the patterns themselves (see Figure 7.10), you can choose the contrasting colors (foreground and background). If you're printing your slides in black and white, patterns are often more useful than colors for distinguishing between two objects.

FIGURE 7.10

Patterns can be useful for distinguishing two different shapes, especially if they're printed in black and white.

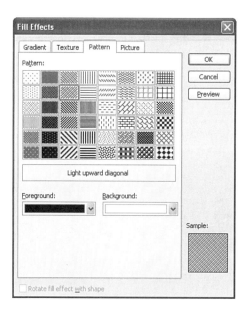

- *Picture*—When used as a fill for a rectangle, this option looks like any other inserted image. But as a background for ovals or irregular shapes, the effect can be quite interesting (see Figure 7.11).

FIGURE 7.11

You can create interesting effects when using picture fills with AutoShapes.

Exploring Special Effects

As if all the options in the preceding sections weren't enough, you can also apply some interesting special effects to drawing objects.

To view shadow options, select an object and then click the Shadow Style button. PowerPoint displays a palette of shadow types (see Figure 7.12). The type of shadow you choose creates a shadow effect for the selected object and changes realistically if you rotate the object. Choose **S**hadow Settings to display the Shadow Settings toolbar, where you can change the depth of the shadow and the shadow's color.

FIGURE 7.12

You add shadows to objects by using the Shadow Style button.

To view 3-D options, select an object and then click the 3-D Style button. Some common orientations are seen on the 3-D Styles palette. If you really want to be in control, select **3**-D Settings to display the 3-D Settings toolbar, where you can change such things as lighting direction, depth, color, and tilt.

Are you having fun yet? I guess I'll have to check back in an hour or two, after you've had some time to play with all these wonderful drawing toolbar options.

Combining Shapes and Other Objects

You might be asking the question "So what?" Sure, you're having fun, but how does this help you create a more effective PowerPoint slide show?

The answer lies in how well you master the many PowerPoint object types—text, graphics, and drawings—to create visually attractive and meaningful slides. And we haven't even talked yet about tables, charts, or diagrams!

Consider the slides shown in Figures 7.28 and 7.29. The basic message for each is textual. The image of the earth adds immediate recognition. The drawing elements make the important things stand out in ways that just aren't possible with text and pictures alone. Figure 7.13 is probably better suited to a more mature audience, and the message is clearly highlighted. Figure 7.14 is a bit more whimsical, but it communicates the same positive message as Figure 7.13.

Background oval

FIGURE 7.13

A professional-looking slide with both textual and visual information, enhanced by the use of a gradient-shaded background.

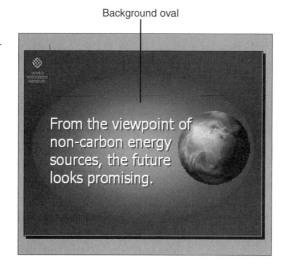

The uses for drawing objects are endless. Consider these examples:

- Add a text label with an arrow that points to the image it's describing.
- Create a gradient-shaded background for an object that might otherwise be difficult to see.
- Draw a thick red circle, with no fill, around a word you want to highlight.
- Combine words with an AutoShape arrow to show directions.
- Use a rectangle, the same color as the background, to cover or hide an image or part of an image.
- Add action settings to invisible objects (no line, no fill) to create hyperlinks.

Callout with gradient fill

FIGURE 7.14

FIGURE 7.14

The same mes-
sage as in Figure
7.13, presented
a bit more
whimsically,
using a callout
and an
AutoShape.

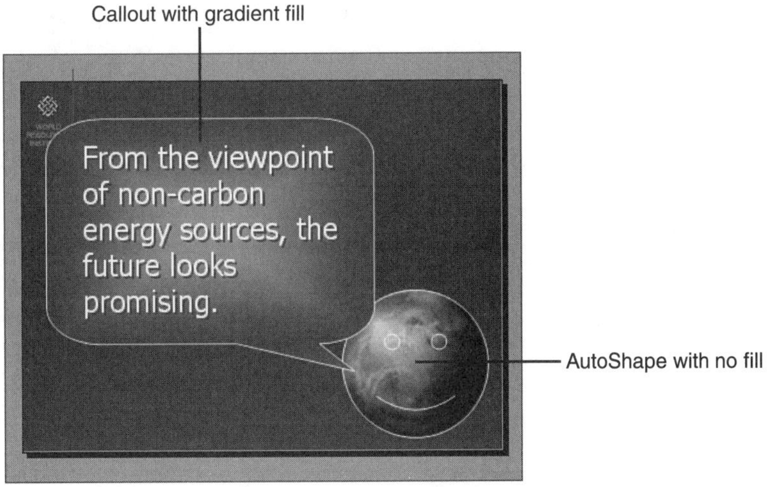

From the viewpoint
of non-carbon
energy sources, the
future looks
promising.

AutoShape with no fill

The value of some of these examples becomes readily evident as you learn how to animate objects—bringing them on or taking them off the screen during a presentation.

➪ To learn about action buttons and action settings associated with drawing
objects, see **p. 221**.

➪ To learn about animating drawing objects, see **p. 197**.

As you work with combinations of drawing and other objects, you sometimes find a
need to use them on other slides or in larger or smaller versions. For example, the
rectangle and oval in Figure 7.15 create the effect of a silo. The oval is layered
behind the rectangle, and both objects have gradient shading. To convert the two
separate drawing objects into one homemade clip art image, you simply group them
together, like this:

FIGURE 7.15

You can create
your own clip
art images by
combining
drawing objects.

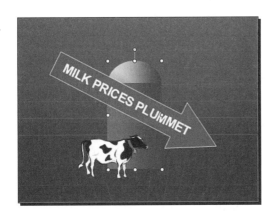

1. Select the first object in the group.

2. Hold down the Ctrl key or the Shift key and select the second object.

3. Release the Ctrl or Shift key.

4. Right-click the group and from the context menu select **G**rouping, **G**roup.

The objects are now grouped together and maintain their proper relationships even when copied to other slides or when sized differently. The silo always looks like a silo, not like two drawing objects.

Using WordArt Objects

Microsoft's WordArt feature is a hybrid of graphics, text, and drawing designs. To insert a word or title as a WordArt object, follow these steps:

1. 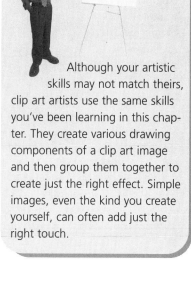 Click the WordArt button. PowerPoint displays the WordArt Gallery (see Figure 7.16).

note

Although your artistic skills may not match theirs, clip art artists use the same skills you've been learning in this chapter. They create various drawing components of a clip art image and then group them together to create just the right effect. Simple images, even the kind you create yourself, can often add just the right touch.

FIGURE 7.16
WordArt provides predesigned shapes and colors that make text really stand out.

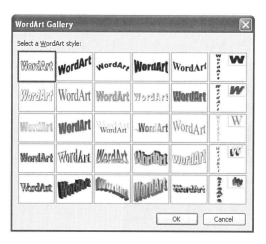

2. Select a style that generally matches what you're looking for. If none seem quite right, start with something close. Click OK, and PowerPoint displays the Edit WordArt Text dialog box.

3. Replace "Your Text Here" with your word or title. Choose a font, font size, and bold or italic.

4. Click OK to insert the WordArt object onto a slide (see Figure 7.17).

FIGURE 7.17
WordArt images
are particularly
useful as a title
or the main idea
on a slide.

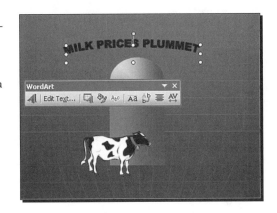

You now can use the WordArt toolbar (refer to Figure 7.17) or the Drawing toolbar to modify the image as you do other clip art images. One particularly useful option on the WordArt toolbar is the WordArt Shape button, which displays a palette of useful shapes that are different from the original shape you chose for your word or title (see Figure 7.18). In any case, you can size, distort, or rotate the image, and you can change the fill color or lines of the text, add shadows, and so on (see Figure 7.19).

FIGURE 7.18
You can use the
WordArt toolbar
to change the
shape or other
features of a
WordArt object.

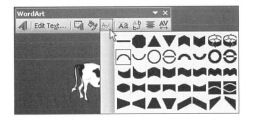

FIGURE 7.19
Starting with
just the basic
palette of
WordArt choices,
you can modify
a WordArt object
to come up with
many different
effects.

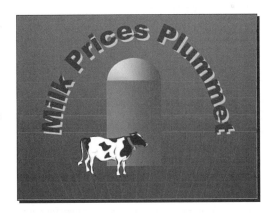

Saving Drawing Images Created in PowerPoint

Perhaps by now you're beginning to believe that you have some artistic ability. In Chapter 6 I told you how to save images as separate graphic image files, but you might have skipped over it, thinking your work just wasn't worth it. If you've changed your mind, I suggest you go back to Chapter 6 and review the procedures outlined there.

▷ To learn how to save images you create as separate graphic image files, see **p. 121**.

THE ABSOLUTE MINIMUM

Drawing objects can help you emphasize, draw attention to, or clarify text or other images on a PowerPoint slide. Learning to create drawing objects can take some time, but your investment in time will pay huge dividends. In this chapter, you did the following:

- You learned how to use the Drawing toolbar to create various lines and shapes.
- You found out how to insert AutoShapes.
- You learned how to change a drawing's borders and fills and how to add shadows and 3-D effects.
- You explored the use of gradient shading.
- You discovered how easily you can create fancy words or titles using WordArt.
- You learned how to group and save drawings.

Chapter 8, "Organizing Information by Using Tables," focuses on tables, which offer an easy and useful way to organize and present detailed information.

8

Organizing Information by Using Tables

What's a table, and why would you want to use one in a PowerPoint slide show? Tables are simply rows and columns of information. Any time you have lots of related facts and figures to present, a table is a useful way of organizing them so that the audience can quickly see and understand how they relate. This chapter explores how to create effective tables in PowerPoint, including some pretty amazing ways to format them, and how to import information to use in them.

Inserting a Table in PowerPoint

Before you create a table, it's a good idea to think about the information you want to present. How will you arrange the data?

For example, say a slide show includes sequential slides describing various products, including their costs, availability, and purposes. As a summary, you create a table similar to the one in Figure 8.1 that gives the audience a better overview of the products.

MASS STORAGE OPTIONS

Product	Cost	Size	Int/Ext	On Sale
SuperGig	$89	80	Internal	Yes
BigMax	$139	160	Internal	Yes
MaxPlug	$149	80	External	Yes
StorMor	$259	500	Internal	Apr 15

Before you create the table, you have to determine whether you want the products in rows and the features in columns or some other arrangement. Sometimes it makes sense to have a single category with lots of items in the rows, and only a limited number of defining features across the columns, as in the table shown in Figure 8.1.

In any case, try to determine the number of columns and rows you need before you create a table. You can add or remove columns or rows later, but a little advance planning can save you work in the long run.

Creating a Standard Table

There are several simple ways to insert a standard table into a PowerPoint slide. If the entire slide is being devoted to the table, the easiest method is to choose the Table layout from the Slide Layout task pane.

To display the Slide Layout pane, choose **Fo**rmat, Slide **L**ayout. Or if the task pane is already open, click the Task Pane drop-down menu and select Slide Layout. Scroll through the list of slide layouts until you see the Title and Table layout. Click this layout to apply it to the slide (see Figure 8.2).

FIGURE 8.2

You can use the Title and Table layout to easily create a PowerPoint table.

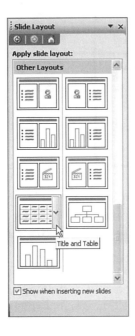

To create a table, double-click the table placeholder. PowerPoint displays the Insert Table dialog box, which asks how many columns and rows you need (see Figure 8.3). You should indicate how many and then click OK to insert the table.

FIGURE 8.3

You use the Insert Table dialog box to establish the initial number of columns and rows in a table.

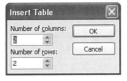

A variation on this approach is to select one of the content layouts—for example, the Content layout or the Title and Content layout. After you select one of these layouts, PowerPoint places a content placeholder on the slide (see Figure 8.4). You then click the table icon in the placeholder, and PowerPoint asks how many rows and columns to insert before it creates the table.

Table icon

FIGURE 8.4

Content layouts
include the
Table layout,
among other
content options.

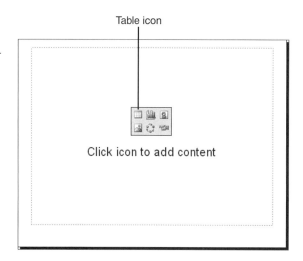

Click icon to add content

If you simply want to add a table to an existing slide, without being constrained by the table placeholder, you can choose **I**nsert, Ta**b**le. PowerPoint displays the Insert Table dialog box (refer to Figure 8.3). Choose the number of columns and rows you need and then click OK.

Finally, you can use the Insert Table button on the main toolbar to add a table to a slide. Click the button to display a grid, and then drag the mouse to select the number of rows and columns you need (see Figure 8.5). If you need more than the 5 columns and 4 rows shown, just keep dragging right or down to expand the grid. The maximum number of columns or rows that you can choose is limited by the resolution of your screen, typically about 20 rows or columns. However, it's unlikely that you'll ever want that many columns or rows in a PowerPoint slide show.

FIGURE 8.5

Using the Insert
Table button is a
quick and easy
way to insert a
table the size of
your choosing.

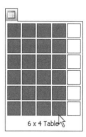

6 x 4 Table

Inserting a standard table by using any of these methods gives you a table within a text box (see Figure 8.6). The columns and rows are evenly spaced. Row heights are determined by the height of the default font.

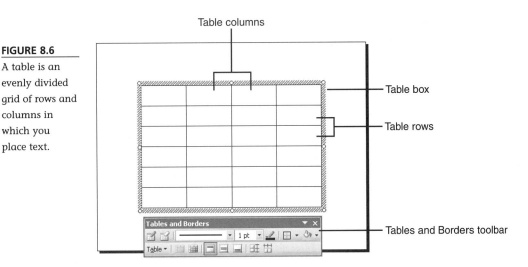

FIGURE 8.6

A table is an evenly divided grid of rows and columns in which you place text.

As shown in Figure 8.6, PowerPoint displays the Tables and Borders toolbar. But before we tackle the options on the toolbar, let's explore some table basics.

Adding Text and Graphic Objects to a Table

Tables use some of the same terminology as spreadsheets (for example, columns, rows). The intersections of columns and rows—the small boxes within tables—are called *cells*.

To add text to a cell, click the cell and begin typing. PowerPoint uses the default font of the design layer chosen. As you add text, you have several options:

- Table cells automatically expand vertically to accommodate the text that fills them. If you keep typing, text wraps to a new line, thus expanding the row and making all cells in that row the same height (see Figure 8.7).

FIGURE 8.7

Text wraps within the constraints of a column and automatically expands the row size.

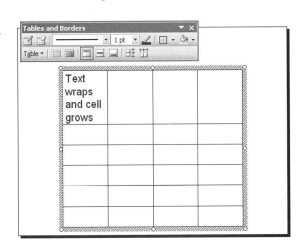

- To advance to the next cell, press the Tab key. You can remove your hand from the keyboard and click the mouse in the next cell—but using the Tab key is easier.

- To back up to the preceding cell, press Shift+Tab. Although you can also use the arrow keys to navigate around the cells, if a cell contains text, using Tab and Shift+Tab to move to the next cell or the previous cell is much quicker.

- If you press Tab at the end of a row, PowerPoint advances the insertion point to the first cell in the next row.

- If you press Tab in the last cell of the table, PowerPoint adds another row and advances the insertion point to the first cell in that row.

Besides typing text in table cells, you can also copy and paste from any Windows program to any cell, and you can copy and paste from one cell to another.

What about other objects, such as graphic images? In a Word document, you can paste an image directly into a table cell, and the cell expands to accommodate it. In PowerPoint, however, tables and images are always separate objects. When you add an image object, you lay it on top of other objects, including tables. Even if you copy a Word table that contains an image into PowerPoint, the table and the image become separate objects in PowerPoint.

In PowerPoint, tables are useful for organizing textual information, but not for organizing graphics or other types of content.

Formatting Tables

If an evenly spaced table is all you need, you've learned all you need to know in order to create one. However, most of the time you need to have some control over the width of columns or the height of rows, as well as over lines, borders, and other formatting features. The following sections describe how to change these aspects of tables.

Understanding the Structure of Tables

Before you begin exploring table formatting, it helps to have a basic understanding of how tables are structured:

- A table consists of at least one row and one column. For convenience, people refer to columns by letter (Column A, Column B, and so on), and to rows by number (Row 1, Row 2, and so on).

- The intersection of a row and column is called a *cell*. For convenience, people use the column and row to name a cell (for example, Cell A1, Cell B5).

- By default, cells are separated by single visible lines. With lines or without, a table's structure still separates the columns and rows.
- By default, a table has no border, but the outside lines of the outside cells make it appear that there is one.
- By default, text is aligned at the top left of a cell.

As you begin modifying a table, you need to keep in mind what you're changing. In no time at all, the whole concept of table structure will seem natural to you.

Using the Tables and Borders Toolbar

When you first create a table, PowerPoint displays a floating Tables and Borders toolbar (refer to Figure 8.7). Sometimes it's easy to modify a table simply by using the mouse or menus. Other times, the Tables and Borders toolbar can be quite handy.

If the Tables and Borders toolbar is not visible, simply click the Tables and Borders button on the main toolbar. If that button is already highlighted, look around, and you might find the toolbar docked somewhere or in another toolbar. If that is the case, simply drag the dotted left end of the Tables and Borders toolbar out into the slide editing area of the screen (refer to Figure 8.7).

You use the top row of buttons on the Tables and Borders toolbar when drawing a custom table. You generally use the bottom row when modifying an existing table. Instead of explaining the toolbar here in detail, the next several sections point out the toolbar buttons that accomplish the tasks being discussed. If you ever have questions about what a button does, you can just hover the mouse pointer over the toolbar buttons to see what they are for or click them to see what happens. You can always use the Undo feature!

Adjusting Columns and Rows

Evenly spaced columns and rows look nice...until you begin to put data in the table cells. It soon becomes evident that some columns need more width than others. If you increase the width of a column, other columns must become smaller. Increasing the size of rows, however, simply makes the table longer. Nevertheless, too many large rows on a PowerPoint slide can also present a problem.

To change the width of a column, follow these steps:

1. Move the mouse pointer to the line that separates the two columns you're going to change. The mouse pointer turns into a double line, with arrows pointing in opposite directions. Figure 8.8 shows column lines being changed.

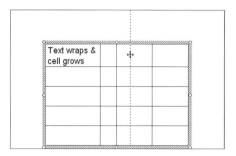

2. Click and drag the line right or left.

3. Release the mouse button to relocate the column line.

4. Repeat these steps until the columns are spaced appropriately for the data they contain.

You can also adjust the height of table rows. To do so, simply follow these steps, but instead of dragging column lines, drag row lines up or down. Note, however, that you can't decrease the height of a row to anything smaller than the height of a single line of text.

There are some aids that can help you measure column widths or row heights (for example, the ruler or grid lines) or to space selected columns or rows evenly (the Distribute Rows/Columns Evenly buttons on the Tables and Borders toolbar). However, although precise table measurements might be important in a Word document, PowerPoint tables are going to be viewed from a projected computer screen. If column and row measurements look good to you onscreen, that's all that really matters.

Besides adjusting the sizes of rows and columns, you might find that you need to add a column or row, or you might need to remove one. To insert a column, follow these steps:

1. Position the insertion point where you want to add the column.

2. Click the Tables and Borders button to display the Tables and Borders toolbar, if it's not already visible.

3. On the Tables and Borders toolbar, click T**a**ble and from the drop-down menu, choose the Insert Columns option you need. Insert Columns to the **L**eft inserts a column to the left of the current location, and Insert Columns to the **R**ight inserts one to the right of the current location (see Figure 8.9).

FIGURE 8.9
After you insert columns or rows, you might need to adjust them to fit on the PowerPoint slide.

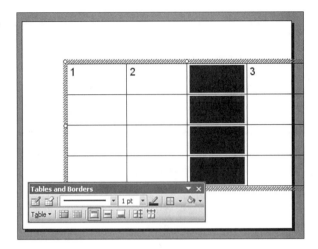

4. Adjust the column widths to make the table fit within the slide's boundaries.

You follow a similar procedure to insert or delete multiple rows or columns. First, select the rows or columns you want to insert or delete. For example, if you want to insert two rows, select two rows in the current table at the location you want to insert new rows. Then from the T**a**ble button on the Tables and Borders toolbar, choose from among the available options (Insert/Delete to the Left, Right, Above, or Below).

Splitting and Merging Cells

Have you ever noticed that many forms, such as invoices, are organized much like tables? Indeed, most of them look like tables, except that some rows or columns seem to have more or fewer cells. To create form-like tables in PowerPoint, you can vary the number of cells in any given row or column of a table. Consider, for example, the table shown in Figure 8.10. Some parts of the table appear to have fewer cells than they should, and others seem to have extra cells. You create this effect by *merging* or *splitting* cells.

 To split a cell, position the insertion point in a cell and click the Split Cell button on the Tables and Borders toolbar. The cell then splits into two equal-sized cells (see Figure 8.11).

caution

When you delete a column or row, PowerPoint also deletes the contents of all the cells in that column or row, without asking if that's okay.

If you accidentally delete a row or column, you can use Undo to get it back.

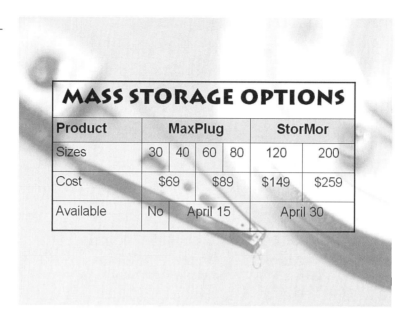

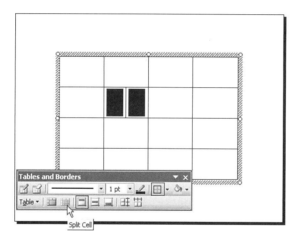

To merge or join two or more cells, click and drag the mouse to select the cells, and then do one of the following:

- Click the Merge Cells button on the Tables and Borders toolbar.

- Right-click the selected cells and from the context menu choose **M**erge Cells.

In Figure 8.10, note that the top row of cells has been merged, and the cells in the last three rows have been split and merged.

If you try to merge cells that can't be merged, the Merge Cells button or menu appears grayed out, and you aren't able to merge the cells. Sometimes you have to merge certain cells first and then merge the resulting cell with other cells.

Modifying Borders, Lines, and Backgrounds

Tables, in and of themselves, help an audience visually organize information you present. However, you can add even more visual help by using colored lines or backgrounds.

By default, PowerPoint table cells are separated by thin single black lines. You can change the lines around a single cell, or you can select several cells, including all the cells in a table, and change several lines at once.

To modify table lines, follow these steps:

1. Position the insertion point in the cell you want to change.

2. Table ▾ Click the Table button on the Tables and Borders toolbar and choose Borders and Fill, right-click the cell and choose Borders and Fill, or choose Format, Table. PowerPoint displays the Format Table dialog box (see Figure 8.12).

FIGURE 8.12

You can change table lines by using the Format Table dialog box.

3. Select the desired line style, line color, and line width.

4. Click the buttons that correspond to the line locations you want to change, or simply click the sample cell diagram to change or add lines. Click a second time to turn off a line.

5. Click OK to apply the changes and return to the slide.

In the Format Table dialog box, you can use **P**review to check out the changes before you apply them, or you can use Cancel to abort the changes. In any case, if you don't like the changes you make, you can use Undo.

You might have noticed the diagonal line options (refer to Figure 8.12). These can be useful in at least a couple ways:

- You can use a diagonal line to divide a cell where you want two pieces of information, for example a check mark if a person is attending, and a number for the number of guests attending with the person.

- You can use two diagonal lines to create a check mark, indicating that a cell is full, selected, or not available.

If you select multiple cells, you can also change the interior lines of the selected cells. For example, you can select all the cells in a table, make the outside lines one style and color, and make all the interior lines another style and color.

On a PowerPoint slide, table lines can sometimes stand out too much. If this seems to be the case on a slide, you can turn off a line or lines to give the appearance of merged cells while maintaining the structure of multiple cells. This technique is useful if you want to organize textual material by using a table structure but without making it look like you're using a table.

Another way to soften the effect of table lines is to use fill colors instead. For example, you could turn off lines altogether and provide shading for alternating rows.

To change cell fills, follow these steps:

1. Position the insertion point in a single cell or click and drag to select multiple cells.

2. Choose F**o**rmat, **T**able. PowerPoint displays the Format Table dialog box.

3. Select the Fill tab (see Figure 8.13, which shows the Fill **C**olor drop-down list box displayed).

FIGURE 8.13

You can change the fill or background of table cells by using the Format Table dialog box.

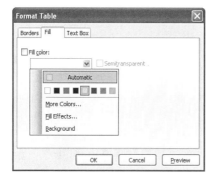

4. Select a fill color from the drop-down Fill **C**olor list box. These are the choices:

    ■ *Automatic*—These are colors that coordinate with the slide design.

    ■ **M**ore *Colors*—These are colors from a Standard or Custom color palette.

    ■ **F**ill *Effects*—These effects include gradient shades of two or more colors.

    ■ **B**ackground—This is a color that matches the slide's background.

5. Select the Semi**t**ransparent check box if you want the slide's background to show through the fill you've chosen.

6. Click OK to apply the changes.

Figure 8.14 shows an example of a fill that sets off the table but also allows the background to show through.

FIGURE 8.14

Semitransparent fills allow the slide's back-ground to show through.

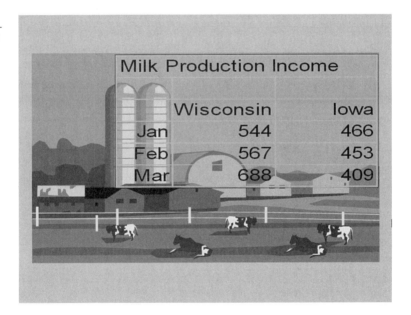

Drawing a Custom Table

Because you seek visual effect rather than technical precision in PowerPoint tables, drawing a custom table can be particularly useful. If you have in mind what you want, you might be able to draw the table from scratch more quickly than you can create a table, split and merge cells, and adjust column widths to get the same effect.

To draw a custom table, follow these steps:

1. 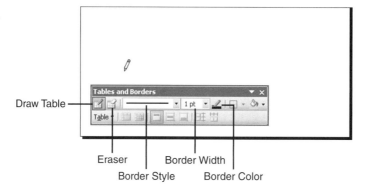 If the Tables and Borders toolbar is not visible, click the Tables and Borders button on the main. The toolbar is displayed, and the mouse pointer turns into a pencil shape (see Figure 8.15).

FIGURE 8.15
You can use the Tables and Borders toolbar to draw a custom table.

Draw Table

Eraser

Border Style

Border Width

Border Color

2. In the slide area, click and drag from where you want one corner of the table to appear to where you want the other corner.

3. Release the mouse button. PowerPoint inserts a blank table.

4. Continue using the Draw Table tool by clicking and dragging where you want vertical, horizontal, or diagonal lines. PowerPoint inserts the lines exactly where you draw them. Figure 8.16 shows an example of a custom table that you could draw by using this method.

FIGURE 8.16
Drawing a custom table enables you to draw columns and rows quickly and easily, just the way you want them.

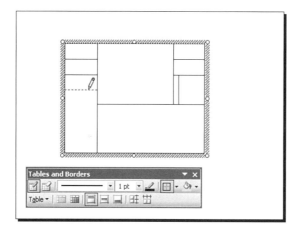

5. 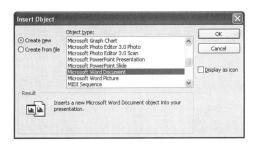 If you want to remove a line, click the Eraser button, move to the line you want to erase, and click to remove the line.

6. Click any of the line style buttons and then click existing lines to change them or draw new lines in the selected styles.

7. When you finish the table, click anywhere outside the table box to turn off the Draw Table tool.

Importing Tables from Word or Excel

If you're familiar with tables in Word or spreadsheets in Excel, you have probably noticed some of the limitations of tables in PowerPoint. For example, you can't perform mathematical calculations in PowerPoint tables as you can in Excel spreadsheets. And you can't use a table in PowerPoint to contain and organize graphic images as you can in a Word table.

Fortunately, you have the option of creating Word tables or Excel spreadsheets inside a PowerPoint slide show.

To create a Word table in PowerPoint, follow these steps:

1. Choose **I**nsert, **O**bject. PowerPoint displays the Insert Object dialog box (see Figure 8.17).

FIGURE 8.17

You can insert Word tables by using the Insert Object dialog box.

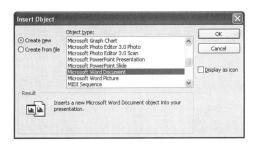

2. Leave the Create **N**ew button selected, and from the Object T**y**pe list, select Microsoft Word Document.

3. Click OK. PowerPoint opens a window on the PowerPoint slide, but it displays menus and toolbars for Word (see Figure 8.18, which also shows a Word table already created).

4. Create a Word table, including text or graphic images, and then click outside the table box to return to PowerPoint.

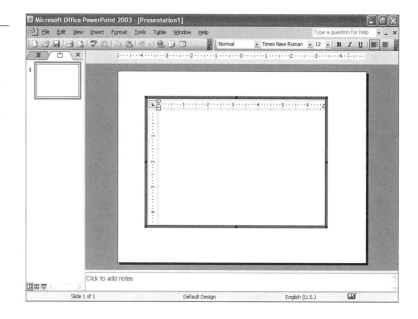

At this point you can move, size, or format the Word object by adding a border, adding a fill background, and so on, although some changes to the table itself might be better done in Word.

To create an Excel spreadsheet in PowerPoint, you follow these steps:

1. Choose **I**nsert, **O**bject. PowerPoint displays the Insert Object dialog box (refer to Figure 8.17).

2. Leave the Create **N**ew button selected, and from the Object T**y**pe list, select Microsoft Excel Worksheet.

3. Click OK. PowerPoint opens a window on the PowerPoint slide, but it displays menus and toolbars for Excel.

4. Create a spreadsheet that includes numbers, labels, or formulas.

5. Click and drag the lower-right corner of the Excel worksheet box to trim the cells you're not using.

6. Click outside the worksheet box to return to PowerPoint.

At this point you can move, size, or format the Excel object by adding a border, adding a fill background, and so on (see Figure 8.19).

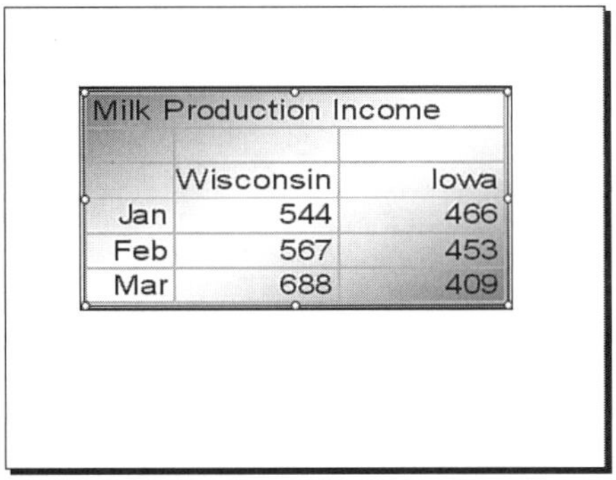

FIGURE 8.19
You can add attractive formatting to an Excel worksheet object in PowerPoint.

Milk Production Income		
	Wisconsin	Iowa
Jan	544	466
Feb	567	453
Mar	688	409

caution

It's tempting to take advantage of Word or Excel to create detailed tables or worksheets. Remember, however, that in a PowerPoint slide, you need to keep the amount of information to a manageable minimum. At the very least, audience members from the back row have to be able to read the table or worksheet text.

Finally, you can import existing Word documents or Excel spreadsheets. However, doing so inserts the entire document, not just a table or part of a spreadsheet. Instead of importing entire Word or Excel documents, it's probably better to create PowerPoint-sized bits of information—for example, a small table or spreadsheet—instead of large documents.

THE ABSOLUTE MINIMUM

Using tables is a great way to organize textual information in ways that the audience members can quickly understand. In this chapter, you did the following:

- You learned how to create simple tables.
- You found out how to move around in a table and add text and other information.
- You learned to adjust and insert columns and rows.
- You explored the use of lines, borders, and fills to enhance table data.
- You created tables by using the Draw Table tool.
- You learned to create Word tables and Excel spreadsheets from within PowerPoint.

Chapter 9, "Presenting Numbers with Data Charts," focuses on how to present numeric information by using data charts.

IN THIS CHAPTER

- Find out how charts can make numbers understandable

- Learn how to use the Microsoft Graph program

- Explore the wide variety of chart types available in PowerPoint

- Learn how to enter chart data and import it from other sources

- Find out how to modify individual chart elements to make them more effective

9

PRESENTING NUMBERS BY USING DATA CHARTS

For those of us who come from relatively nontechnical, nonnumeric backgrounds, the very thought of creating data charts causes fear and trepidation. You might ask "What is an x-axis anyway?" or "Why do I want an area chart instead of a pie chart?" Or perhaps you're even asking whether you want to create a data chart at all.

In my experience, *data charts*—graphic representations of numeric information—can be quite useful in sometimes rather unexpected ways. But most of all, they help an audience understand how numbers relate to each other. They show trends and patterns, and in other ways they put a visual face on otherwise nondescript lists of numbers. In Chapter 8, "Organizing Information by Using Tables," you learned how to present numbers in tables. Although that helps an audience sort out numbers, data charts can really bring those numbers to life.

If you're already a numbers and charts type of person—for example, if you already create charts by using Excel or some other program—you'll find it easy to understand what's presented in this chapter. But even if you're new to numbers and charts, you'll find that PowerPoint makes it easy to create powerful, effective, and memorable data charts.

Inserting a Data Chart

The first step in creating a chart is to decide how you want to insert the chart object. Several PowerPoint layouts use the content placeholder, which includes an icon for creating a chart. For example, to create a slide that contains a title and a chart, follow these steps:

1. Choose F**o**rmat, Slide **L**ayout to display the Slide Layout task pane.

2. Scroll through the list of layout types until you find one that provides for content, such as the Title and Content layout.

3. Click the layout to add placeholders to the slide (see Figure 9.1).

Insert Chart

FIGURE 9.1

Content place-
holders enable
you to quickly
insert a data
chart.

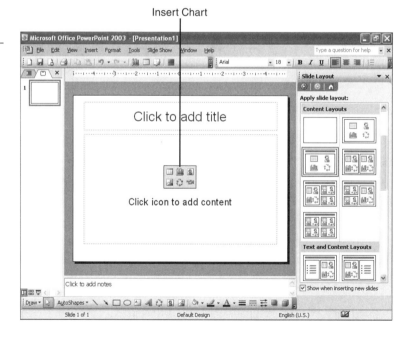

4. Click the Insert Chart icon (refer to Figure 9.1) to start the Microsoft Graph program, which automatically creates a bar chart. A separate datasheet that

contains sample numbers also appears (see Figure 9.2). At this point, you can edit the data, change the chart type, and more, all of which we'll explore in this chapter.

FIGURE 9.2

The Microsoft Graph program provides several tools specifically designed for working with charts.

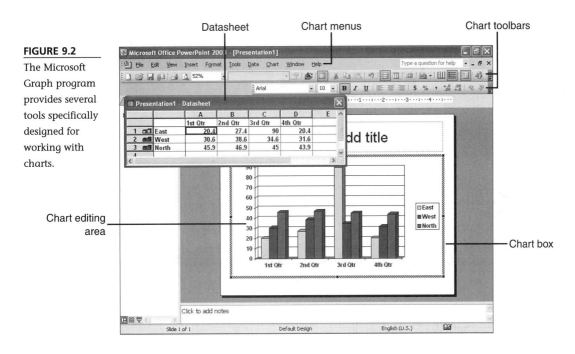

5. To return to the PowerPoint slide, click outside the chart box. PowerPoint closes the Microsoft Graph program and displays the completed chart as a PowerPoint object (see Figure 9.3).

FIGURE 9.3

Charts are objects on a PowerPoint slide.

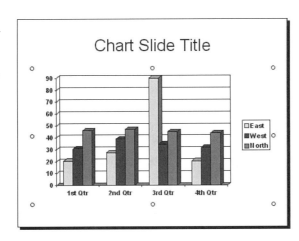

If you want to insert a chart as an object in a PowerPoint slide, without using a predefined layout, simply click the Insert Chart button on the toolbar. PowerPoint opens a chart editing screen and also displays its datasheet.

An Overview of the Microsoft Graph Program

When you open a PowerPoint chart, your eyes are so dazzled by the fancy chart that you might miss the fact the PowerPoint has actually taken you into an entirely different program: Microsoft Graph. After you use the Graph program to create a chart, you click outside the chart box to return to PowerPoint. To get back to the Microsoft Graph program, you double-click the chart.

You need to become familiar with the Microsoft Graph program so you'll know where to find things and what to do with them. To begin our exploration of Graph, we'll discard the cumbersome moniker *Microsoft Graph program* and refer to this program simply as *the chart program* or *the chart editor*. After all, that's what the Graph program is for—creating and editing charts.

When you have the chart editor open, besides seeing the datasheet and chart editor, you'll likely notice that the menus and toolbars have changed (refer to Figure 9.2). Here are some examples:

- The Slide Show menu disappears.
- Two new menus, **D**ata and **C**hart, appear.
- Other menus retain the same names but contain different and fewer menu choices.
- Two new toolbars appear, with some familiar, but also some new, buttons.

Take a few moments to click the **C**hart menu items to see what's there and to hover the mouse over the toolbar buttons to see what they are for. We'll explore several of the features and tools you see here throughout this chapter. (If you're working on a chart slide and you don't see the menu items you expect to see, look at the menu and toolbars to see whether you're in the chart editor or in the PowerPoint slide editor.)

Understanding Chart Types and Purposes

Perhaps one of the most difficult tasks you face is to determine what type of chart you need to create. Essentially, you need to decide how the numbers can best be presented to communicate the right message. Sometimes you're limited by the numbers you have at your disposal. You can even be hampered by having too much information, in which case you have to decide what's most important to represent.

Consider, for example, Figures 9.4 and 9.5. If you're interested in showing how the travel budget is eating up everything else, a bar chart showing travel expenses isn't going to help much, especially because the high equipment cost in the third quarter is what grabs the viewer's attention. However, a pie chart that shows nearly 40% of the budget being devoted to travel indeed can convey the appropriate message, especially if you enhance that portion of the pie by *exploding* the slice (that is, pulling it away from the other slices) or by adding a color or pattern that stands out.

FIGURE 9.4

Bar charts, although commonly used, may not be the most appropriate charts to use.

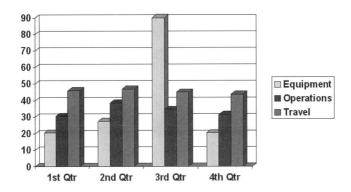

FIGURE 9.5

A pie chart with an exploded slice of data draws your attention to that chart element.

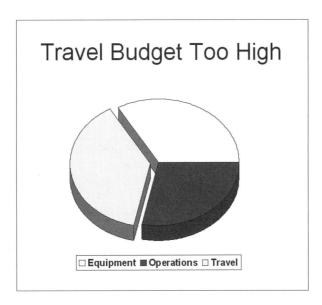

PowerPoint offers a comprehensive variety of chart types to match nearly any kind of data or presentation need. To select a chart type, follow these steps:

1. Access the chart program by double-clicking an existing chart or by creating a new one.

2. Choose **C**hart, Chart T**y**pe. PowerPoint displays the Chart Type dialog box (see Figure 9.6).

FIGURE 9.6

You can choose from many chart types in the Chart Type dialog box.

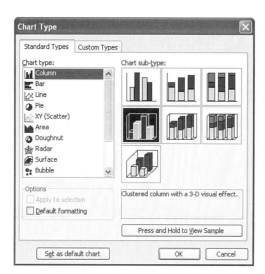

3. Scroll through the list of chart types in the Chart Types list box until you find a type you're interested in. Click the chart type to display various examples in the Chart Sub-**t**ype area on the right side of the dialog box.

4. Click an item in the Chart Sub-**t**ype area. PowerPoint displays a brief description in the box beneath the subtypes. Sometimes these descriptions also help you understand how a chart is used.

5. If you want to see what a chart looks like before you select it, click and hold the Press and Hold to **V**iew Sample button.

6. Click OK to apply the chart type to your current chart.

I won't bore you with the details of each chart type. You can easily click each type in the Chart Type dialog box to see what it looks like and what it's used for.

However, you should note the following tips as you select and prepare a chart:

- Make sure the data matches the chart type. If you have only one data series, a pie chart might be in order. If you have several series to compare, a bar chart or line chart might work.

- Eliminate data that's irrelevant to what you're trying to communicate. For example, a dozen different categories in a pie chart are likely to overshadow the one category you want to emphasize. You should combine relatively unimportant categories. The categories Phone, Office Supplies, and Photocopying Expenses, for example, could be combined in one category, Operations.

- Make sure you understand the chart type you're using and, even more importantly, that your audience does, too! If a chart speaks only to those familiar with how it works—for example, the radar chart— you might find that some audience members don't have a clue as to what you're talking about. In such cases, a picture is worth considerably less than a thousand words.

- If you're using a chart in a presentation, you can use colors to help enhance visual understanding. But if you print a chart on a black-and-white printer, readers might not be able to distinguish between one series and another. Instead of using colors, use patterns such as lines or dots so that the differences between parts of the chart are visible in black-and-white print-outs and overhead transparencies.

- Consider animating a chart, to display information bit-by-bit.

> **tip**
>
> Getting just the right kind of chart can be tricky. Sometimes it helps to take a plain old pencil and piece of paper and roughly sketch what you think you'd like to show. That'll give you an idea whether a particular chart will effectively illustrate the data.
>
> If you spend a lot of time on a chart in PowerPoint before you're sure whether it will work, you might find yourself sticking with a less-than-effective design just because you don't want to have to start over again.

⇨ For information on animating data charts, see **p. 217**.

Entering Chart Data

The basis for any chart is the data found in the chart's datasheet. You must start with accurate numbers and then make sure you arrange the numbers to match the chart type you're creating.

The simplest way to enter chart data is to type data directly into the chart's datasheet. You can also copy and paste numbers from other sources. First, however, you have to clear or modify the sample data that PowerPoint initially displays in charts.

If you're not comfortable creating a chart from a blank datasheet, you should first try selecting a chart type and modifying the sample data. After you get a feel for how the data and axis labels relate to the chart, you can clear the datasheet and build the chart from scratch.

To modify an existing datasheet, follow these steps:

1. Access the chart program by creating a new chart or double-clicking an existing one.

2. If the datasheet is not visible, choose **V**iew, **D**atasheet. PowerPoint displays the datasheet.

3. Click a cell that contains a label and type a replacement label. When you start typing, the existing data disappears. The chart also updates automatically (see Figure 9.7).

FIGURE 9.7

As you make changes to a chart's datasheet, the chart automatically updates.

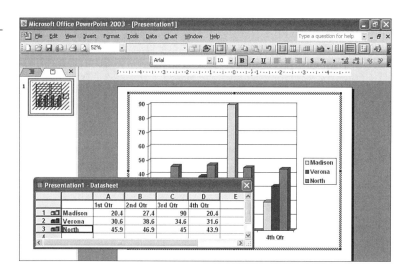

4. Move to the next label and change it. Although you can click each cell you want to change, you can also just move from cell to cell by using the arrow keys.

5. Finally, type in the datasheet cells the numbers that correspond to the intersection of labels (Sales for January, and so on).

6. If you end up with leftover sample rows or columns, move the mouse pointer to the number of the extra row or the letter of the extra column and click to select it (see Figure 9.8). Then press Delete or right-click and from the context menu choose **D**elete to remove the entire row or column.

		A	B	C	D	E
		1st Qtr	2nd Qtr	3rd Qtr	4th Qtr	
1	Madison	20.4	27.4	90	20.4	
2	Verona	30.6	38.6	34.6	31.6	
3	North	45.9	46.9	45	43.9	
4						

Presentation1 - Datasheet

To clear an entire datasheet and create a new one from scratch, follow these steps:

1. Access the chart program by creating a new chart or double-clicking an existing one.

2. If the datasheet is not visible, choose **V**iew, **D**atasheet. PowerPoint displays the datasheet.

3. Move the mouse pointer to the upper-left button of the datasheet (above the numbers column and to the left of the letters row).

4. Click once to select all the cells in the datasheet. (Remember that *cells* are the intersections of rows and columns that contain datasheet data.)

5. Press Delete to clear the datasheet.

6. Enter the labels for the x-axis at the top of the letters columns (A, B, C, and so on). The x-axis runs across the bottom of a bar chart and usually represents points in time (months, years, and so on, as shown in Figure 9.9).

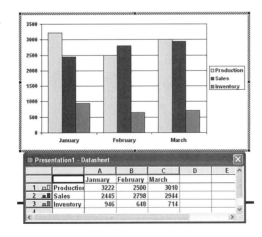

		A	B	C	D	E
		January	February	March		
1	Production	3222	2500	3010		
2	Sales	2445	2798	2944		
3	Inventory	946	648	714		

Presentation1 - Datasheet

7. Enter the labels for the series elements next to the numbers rows (1, 2, 3, and so on). *Series* are items that change from one point to the next along the x-axis, such as production figures, sales for a region, and inventory on hand (refer to Figure 9.9).

8. Enter the numbers that correspond to the labels. For example, if you produce 3,222 automobiles during January, 2,500 during February, and so on, enter these numbers (refer to Figure 9.9). By default, the y-axis numbers automatically adjust from 0 at the bottom to a rounded number just higher than the largest number in the cells at the top.

After you get the labels and numbers right, you can start to think about how the chart looks and whether it's communicating what you want it to.

Modifying Chart Elements

With the data and labels in place, you're now ready to make sure the chart looks good and communicates effectively. That's where formatting the chart elements comes in.

The first task in modifying chart elements is to verify that the chart type conveys the information in the best way possible. For example, say you create a bar chart to illustrate trends at the Rolling Thunder Motorcar Company (see Figure 9.10). You notice that the chart really doesn't make certain trends clear: It doesn't clearly show that sales are up and inventory is down.

FIGURE 9.10

This bar chart doesn't clearly represent important sales or inventory trends.

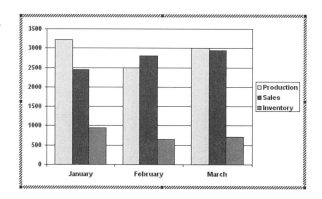

Choose **C**hart, Chart T**y**pe. The Chart Type dialog box appears (see Figure 9.11). In this dialog box, click various bar chart subtypes to see if any of those would work better than the type you are currently using. If none of them do, you should try another chart type.

You might eventually decide that a simple line chart shows trends better than some of the fancier types of charts (see Figure 9.12). Even the three-dimensional versions of the line charts seem to distract from the simple power of a standard line chart.

FIGURE 9.11

You can preview chart types to find the one that best fits your data.

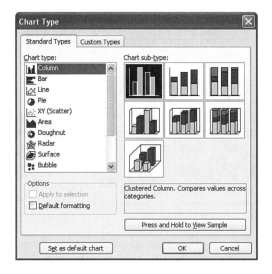

FIGURE 9.12

Sometimes a simple line chart works better than other, fancier, chart types.

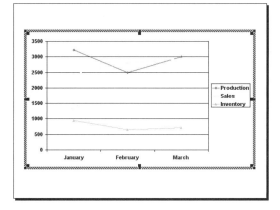

Next you need to choose from various options for the chart, including title, axis titles, and gridlines. To change chart options, follow these steps:

1. Choose **C**hart, Chart Opt**i**ons. PowerPoint displays the Chart Options dialog box (see Figure 9.13).

2. Each tab of the Chart Options dialog box offers various useful options that apply to the entire chart (see Figure 9.14, which illustrates several of these options):

   ■ *Titles*—You can add an overall title above the chart or you can add titles along the bottom (by filling in a name in the **C**ategory (X) Axis text box) or along the side (by filling in a name in the **V**alue (Y) Axis text box).

FIGURE 9.13
Chart options
apply to an
entire chart.

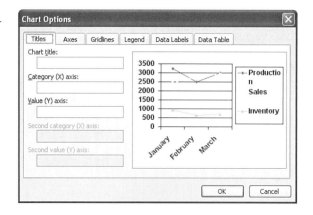

FIGURE 9.14
You can add
titles, labels, and
other options,
although using
too many
options can be
confusing.

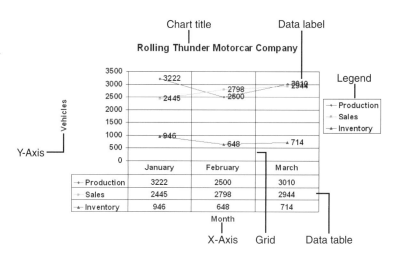

- *Axes*—You can choose to display or not display axis labels on either or both axes.

- *Gridlines*—You can display major or minor gridlines to make data points easier to correlate with corresponding axis labels.

- *Legend*—You can specify where the legend should appear, if at all.

- *Data Labels*—You can add labels that contain actual numbers at the data points in a chart. This can clutter up a chart, so you need to make sure the chart benefits from the labels before you use this option.

- *Data Table*—If you think a chart would benefit from displaying the contents of the datasheet, you can insert a data table.

3. After you choose chart options, click OK to apply them to the table.

If the results aren't quite what you hoped for, you can go back and change them again or simply click Undo.

When you have the right chart type and you've added overall chart options, you're ready to modify individual chart elements (for example, to make them more visible). For example, the lines in Figure 9.12 are too thin and the marker points too small to really distinguish which lines are which. On a color screen, PowerPoint shows the lines in red, yellow, and green, but a black-and-white printout shows hardly any difference at all among the line types.

To modify a series element (for example, the Sales series), follow these steps:

1. Access the chart editor by double-clicking the chart.

2. Move the mouse pointer to the series element you want to change. PowerPoint displays a help flag to help you identify the element (see Figure 9.15).

FIGURE 9.15

You can see what different chart elements are by simply pointing at them with the mouse.

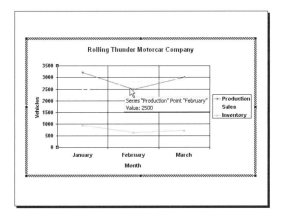

3. Double-click the element to display the Format Data Series dialog box (see Figure 9.16).

4. Choose the changes you'd like to make. For example:

   ▪ Change the line's color, thickness, or style.

   ▪ Specify whether the line changes should be smooth or angled

   ▪ Choose a marker style and its colors.

   ▪ Set a size for the marker (usually larger).

   ▪ Add a three-dimensional shadow to the marker to make it more visible.

5. Repeat steps 3 and 4 for each series element.

6. Click OK to return to the chart and see your changes (see Figure 9.17).

FIGURE 9.16

You can format individual elements, such as data series elements, by using corresponding dialog boxes.

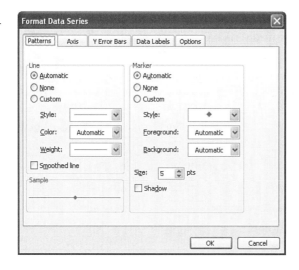

FIGURE 9.17

Changes to individual chart elements can make them more visible.

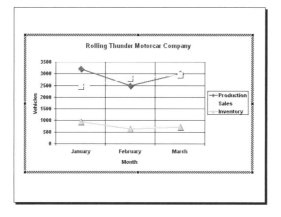

You probably noted that the Format Data Series dialog box has several tabs of options. If you're into fancy charts, you can go ahead and explore those tabs. For the rest of us, the modified chart should do for now.

You can modify chart elements easily. Just double-click something you'd like to change, and a dialog box pops up to help you change it. You can also change a number of elements by clicking corresponding buttons on the toolbar. Among the things you can change are the following:

■   You can click to select a chart element and then click the Format button on the toolbar. When you point at the button, the screen tip indicates the element you have selected to modify. Clicking the button brings up the same dialog box you get if you simply double-click the element directly in the chart.

■ ⊞ You can click the Data Table button to insert a table that contains the datasheet data (refer to Figure 9.14). Generally, the point of a chart is to avoid having to present too many numbers, but sometimes this detail can help the audience add substance to the general ideas conveyed by the chart.

■ ◪ You can quickly try out different chart types by selecting one from the Chart Type drop-down palette.

■ ⊞ You can add or remove category axis (that is, x-axis) gridlines.

■ ☰ You can add or remove value axis (that is, y-axis) gridlines.

■ ⬠ ⬠ You can select the x-axis or the y-axis and click the Angle buttons on the toolbar to rotate axis labels 45 degrees (see Figure 9.18). This is particularly useful if you have long labels and several categories. If you don't angle the labels and the labels do not fit as they're placed, PowerPoint simply displays every other label or every third label to make them more readable. Angling the labels makes it possible to display every axis label. You can also double-click an axis label, and under the Alignment tab of the Format Axis dialog box, you can fine-tune axis label angles.

FIGURE 9.18

You can angle axis labels if there's not enough room for them to display horizontally.

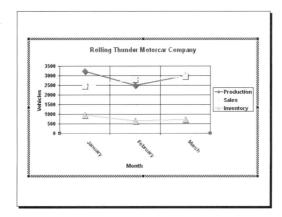

■ You can select a y-axis label and use several buttons on the toolbar to format the numeric information. For example, you can format for currency or percentage, you can add commas, and you can increase or decrease the number of zeros following decimal points.

Exploring Special Chart Formatting Options

The preceding section focuses on bar and line charts. However, some other chart types have features that deserve special treatment.

Pie charts are particularly attractive when they're shown in three dimensions. If you want to change the default angles of a three-dimensional object, follow these steps:

1. Double-click the three-dimensional chart to open the chart editor.

2. Choose **C**hart, 3-D **V**iew. PowerPoint displays the 3-D View dialog box (see Figure 9.19).

FIGURE 9.19

You can decide how a 3-D object should look by using the 3-D View dialog box.

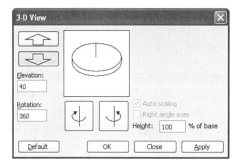

3. Adjust the object's elevation (that is, how squarely it faces you or how much it lies down).

4. Adjust the object's rotation. For example, if you want a certain piece of the pie to appear closer to the viewer, you can rotate the pie until that piece is in front, also making it look larger. (Who says you can't mess with statistics?)

5. Click OK to apply the changes to the object.

As mentioned earlier in this chapter, you can explode a pie or a single section of a pie chart. It sounds messy, but it's really not. To explode a piece of a pie chart, just click any section of the pie and drag it outward. All the pieces move away from the center equally. To regroup the slices, drag any of the pieces toward the center of the pie. To explode a single piece of a pie chart, click the piece once and then after a moment, click it again to select just that section. Then drag the section away from the center (see Figure 9.20).

Combination charts can also be effective. A *combination chart* is a chart that uses more than one type of series element to distinguish between the types of data being displayed. For example, you might use a bar chart for one element of data, a line chart for another, and an area chart for yet another (see Figure 9.21).

FIGURE 9.20

You can explode all slices or single slices of a pie by dragging them away from the center of the pie.

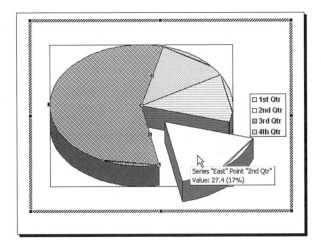

FIGURE 9.21

You can combine several chart types in one chart to make series elements stand out.

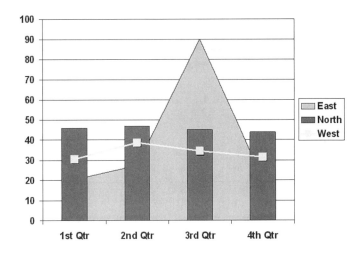

To change the chart type for a single series element, simply select the element, choose **C**hart, Chart T**y**pe, and select the chart type you want. Finally, select Apply to **S**election and then click OK. Note that you cannot combine 2-D and 3-D elements in the same chart.

Working with Charts As Objects

Charts are only part of the PowerPoint presentation picture. After you create a chart, it needs to be integrated with the slide design and other objects on a slide.

As an object, a PowerPoint chart can be moved or sized, and you can add borders and fills to the chart. However, you cannot rotate chart objects. As you size a chart, you probably want to drag the corner sizing handles to size the chart proportionally. And if you do change the chart's size, be sure to preview the slide in Slide Show mode to make sure it looks good and is readable even from a distance.

Finally, you can add text, AutoShapes, or clip art to complete a slide (see Figure 9.22).

FIGURE 9.22

You can increase a chart slide's effectiveness by adding clip art, text, and other supporting objects.

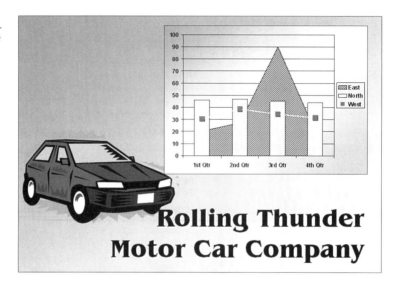

THE ABSOLUTE MINIMUM

Using data charts is a great way to present numbers visually so that viewers can more easily grasp their meaning. In this chapter, you did the following:

- You learned how to insert data charts into a PowerPoint slide.
- You found out that the Microsoft Graph program is a powerful tool for modifying data charts.
- You explored different chart types.
- You learned how to modify entire charts as well as individual chart elements.
- You learned how to combine charts with other slide objects.

In Chapter 10, "Using Diagrams and Organization Charts," you'll learn ways to visually represent textual information by using diagrams and organization charts.

In This Chapter

- Find out how diagrams can help conceptualize words

- Learn how to organize and format diagram elements

- Explore the use of organization charts in all kinds of organizations, not just in business settings

- Learn how to enter organization chart data

- Discover how to customize an organization chart

10

Using Diagrams and Organization Charts

In Chapter 9, "Presenting Numbers by Using Data Charts," you learned how to present numbers visually by using data charts. You can also present ideas visually by using diagrams. Certainly you can use graphic images to communicate ideas, but diagrams also help to show relationships between ideas or concepts. Consider, for example, Figure 10.1, which shows conceptually that more people buy cars that cost less than buy cars that cost more.

Another type of specialized diagram is an organization chart, which typically shows relationships between people but can also show relationships between products, plant or animal groups, or political groups, to name just a few examples (refer to Figure 10.1).

FIGURE 10.1
Diagrams help illustrate relationships and concepts and organization charts can illustrate relationships other than those found in business organizations.

Adding a Diagram

Adding a diagram to a PowerPoint slide is simple. You can insert a diagram directly onto the slide or you can choose a content layout and create the diagram in the content placeholder. To insert a diagram directly onto a slide, follow these steps:

1. Choose **I**nsert, Dia**g**ram or click the Insert Diagram or Organization Chart button on the Drawing toolbar. PowerPoint displays the Diagram Gallery (see Figure 10.2).

FIGURE 10.2
PowerPoint offers organization charts and five types of diagrams.

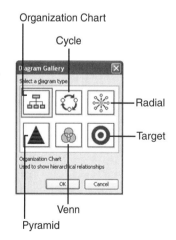

2. Click a diagram type. PowerPoint provides a brief description of the diagram type beneath the gallery of diagrams.

3. Click OK to insert the diagram into PowerPoint. PowerPoint displays not only the diagram but also the Diagram toolbar (see Figure 10.3).

FIGURE 10.3

The Diagram toolbar is extremely useful for modifying and working with diagrams.

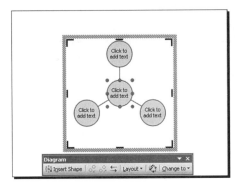

You now can use the *diagram box* (the placeholder box that contains the diagram) to create and modify your chosen diagram style.

The diagram box works much like other PowerPoint objects in that you can move it and change its order relative to other objects on the slide. However, by default, the box works more like a text box than like other objects in that as you change it, the chart inside doesn't change size. The sizing handles also have a different look (refer to Figure 10.3). If you drag any of the corner or side sizing handles outward, the size of the diagram box expands. When you release the mouse, however, the diagram inside simply centers itself in the new box, but it doesn't expand. If you drag the sizing handles inward, you find that you can't go any farther than the diagram itself.

To expand or shrink a diagram along with the diagram box, follow these steps:

1. Select the diagram box to display the Diagram toolbar (refer to Figure 10.3).

2. Click the **L**ayout button on the Diagram toolbar and choose S**c**ale Diagram. The diagram now displays normal sizing handles.

3. Drag the sizing handles to expand or shrink the diagram.

4. Click inside the diagram to return to the normal diagram box, or click outside the box to return to the slide.

Understanding Diagram Types and Purposes

As with data chart types, you have to determine whether a diagram type is right for the kind of ideas or concepts you're trying to communicate.

With the exception of the Venn diagram, I suspect you can pretty much figure out what each type of diagram is used for. Nevertheless, a brief description might help you choose the right one:

- *Organization chart*—We'll explore this option separately later in this chapter.

- *Cycle*—This type of diagram is used to show a repetitive or cyclical process. You might show a cycle in nature, such as rain to lakes to clouds and back to rain again. Or you might show an economic cycle or an editorial revision process.

- *Radial*—In this type of diagram, one item is the most important. Other items relate to but are secondary to it. Some examples might include a dictator to whom everyone answers directly or a network server and its connections or peripherals.

- *Pyramid*—You can illustrate a couple of different things with a pyramid. For example, the levels could correspond to numeric quantities, with larger quantities at the base and smaller ones at the top. Or you could indicate fundamental, or first-step, items at the bottom, with finished products or results at the top.

- *Venn*—This diagram type is used to show overlapping areas between elements. For example, you could use it to show how three government agencies have responsibilities for some of the same people or services. The overlaps can indicate just how much overlap there is, and the diagram can even identify the areas of overlap.

- *Target*—With this type of diagram, you can illustrate ideas that lead to a central idea or steps toward a targeted goal. Usually the most important of the ideas is at the center. The center of a target diagram could also represent the "right" answer, with the outside circles representing good ideas that aren't quite right.

Adding and Organizing Diagram Information

After you insert a diagram (refer to Figure 10.3), you can modify it. For now, let's talk about the radial diagram. Much of what you learn with one diagram type also applies to others. Later in this chapter you'll learn about specific issues related to other diagram types.

> **tip**
>
> Before you begin working on a diagram, consider sketching a diagram with paper and pencil, keeping in mind the basic diagram types available to you in PowerPoint. When you find something that works, create it in PowerPoint. You'll waste less time and use the diagram more appropriately if you do.

Although you might be tempted to worry about things like colors and shapes, focus first on the content of your diagram. For example, Figure 10.3 shows a central object and three peripheral objects. Its goal is to show the relationship between a network server and four objects: a printer, a desktop computer, a laptop computer, and the Internet.

To add a shape to a diagram, simply click the **In**sert Shape button on the Diagram toolbar. You can also right-click the shape and from the context menu choose **In**sert Shape. By default, the diagram is controlled by the AutoLayout feature, so when you add a shape, PowerPoint also adds a connecting line and adjusts all connected shapes proportionally (see Figure 10.4, which shows a diagram with text added).

FIGURE 10.4

PowerPoint's AutoLayout feature adjusts a diagram automatically as you add or remove elements.

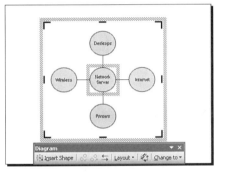

You can continue to add shapes as needed, or if you decide you need to remove one, you right-click the shape and choose **D**elete Shape. Note that you must click the very edge of the shape, or you won't get the context menu that allows you to insert or delete a shape.

You're now ready to begin adding textual information. The text placeholders tell you what to do, so click and begin typing. For example, type Network Server in the center circle, and type the connecting devices in the other circles (refer to Figure 10.4).

If you type a lot of text, you'll notice immediately that the text does not wrap like it does in normal text boxes. For example, if you want "Network Server" to fit within the circle, you need to press Enter after "Network" and type "Server" on a second line.

You should try to keep your text brief—for two reasons. Too much text is hard to digest, and very small text is hard to read. However, if your text doesn't fit within a shape, you can select the text and change the font or font size as needed. You can also enlarge shapes. You'll learn more about this option in the next section, "Formatting Diagram Elements."

After you add text to the various diagram elements, you can also change their order. For example, you might decide you want the Internet circle (refer to Figure 10.4) to appear at the top of the diagram instead of at the right side. Although you could delete the text and type it over, there's an easier way.

To change the order of a diagram element, follow these steps:

1. Select the element you want to change. Note that some elements cannot be changed in this manner (for example. the center element in a radial diagram).

2. Click these buttons, as appropriate, on the Diagram toolbar:

   ■ [icon] Move Shape Backward moves the element counter-clockwise.

   ■ [icon] Move Shape Forward moves the element clockwise.

   ■ [icon] Reverse Diagram reverses the order of elements. For example, Top to Bottom changes to bottom to top on the pyramid diagram.

Formatting Diagram Elements

[Arial ▼] PowerPoint provides a gallery of predefined diagram styles that apply to any of the diagram types you insert. To access this gallery, select the diagram and then click the AutoFormat button on the Diagram toolbar. PowerPoint displays the Diagram Style Gallery.

The default style is nicely understated. Some of the other styles, however, add pizzazz and sometimes even border on the garish. Click each style to see what it looks like in the preview box. When you find one you like, click **A**pply. Figure 10.5 shows three styles: thick outline, gradient, and square shadows.

You can also format individual diagram elements the same way you do other graphic images, with a few limitations. For example, to change the line or the fill of a diagram shape, follow these steps:

1. Select a diagram shape. If you see a hash mark box around the shape, you need to click the edge of the box to display what look like sizing handles (refer to Figure 10.3). Note that each handle contains a small x, which simply means that at this point you can't really use it for sizing the object.

2. Right-click inside the diagram box, but not on the diagram itself, to display the context menu. If Use A**u**toFormat is checked, click it to deselect it. If it's already unchecked, click elsewhere to close the context menu.

3. Double-click the shape or right-click and choose Format Aut**o**Shape. PowerPoint displays the Format AutoShape dialog box.

FIGURE 10.5

PowerPoint's
automatic
diagram styles
range from sub-
tle to loud, to
match the tone
of almost any
slide show.

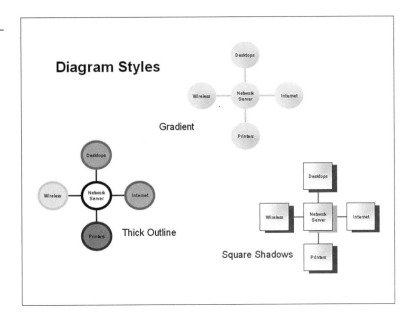

4. Change the fill color, gradient shading, pattern, or picture as desired.

➪   For details on changing AutoShape fill colors or lines, see **p. 130**.

5. Change the line color, style, and thickness, as desired.

6. Click OK to apply changes to the shape.

If you want to change several shapes at the same time and in the same way, select them all by holding down the Shift key or the Ctrl key while clicking them. Then fol- low steps 3–6 above.

You can also use the Drawing toolbar to quickly make changes to diagram elements. Simply select the element(s) you want to change and choose from options on the toolbar such as fill, line, or text color, and line, shadow, or 3-D styles.

You can also change a shape by choosing D**r**aw, **C**hange AutoShape from the Drawing toolbar.

By using these options you can come up with nearly any look you want. But be careful: You can also waste a lot of time playing with options that may add glitz but little communicative substance to a diagram.

Already you've seen that individual shapes can't be sized or moved. That's because by default diagrams are controlled by the AutoLayout feature, which simply forces the diagram objects to certain predetermined locations. If you turn off this feature, you can modify nearly any object in the diagram.

To turn off the AutoLayout feature, click **L**ayout on the Diagram toolbar and then click **A**utoLayout. If you later select AutoLayout again, shapes and connectors are restored to their original location, and changes you have made are wiped out.

Figure 10.6 shows some of the things you can do with AutoLayout turned off. For example, you can do the following:

- Size and distort shapes and lines by dragging their sizing handles
- Move shapes and lines within the diagram box
- Copy shapes and lines

FIGURE 10.6

If you turn off AutoLayout, you can reconfigure diagram elements by hand.

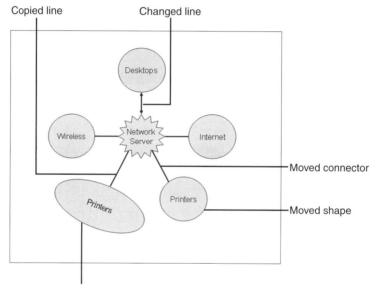

Copied line

Changed line

Moved connector

Moved shape

Copied, distorted, rotated shape

Note these peculiarities:

- You cannot rotate a diagram shape, although you can rotate a copied diagram shape.
- Text continues to move with the shapes.
- If you delete a connector, you also delete the associate shape and text, even if you've moved them so they appear disconnected.

At this point you might be wondering why you'd want to make these changes. Let's take a look at one possible reason for turning off the AutoLayout feature. Suppose you're creating a Venn diagram to illustrate breadth of responsibilities among three different groups. By turning off AutoLayout, you can increase the size of the most influential of the groups and move it to overlay a larger portion of a smaller, dependent group. You could even separate another group entirely, adding a dotted connector line to show a collaborative relationship (see Figure 10.7).

FIGURE 10.7

Turning off AutoLayout enables you to modify the size and location of diagram ele-ments to more accurately illus-trate your point.

Inserting an Organization Chart

Organization charts, often referred to as *org charts*, are diagrams, but their purpose is explicitly to show organizational relationships. You might assume that such charts are used only in a business setting to show who's the boss and how he or she is related to others in the organization. However, organization charts can be used for groups or clubs, churches, government, and in any other instance to visualize reporting lines. You can even use them to show hierarchical relationships, such as in the plant or animal kingdoms.

To insert an organization chart, follow these steps:

1. Choose **I**nsert, Dia**g**ram or click the Insert Diagram or Organization Chart button on the Drawing toolbar. PowerPoint displays the Diagram Gallery (refer to Figure 10.2).
2. Click the Organization Chart icon if it's not already selected.
3. Click OK to insert an organization chart. PowerPoint displays not only the chart, but also the Organization Chart toolbar (see Figure 10.8).

You can now use the *organization chart box* (the placeholder box that contains the organization chart) to create and modify your chosen organization chart style.

The organization chart box works much like other PowerPoint objects in that you can move it and change its order relative to other objects on the slide. In fact, unlike with diagram and text boxes, dragging the sizing handles on an organization chart box enlarges or reduces the chart *and* the text within the chart boxes.

FIGURE 10.8

You can use the Organization Chart toolbar to quickly add positions or to modify chart elements.

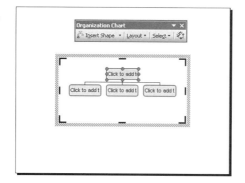

Understanding How an Organization Chart Is Organized

An organization chart is similar to a diagram, but it always requires someone or something at the head. From that point on, you can add assistants or subordinates. Except for the head, anyone can also have co-workers, as well as assistants and subordinates...if the budget allows! Figure 10.9 shows examples of relationships in an organization chart.

FIGURE 10.9

Organization chart terminology relates to employee relationships, but chart elements can also be used to show other kinds of relationships.

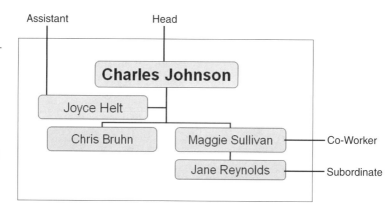

Organization chart layouts fall into four basic types. To see and change these types, click the drop-down menu on the **L**ayout button on the Organization Chart toolbar (see Figure 10.10).

- **S**tandard—The organization chart lines branch out in two directions and then down to the next tier of the organization.

- **B**oth Hanging—The organization chart lines go down first and then spread out sideways to both sides for persons of equal rank.

- **L**eft Hanging or **R**ight Hanging—The organization chart line goes down and then all the items in the same tier are either at the left or the right, respectively.

Each organization chart level can have its own layout style, making it possible to fit more positions in a limited amount of space.

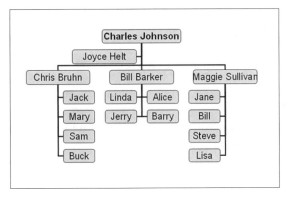

The layout you choose sometimes has more to do with how many items you have to fit in the chart than it does with rank. However, you also need to choose a layout that shows as clearly as possible the relationships between various items in the chart.

Entering Organization Chart Data

What comes first: the organization or the people in it? Let's explore how to add names of people first, and then in the next section you'll add, delete, and move positions.

To add text to an organization chart box, do as the box says: "Click to add." PowerPoint opens a text box that fits inside the shape you selected, and it centers the insertion point both horizontally and vertically. However, this isn't any ordinary text box. Here's what happens as you add text:

- Text does *not* wrap within the text box.

- You can press Enter to force a new line, but the organization chart box does not expand to accommodate the text.

- If you type too much text, PowerPoint displays the text outside the box. If you click the Fit **T**ext button on the Organization Chart toolbar, PowerPoint reduces the font size so that it all fits, even if the result is unreadable because it's so small. This also reduces proportionally the font size of text in the rest of the organization chart. You should avoid long lines of text.

- If you must type lots of text in a box, you might prefer to select the text in that box and change its font size instead of choosing Fit **T**ext. This prevents the reduction in font size of text in other boxes.

- Text options such as spelling or style options are active in these text boxes, just as they are for any text you type in a slide.

Adding text takes some getting used to, especially if you plan to include a lot of positions or if positions have long names.

Modifying Organization Chart Elements

I suspect there aren't many organizations that have as few people as are shown in the default PowerPoint organization chart (refer to Figure 10.8). Therefore, you need to add members of your organization and make their relationships clear. Fortunately, adding, deleting, and moving members is easy. All you have to do is select the point of the organization that you plan to modify and then remember three basic types of relationships.

To add a member, click a box in the organization chart to which the person will be linked and then click the I**n**sert Shape drop-down menu on the Organization Chart toolbar to select one of these three relationship types (see Figure 10.11):

FIGURE 10.11

Select a chart member before inserting a related position.

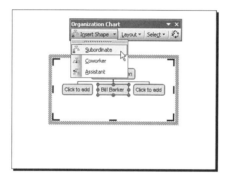

- **S**ubordinate—Typically, this shape is appended beneath the currently selected position. The line connecting the two usually signifies a subordinate role or that the added person reports to the person he or she is appended to.

- **C**oworker—Typically, this shape is appended to the same position as is the selected position. The new box and the selected one report to the same person.

- **A**ssistant—An assistant can be defined in a number of ways. Generally, although the assistant has the "ear" of and a special relationship with the "boss," those who report to that boss don't have to go through the assistant (unless, of course, you work at the White House).

As you add individuals to the organization, the size of the shapes and the text they contain gets smaller, to make room for everyone.

After you create a chart, it's also easy to move people around, reorganizing and promoting, demoting, hiring, and firing as you will. But don't let the power go to your head...this is only an exercise!

To move part of an organization, follow these steps:

1. Click the top person in the group you want to move.

2. If the selected person also has subordinates, you must first select the entire branch. Choose Sele**c**t from the Organization Chart toolbar and then choose **B**ranch. PowerPoint selects the whole branch (see Figure 10.12).

3. Drag the top person in the branch directly on top of the person to whom he or she will report (for example, the State Beat group).

tip

If you need to create a detailed organization chart but have limited space to do so, you can consolidate areas of the chart by showing departments rather than individuals. You can also create the top-level employees (for example, department heads) and then indicate that "Department X" continues on slide *nn*. Then on slide *nn*, the department head shows as the head of that slide's organization chart.

FIGURE 10.12

To move a position that has subordinates, you must first select the entire branch.

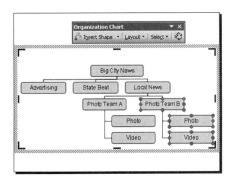

4. Release the mouse button to move the group (see Figure 10.13). If you get it wrong, try again or use Undo to start over.

Note that you can't move an individual and leave subordinates hanging by themselves. If you move a person, you have to move his or her entire branch.

However, if you delete a position, you automatically promote subordinate positions. If you want to remove a person but maintain the organizational relationships, delete the text from the shape—don't delete the shape itself.

FIGURE 10.13

When you move a branch, the AutoLayout feature automatically adjusts the location and shape of lines and boxes for the entire chart.

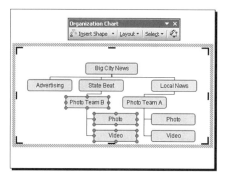

Play around a bit by adding, deleting, and moving positions. With a little practice, you'll be able to create accurate organization charts in no time at all.

Formatting Organization Chart Elements

PowerPoint's default organization chart elements are like other diagram chart elements because they depend on the background design being used. You can modify an entire chart by using the AutoFormat option:

1. Select the organization chart.

2. Click the AutoFormat button on the Organization Chart toolbar. PowerPoint displays the Organization Chart Style Gallery, which is similar to the Diagram Style Gallery, but which includes additional options.

3. Click diagram styles to preview what they look like. For example, one style that is used only for organization charts is the Brackets style (see Figure 10.14).

FIGURE 10.14

Using predefined organization chart styles can save you time.

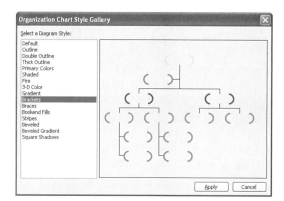

4. Click **A**pply to change the organization chart style.

You can also format individual organization chart boxes and lines, but first you have to turn off the AutoFormat feature. To change an individual shape, follow these steps:

1. Right-click the organization chart. If the context menu doesn't display Use AutoFormat, right-click somewhere else until it does.

2. If Use AutoFormat is checked, click it to deselect it. If it's already unchecked, click elsewhere to close the context menu.

3. Click a shape in the organization chart that you want to change (for example, the head of the organization; see Figure 10.15). Changes you can make include the following:

   ■ Double-click the edge of the shape to display the Format AutoShape dialog box, where you can change line colors and styles, shape fills (including gradients), and more.

   ■ Choose Draw, Change AutoShape on the Drawing toolbar and select a different shape.

FIGURE 10.15

You can change individual organization chart elements to make them stand out or to distinguish among various personnel types.

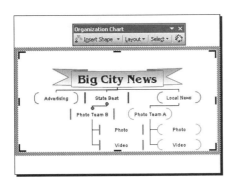

4. To further customize the shape, choose Layout from the Organization Chart toolbar and deselect AutoLayout. This allows you to do the following:

   ■ Resize or distort the shape by dragging the shape's sizing handles.

   ■ Use the shape's yellow diamond-shaped glyphs to modify angles or other features of the shape.

5. Select text or the entire shape and change the font, font size, or other font attributes.

You can also change connecting lines, individually or altogether. To change a line, follow these steps:

1. Click the line to select it and to display its edit points (refer to Figure 10.15).

2. Use the Drawing toolbar to change the line's color or to apply other line styles.

To change all lines in the organization chart at once, choose Sele**c**t, All **C**onnecting Lines from the Organization Chart toolbar. Then apply changes as you do for single lines.

Finally, you can connect chart shapes just about any way you'd like to by modifying the AutoShape connector lines (see Figure 10.16).

➡ For details on using AutoShape connector lines, see **p. 127**.

caution

If you make changes to organization chart shapes or lines and then turn on AutoLayout or AutoFormat, most of the changes you have made revert back to the original format and style.

When you decide to customize chart elements, leave AutoLayout and AutoFormat off, unless you intend to wipe out your changes.

FIGURE 10.16

Organization charts can be made to fit unusual organizational structures.

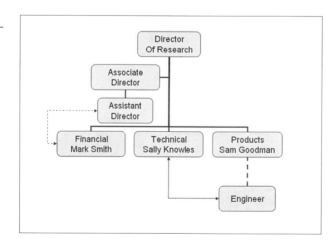

The Absolute Minimum

Diagrams and organization charts are two excellent ways of presenting relationships among concepts, facts, or people. In this chapter, you did the following:

- You learned to create effective diagrams to illustrate concepts.
- You found out that each diagram type has a unique purpose.
- You learned how to format diagram elements.
- You explored the use of organization charts for business and other situations.
- You learned to add, delete, and move organization chart elements.
- You learned how to change chart shapes and lines.

In Chapter 11, "Animating Slide Show Objects," things really jump as you learn to animate PowerPoint objects.

PART III

MAKING THE SLIDE SHOW ACTIVE AND INTERACTIVE

In This Chapter

- Find out what animation is and why you want to use it in slide shows

- Learn how to use preset animation schemes

- Find out how to apply slide transitions

- Explore how to animate nearly any object, including bullets, text, and graphic images

- Learn how to add sound effects to slide transitions and animations

- See how to animate data charts and diagrams

11

Animating Slide Show Objects

The word *animation* probably conjures up visions of Mickey Mouse or Woody Woodpecker. In cartoon animations, a sequence of still pictures shown rapidly gives the illusion of motion.

In PowerPoint, animations also create the sense of motion. Fortunately, however, you don't have to create a sequence of still pictures to get this effect. You simply tell PowerPoint where an object starts to move and where it ends, and PowerPoint does the rest.

This chapter explores the use of animations. Beyond discussing the mechanics of making things move, it also talks about *why* you use animations and what they can do to help improve presentations.

Understanding What Animation Can Do

In a sense, old-fashioned slide shows are animated. That is, you jump from one picture to the next, to the next, and so on. But in the world of PowerPoint, you do that and much more. You can, for example, do the following:

■ You can determine how slides transition from one slide to the next, including the use of fades, wipes, dissolves, and so on. If you're not sure what these terms mean, don't worry: We'll talk more about them later in this chapter.

■ You can determine how objects appear onscreen. Words, phrases, or graphic images can appear at the same time as the slide appears, or they can be made to appear sometime after the slide begins. For example, you could show the title "Birds of Prey" and then add the bullet "Eagle," then a picture of an eagle (see Figure 11.1), and finally, after you discuss that bird, you can add "Hawk," followed by another picture, and so on.

FIGURE 11.1

Adding bullets and graphic elements one at a time helps keep the audience focused.

■ You can determine how long pictures remain onscreen and how they exit. For example, in the preceding example, you could make the eagle fly away before you talk about the hawk.

■ You can make things move from one point onscreen to another. For example, you could trace a bird's migration path by having a pointer actually move along the path.

■ You can use animations to simulate pointing, drawing, growing, and so on. For example, if you have a line that connects a label at the left to an image at the right, when you wipe right, it appears that you're actually drawing the line from the label to the image. Or you could make an arrow fly in from the left to make it appear that you're shooting the arrow.

Before we go much further, let's get something clear: Animations can be great fun, but they can also be annoyingly distracting. While there can be a place for gratuitous animation, there's even more use for properly applied animations. For example, a word falling onto the slide with a bomb sound might wake your audience up. But an animation that adds a slowly moving arrow between Wisconsin and California to illustrate a gradual shift in milk production dominance can help audience members understand and remember what they see.

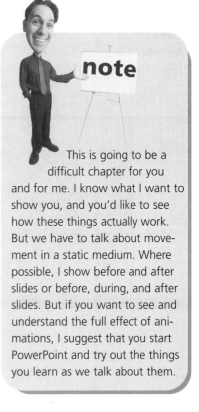

note

This is going to be a difficult chapter for you and for me. I know what I want to show you, and you'd like to see how these things actually work. But we have to talk about movement in a static medium. Where possible, I show before and after slides or before, during, and after slides. But if you want to see and understand the full effect of animations, I suggest that you start PowerPoint and try out the things you learn as we talk about them.

Using Preset Animation Schemes

Animated cartoon illustrators spend weeks creating individual drawings to produce just a couple animated minutes on film. Fortunately, PowerPoint makes it much easier to create effective and professional-looking animations. One way is by using *animation schemes,* which are predefined animations applied to transitions, titles, and bullets in a PowerPoint slide.

Many slides are bullet slides, and you often need to make one bullet appear at a time; using animation schemes is a quick way to accomplish this. To apply an animation scheme to the text of a slide, follow these steps:

1.   ⌨ Slide Show   Choose Slide Show, Animation Schemes. PowerPoint displays the Slide Design task pane, with Animation Schemes selected. You can instead click the Design button, and then in the task pane, click Animation Schemes (see Figure 11.2).

FIGURE 11.2

You use the task pane to work with animation schemes.

2. Choose an animation scheme from these categories (you may have to scroll to see all the categories):

   ■ *Recently Used*—This includes schemes you've just used, so you don't have to search for them each time.

   ■ *No Animation*—This scheme turns off animation on the slide and is sometimes the best choice.

   ■ *Subtle*—This scheme involves gentle animations, such as wipes, fades, and dissolves. In most cases these are appropriate and may even be less distracting than no animation at all where slides jump from one to the next.

   ■ *Moderate*—This scheme helps you get a little more attention, with text that ascends, descends, zooms, or spins in. Generally, however, the effects in this scheme are still relatively subtle.

   ■ *Exciting*—Although the effects in this scheme offer the most pizzazz, you should reserve these animations for unusual situations, such as a self-running slide show at a trade convention booth. The novelty of these animations wears off quickly.

3. If the AutoPreview check box is checked, PowerPoint plays the animation once, but you can click the Play button at the bottom of the task pane to repeat the animation.

4. Click Slide Show to see how the animation works in a real slide show. The preview automatically plays all the transitions, but in the Slide Show view you can see what's automatic and what's not.

5. If you want to apply the same animation scheme to all the slides in a slide show, click the Apply to All Slides button.

That's easy, isn't it? Try several different animation schemes to see what they do, and you'll soon have a sense of what is meant by subtle and exciting. You'll also soon notice that not everything moves in PowerPoint like you'd like it to. For example, although schemes animate bullets, graphic images automatically appear when the slide appears, and they may not appear in the sequence in which you want to show them.

> ## caution
>
> Selecting different animation schemes for each slide in a slide show might seem interesting to you, but it can also be distracting to the audience. Audience members will be wondering how the next slide is animated instead of focusing on what you're trying to tell them.
>
> Glitz can become the spinach-in-the-teeth of an otherwise charming presentation.

Choosing Slide Transitions

One of the biggest differences between a standard slide show—using 35mm slides and a slide projector—and a PowerPoint slide show has to do with the way you can transition from one slide to the next. Certainly, in PowerPoint you can have each slide simply appear, replacing the previous slide. But why? Even the most conservative presentation can benefit from subtle slide transitions to help the audience move smoothly from one topic to the next.

You can apply a slide transition to a single slide or to an entire slide show. Usually I find it best to select a transition I like, apply it to all slides for consistency, and then change individual slide transitions only when absolutely necessary.

To add or change a slide transition, follow these steps:

1. Go to the slide where you intend to add a transition.

2. Choose Slide Show, Slide Transition or right-click the slide and then choose Slide Transition. PowerPoint displays the Slide Transition task pane (see Figure 11.3).

3. From the list, select any of the many options from No Transition to Random Transition. Each time you click a transition, PowerPoint previews the effect on the currently selected slide.

FIGURE 11.3

You use the Slide Transition task pane to add or change slide transitions.

4. Modify the transition by changing its speed (fast, medium, or slow).

5. Add a sound effect (you'll learn more about this later).

6. Specify how you want the slide to advance:

   ▦ *On Mouse Click*—This is the default option, and it means that you have to do something to make the slide advance (for example, click the mouse, press the spacebar).

   ▦ *Automatically After*—Selecting this box means that you can specify exactly how long the slide remains before moving to the next slide. This helps you time a self-running show or pace yourself should you get too long-winded.

   If you leave both of these boxes checked, you can advance the slide before time's up. But if you uncheck the On Mouse Click box, you have to wait the full amount of time.

7. If you want to apply the transition, speed, sound, and timing that you have selected to the entire slide show, click Apply to All Slides.

Slide transitions can add just the right touch of professionalism to a slide presentation. However, watch out for the following, especially in a live presentation as opposed to a self-running show:

- Transition speed should not be so slow that you find yourself waiting for the slide to advance.

- Using sound effects on slide transitions generally is not a good idea. Once in a while, for special impact, a sound effect might be appropriate.

- Try to avoid using the Random Transition option. You will find yourself wondering what kind of transition will take place next. You don't need this kind of distraction, and if it bothers you, you can be sure it also bothers your audience.

Creating Custom Animations

Using slide transitions and animation schemes are good ways to begin making a slide show more alive. But if you really want to make a presentation move to *your* drumbeat, you need to learn how to use custom animations. In fact, when you become familiar with animating individual slide elements, you'll find yourself using animation schemes less often, so that you don't end up with animations you're not interested in using.

Animating Bullets

Typically, you don't want to get too carried away with bullet animations. You simply want to get the information onscreen, in the proper order, and with the proper timing. You might want to add a sound effect, or make the slides appear with a special transition, but you certainly don't want to make each bullet come on the scene differently. Nevertheless, you can learn about the elements of custom animations by working first with bullets.

To customize a slide's bullet text, follow these steps:

1. Click the bullet box. If you select text for a single bullet, you create a custom animation for that bullet only. Click the edge of the box to make sure you're applying animations to all bullets in the bullet box.

2. Choose Slide Show, Custom Animation, or right-click the bullet box and choose Custom Animation. PowerPoint displays the Custom Animation task pane (see Figure 11.4).

FIGURE 11.4

The Custom
Animation task
pane enables
you to animate
individual
PowerPoint
objects.

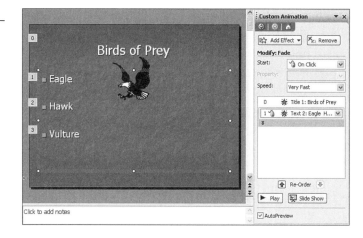

3. Click the Add Effect button. PowerPoint displays a palette of animation types (see Figure 11.5), which includes the following:

FIGURE 11.5

Animation types
fall into four
categories.

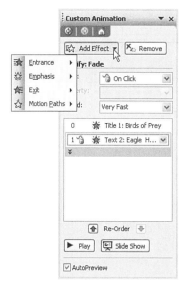

■ *Entrance*—This category assumes that the bullet is offscreen and makes
an entrance, ending up in its place in the bullet list.

■ *Emphasis*—When you select this category, the bullet is already onscreen,
but it does something such as grow, change color, or spin, to let the
audience know it's the bullet you're talking about.

- *Exit*—When you select this category, the bullet leaves the screen on its turn. This isn't usually too practical for bullet slides, but it can be for other objects.

- *Motion **P**aths*—When you select this category, the bullet is already onscreen, and it moves along a predefined path, either to a new location or to its original location. For example, each bullet could move to the right, one at a time, like soldiers stepping forward out of rank. Motion path animation calls attention to the bullet you're talking about.

4. Point to the menu type you're interested in. PowerPoint displays a list of basic choices (see Figure 11.6).

FIGURE 11.6

Each animation category includes a standard set of animation styles.

5. Click **M**ore Effects to choose from an extensive list of basic, subtle, moderate, and exciting animations (see Figure 11.7). As you click each one, you also preview it.

6. Click OK to apply the animation to all the bullets in the box.

The slide now displays numbered boxes that indicate the order in which the objects appear on the slide (see Figure 11.8). The task pane also displays additional choices for modifying the animation, depending on the style you selected:

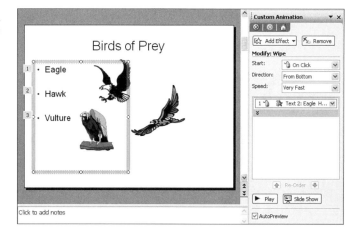

- *Start*—You can select when the animation should begin: when you click the mouse, at the same time as the previous animation, or immediately following the previous animation.

- *Direction*—You can choose the direction from which to enter. For example if you've selected wipe or fly in, you can enter from the bottom, top, left, or right sides.

- *Speed*—The speed of the animation can vary from very slow to very fast.

When you first add an animation to bullets, the animation applies to all the bullets as a group. In the task pane, PowerPoint displays only the first of the bullets. However, you can click the double arrow beneath the transition to expand the contents to display each bullet (see Figure 11.9). You can click the double arrow again to hide the contents.

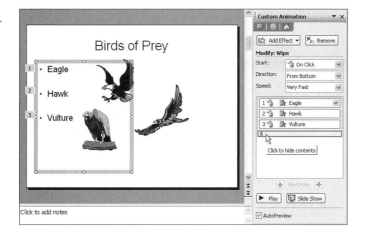

Changes you make to a group apply to all the hidden elements in the group. In fact, you can make some important changes by clicking the drop-down arrow at the right of the animated group and choosing **E**ffect Options. Or you can double-click the animation in the list. PowerPoint displays a dialog box that is named for the animation style you're changing—for example, Wipe (see Figure 11.10). The choices you see in this dialog box vary, depending on the animation style. Poke around to find out what you can do with the animation style you've selected. Wipe options, for example, include the following:

FIGURE 11.10

The name of the animation effects dialog box depends on the animation style selected.

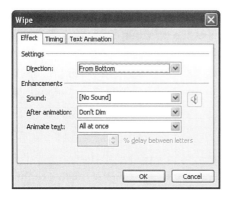

- On the Effect tab you can change settings such as the direction of the wipe or you can add enhancements such as sound, what to do after the bullet finishes its animation, or whether to animate a bullet all at once, by word, or by character.

- The Timing tab (see Figure 11.11) lets you indicate how to start the animation, how long to wait before the animation starts (for example, after a previous animation), whether and how many times to repeat the animation, and whether to rewind when the animation is done playing. (Rewinding simply means going back to where the slide show was before the animation played, which in the case of the wipe means that the bullet disappears again.)

FIGURE 11.11

You use the Timing tab to delay an animated object's entrance.

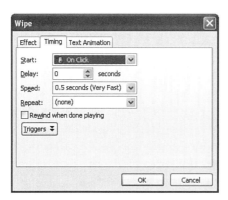

- The Text Animation tab (see Figure 11.12) contains two very important options:

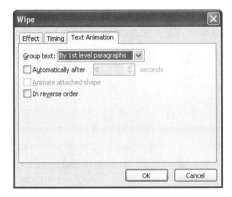

- By default, bullets are grouped by first-level paragraphs, which means that a main bullet and all its subbullets appear together. Choosing By 2nd Level Paragraphs enables you to animate subbullets one-by-one as well.

- You can make bullets appear in reverse order so that the last one appears first, as in a countdown list.

Finally, you can change individual bullets, although you should make sure there's a purpose in doing so. To change a single bullet, click the double arrow beneath the animation in the task pane to expand the contents. Then click the individual bullet you want to change and modify it just as you would a group of bullets, as described earlier in this section.

There really are so many choices that it's impossible to cover all the variations here. Play around and try things out. The more you do, the sooner you'll find a handful of animations that work well for you. Then you can begin to apply animations to your slides quickly and effectively.

Previewing Custom Animations

So far in this chapter you have learned that animations automatically play as you select them and that you can click the Play button to preview them again. The only problem with these previews is that you see only the effects and their order. You don't see other options, such as how the animation starts or how much time passes between animations.

To truly preview a slide's animations, including the transition that leads into it, you need to click the Slide Show button at the lower right of the task pane. PowerPoint then displays that slide as it appears in the slide show. You can click the mouse or press the spacebar to advance from animation to animation or to advance to the next slide. If you've used special timings, those also play automatically. Press Esc to return to the PowerPoint editor.

Using Sound Effects

I've hinted for some time that I'd talk about sound effects. Are you ready? Sound effects are nothing more than digital sound clips that you associate with animation events. For example, you can specify that a fanfare should play each time a positive bullet appears and that a groaning sound effect should play with each negative bullet by associating sound effect files with each corresponding bullet.

To associate a sound effect with a bullet, follow these steps:

1. If you haven't already added an animation, do so, either by using a scheme or a custom animation.

2. Click the bullet box, and choose Sli**d**e Show, Custo**m** Animation to display the Custom Animation task pane (refer to Figure 11.12).

3. If you want to apply the same effect to all the bullets (which is a good idea), click the double arrow beneath the group of bullet animations to hide the contents.

4. Double-click the animation or click the drop-down list box to the right of the animation and choose **E**ffect Options. PowerPoint displays the effects dialog box for the selected animation style.

5. Click the **S**ound drop-down list box to see a list of standard sound effects and then choose one (see Figure 11.13). We'll come back to this to explore a couple other options in a moment.

FIGURE 11.13

It's easy to add simple sound effects to animated objects.

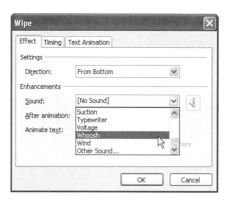

6. Click OK to apply the sound effect and to preview the animation and sound together.

In the animation effects dialog box (refer to Figure 11.13), you can select a sound clip of your own. For example, you could use the Windows recorder to record your own voice and then select that sound in this dialog box. You could also digitize a clip of music or a portion of a famous speech and then select it here. You could even search the Internet to find specialized sound effects, remembering, of course, to observe copyright laws.

To add a sound of your own to an animation, you follow these steps:

1. Choose Slide Show, Custom Animation to display the Custom Animation task pane.

2. Double-click the animation to display the animation effects dialog box (refer to Figure 11.13).

3. Click the **S**ound drop-down list box, scroll down the entire list, and click Other Sound. PowerPoint displays the Add Sound dialog box, which is the same as the Open dialog box.

4. Browse your hard drive to the location where you keep your sound files (for example, My Music). Note that PowerPoint can play only .WAV sound files. It cannot play .WMA, .MP3, or other popular types of sound files.

5. Select the sound file and click OK. The sound plays once.

6. Click OK again to associate the sound with the animation style.

Sound effects used along with bullet animations need to be used with a purpose. For example, you could associate a clip from Martin Luther King's "I Have a Dream" speech with a bullet point that reads "Martin Luther King." Typically, however, novice presenters tend to go overboard in using sound effects for bullet animation. I know because I did it, too. It's just so much fun. You quickly learn, however, that unless a sound effect helps communicate better, it's best not to use it. Nevertheless, what you've learned here works even better with other animated objects such as graphic images or individual text boxes.

Animating Graphic and Text Objects

As easy as it is to animate bullets, animation can often be even more powerful and effective when used with individual slide objects such as graphics or text boxes. For example, after displaying a bullet for the eagle on the Birds of Prey slide, you could make a picture of an eagle appear. You could even associate a sound of an eagle as the object appears.

To animate an individual PowerPoint object, follow these steps:

1. Select the object. Its sizing handles appear.

2. Choose Slide Show, Custom Animation to display the Custom Animation task pane.

3. Click the Add Effect drop-down list box to choose an effect from one of the four effect categories, such as Fly In, from the **E**ntrance category.

4. Modify how the object is to appear—for example, from the right, slowly, or when you click the mouse.

5. Double-click the animation to access the animation effects dialog box (refer to Figure 11.13) and further modify the animation (for example, add a sound effect). Click OK to close the dialog box.

Repeat these steps for all objects you want to animate. You can even add more than one animation to an object. For example, you could have a bird appear, and its next animation could be to exit. You can animate lines or circles that highlight important points. You can add objects one-by-one to create a group or collage. Figure 11.14 illustrates some possible animations. The bullet appears by itself. On a mouse click, the eagle flies in from the right. Another mouse click makes a circle and arrow wipe right to simulate pointing at the image.

FIGURE 11.14
Animations can do the same things you can do at a chalk-board, only better.

In short, think about each slide the way you've always wished you could present a slide; display items the way that makes the most sense for what you're trying to communicate.

Customizing Animation Order and Timing

It's one thing to have things appear onscreen, but it's quite another to make them appear when you want them and in the order you want them. Fortunately, PowerPoint makes it easy to adjust animation order as well as animation timing.

Consider, for example, Figure 11.15, which you see after you access the Custom Animation task pane:

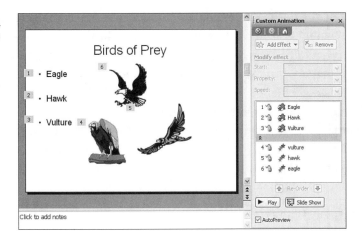

FIGURE 11.15

Numbered boxes indicate the animation order of onscreen objects.

■ On the slide, small boxes appear with numbers that indicate the order in which the objects animate. These numbers correspond to the order in which you added an animation effect.

■ In the task pane, the expanded list of animations corresponds to the numbered boxes.

■ Clicking or pointing at an animation in the task pane displays information about the animation (for example, On Click, Fly In). The visual icons also help you see what happens.

To change the animation order, follow these simple steps:

1. On the slide, click the number of the object whose order you want to change. You can also click the animation listing in the task pane.

2. Click the Re-Order buttons in the task pane to move the object up or down in the list. The animation order numbers for all objects automatically adjust to their new sequence.

Some animations work best if you click to make them start. For example, you might want to click to start each bullet item to ensure that you have enough time to talk about one before you display the next. However, if you have lots of animations, having to click each animation to advance can be tedious and unnecessary. For example, after a bullet appears, you can have its associated graphic image appear automatically. You can even have the graphic exit automatically when the next bullet item appears. You are the best judge as to what needs to appear when and how automatic you should make the bullets.

You can find the following timing options by clicking the drop-down list at the right of the animation in the task pane list or by clicking the Start drop-down list box:

- *Start on **C**lick*—This option, the default, simply means you have to initiate the animation by clicking or otherwise advancing (by using the spacebar, Page Down, and so on).

- *Start **W**ith Previous*—This option ties the object to the animation directly preceding it. When that animation begins, so does this one.

- *Start **A**fter Previous*—This option ties the object to the animation directly preceding it. However, the order is sequential. As soon as the preceding animation ends, this one begins.

Note that Start **W**ith Previous and Start **A**fter Previous change the animation order number so that both objects have the same number. One action (mouse click) causes both objects to do their thing.

Often, it's useful to add a timed delay to an automatic animation. This gives the audience a chance to mentally absorb one bit of information before you add another. For example, you could make a graphic image appear, followed in a couple seconds by a text box description. To add a delay, follow these steps:

1. Select the animated object in the task pane list.

2. Click the drop-down list box at the right of the object and choose Start **A**fter Previous.

3. Click the same drop-down menu and choose **T**iming. PowerPoint displays the animation effects dialog box for the animation style being used (see Figure 11.16).

FIGURE 11.16

You use the Timing tab in the animation effects dialog box to specify how long an object should wait before starting its animation.

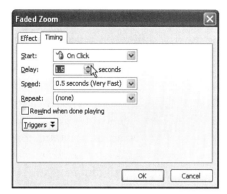

4. Increase or decrease the delay by clicking the up or down arrows or by typing the delay in number of seconds, in half-second increments.

5. Click OK to apply the timing delay.

Figures 11.18 through 11.21 illustrate an animation progression. While Figure 11.17 is showing, you announce and introduce the topic.

FIGURE 11.17

You introduce the slide show by showing only the title.

On the first mouse click, the bullet "Eagle" appears, and after two seconds, an eagle image flies in from the right, accompanied by a wind sound effect that simulates fly-ing (see Figure 11.18).

On the next mouse click, the eagle flies out to the left, and at the same time, the bullet "Hawk" appears. After two seconds, a hawk image flies in from the right, again accompanied by the wind sound effect (see Figure 11.19).

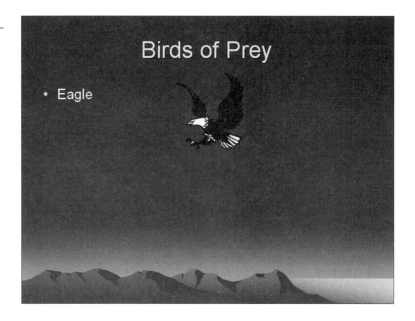

On the final mouse click, the hawk flies out to the left, and at the same time the bullet "Vulture" appears. After two seconds, a vulture image zooms in from a fade. Because the vulture is sitting, flying in wouldn't be appropriate. The vulture is also perfectly still, so no sound effect is required (see Figure 11.20).

FIGURE 11.20

The hawk
leaves, and a
vulture appears.

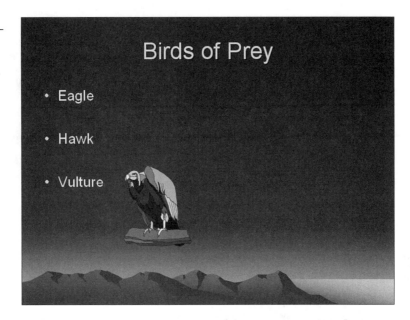

Believe me when I say that these animations are a lot more fun to watch on a computer than they are in this book. Nevertheless, you should be able to see that animation options are nearly as limitless as you want to make them. No longer do you need to think in terms of sequential slides to simulate changes onscreen. Nor do you have to resort to a chalkboard to show changes or add emphasis to illustrations. A few well-prepared, animated slides not only can help you get your point across better, but they can save lots of time by helping you illustrate your points quickly and clearly. If you've ever tried to explain a concept or procedure instead of illustrating it, you'll understand how an animated PowerPoint slide can make a positive difference.

Animating Charts and Diagrams

Like other types of slides, data charts and diagrams can also benefit from animation. However, instead of selecting and animating individual objects, you treat chart and diagram objects as a group, animating parts in sequence.

Consider, for example, a bar chart that illustrates your company's sales figures for the entire year. At a board meeting, you want to talk about sales progress over each quarter, but you want to do so by quarter, not revealing activity for the entire year. You can apply animation to a data chart by following these steps:

1. Select the data chart so that its sizing handles appear.

2. Access the Custom Animation task pane.

3. Click the Add Effect button and choose an animation style. Some styles are not allowed in data charts and are grayed out. For a bar chart, a simple wipe is often effective, and by default a chart's animation wipes from the bottom up.

4. Double-click the animation in the task pane to display the animation effects dialog box.

5. Select the Chart Animation tab (see Figure 11.21).

FIGURE 11.21

Use the Chart Animation tab in the animation effects dialog box to specify which elements to animate.

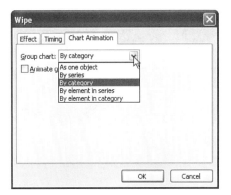

6. By default, the entire chart appears as a single object when it is animated. Click the **G**roup Chart drop-down list box to access the following animation choices:

   ▪ *Display a Whole Series at Once*—For example, you can display the East region's performance, followed by the West region's, and so on.

   ▪ *Display a Whole Category at Once*—For example, you can show the first quarter, followed by the second quarter, and so on.

   ▪ *Display Either a Series or a Category One Element at a Time*—For example, you can display the East first quarter, then the East second quarter, and so on.

7. Uncheck **A**nimate Grid and Legend. This allows the grid and legend to appear immediately. Otherwise, you have to click to animate them before you can animate the chart's data.

8. Click OK to apply the changes.

Figure 11.22 shows the chart after displaying the third-quarter results. Clicking once more displays the fourth-quarter results.

FIGURE 11.22

Presenting just
one data set at a
time helps view-
ers focus on
important
details, such as
the East's huge
increase in the
third quarter.

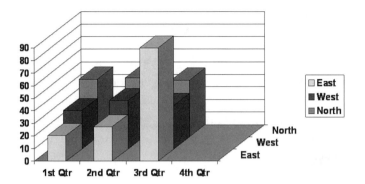

You animate diagrams in a similar manner. Consider, for example, an organization chart that shows two major branches or sections of the organization. Suppose you want to reveal one branch of the organization at a time. To animate a diagram, follow these steps:

1. Select the diagram so that its sizing handles show.

2. Access the Custom Animation task pane.

3. Click the Add Effect button to select an animation style.

4. Double-click the animation to access the animation effects dialog box.

5. Click the Diagram Animation tab. Each diagram type displays different animation options. For example, you can click the **G**roup Dialog drop-down list
   box to see the options for the organization chart (see Figure 11.23).

FIGURE 11.23

Diagram ani-
mations vary
depending on
the type of
diagram.

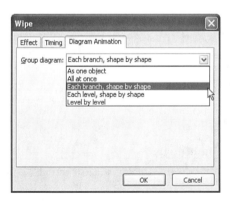

6. Select a method and an order in which to display elements of the organization chart (for example, Each Branch, Shape by Shape).

7. Click OK to apply the animation effects.

You want to display an entire branch at once, but unfortunately that isn't one of the options. Instead, you have to click to display each position in the branch, one-by-one. You can change individual elements by clicking the double arrow to expand the contents. Then you change the animation for each of the positions in the State Beat branch to start with the State Beat shape. This is a little more work, but it illustrates how flexible PowerPoint can be in letting you animate nearly anything in any order or timing.

Figure 11.24 shows the organization chart with its animation order numbering. Note that each item in the State Beat branch is numbered 3, which simply means that the third animated object is the entire State Beat branch.

FIGURE 11.24

You can modify individual diagram elements to make them appear how and when you want them to.

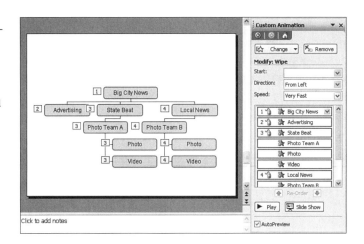

THE ABSOLUTE MINIMUM

One of the PowerPoint's greatest strengths is its capability to animate text and graphic objects, thus getting away from static presentations such as those found in books or in 35mm slides. In this chapter, you did the following:

- You found out what animations are and how to use them.
- You learned how to apply animation schemes.
- You learned about slide transitions.
- You explored the power of custom animations for bullets, text, and graphic images.
- You learned how to add sound effects.
- You discovered how you can animate charts and diagrams.

In Chapter 12, "Letting Action Settings Work for You," you'll learn how to make useful things happen when you click slide objects.

In This Chapter

- Find out what action settings are and how they can help you create a dynamic slide show

- Learn how to add action settings to PowerPoint objects

- Explore the use of action buttons

- Learn how to add action settings to text by using hyperlinks

- Discover how to create a nonlinear presentation

12

Letting Action Settings Work for You

One of the more serious drawbacks of a traditional slide show is that it locks you into a sequential presentation, one slide after another. If your presentation is strictly an exposition, with no questions or side trips allowed, that might not necessarily be so bad. But if you already present in any kind of teaching or training environment, you know that such presentations are rarely sequential.

Can PowerPoint be used in a nonlinear fashion? And if so, how? Indeed, it can. This chapter explores the use of action settings, which are tools that help you jump from what you're doing to something else, whether or not that something else is next on your planned agenda.

Using PowerPoint to Launch Actions

No longer are you forced to march through a presentation one step at a time. With PowerPoint, you can create a variety of action settings that enable you to move around freely. You can associate action settings with nearly any PowerPoint object, so that when you click the object during a slide presentation, the specified action takes place.

Creating Slide Navigation Tools

One of the most useful applications for action settings is for slide show navigation. If you're moving from Slide 1, to Slide 2, and so on, getting lost isn't too likely, and having ways to find where you are isn't terribly important. But suppose you have a slide that can take a discussion in several different directions. The topics slide in Figure 12.1 is an example of such a slide.

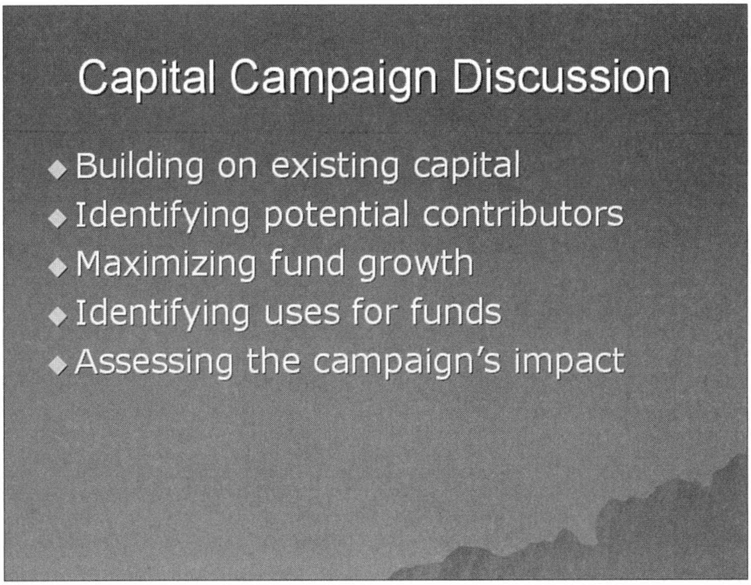

FIGURE 12.1

A topics or agenda slide can serve as a departure point for a discussion-based slide presentation.

Capital Campaign Discussion

- Building on existing capital
- Identifying potential contributors
- Maximizing fund growth
- Identifying uses for funds
- Assessing the campaign's impact

If you have set action settings for each of the bullet items, the slide becomes a "menu" or "home" slide. Click an item to jump to the slide that begins the section of slides related to that item. Then, on the last slide of that section, create an action setting that returns to the "menu" or "home" slide.

In a sense, you can make a slide show work much like a well-designed Web page: You can click links to go to areas that interest you, knowing that you'll always be able to find your way back home.

Another useful application for slide navigation is to create hidden slides that normally won't be viewed as you progress through the slide show. However, if a question or situation arises that calls for the information found on a hidden slide, you can jump to that slide. Otherwise, PowerPoint just skips right over the slide without the audience seeing it and asking, "But what about that slide you just passed?"

Launching Other Programs

PowerPoint is a great tool, but it can't do everything for you. Suppose, for example, that you have a specialized computer-based instrument tool that you want to demonstrate. Instead of having to close PowerPoint, you can create an action setting that jumps to and starts that program. When you close that program, you automatically return to PowerPoint.

What you can link to is nearly unlimited: a spreadsheet, a word processor, a database program, a photo editing program—any program that you might use outside PowerPoint.

Linking to the Internet

One of the most common uses for action settings is to open a Web browser and go to a location on the World Wide Web. For example, say you're talking about your trade agreements with Argentina (see Figure 12.2). You click an image on the slide that has an action setting, which in turn opens a browser and takes you directly to the Web page for YPF, Argentina's national petroleum company.

FIGURE 12.2

Clicking an action setting link on one slide causes PowerPoint to jump directly to another slide.

Linking to the Internet through PowerPoint expands a presentation's scope and power. Instead of trying to re-create information on slides and never being sure that it's up-to-date, you can jump directly to the Web sites that contain the latest, most complete information.

Adding Action Settings to PowerPoint Objects

Adding action settings to PowerPoint objects is quite simple. You begin by selecting an object to which you attach the action setting. Such objects can be text boxes, graphic images, drawings, charts, and so on. After you identify the object, follow these steps:

1. Select the object.

2. Choose Slide Show, Action Settings. PowerPoint displays the Action Settings dialog box (see Figure 12.3).

3. Choose an action setting and click OK.

The Action Settings dialog box offers lots of options; let's take a look at how they work.

caution

As intriguing as it is to link to the Internet, this does require that your computer be connected to the Internet while you're presenting a slide show. As anyone who uses the Internet knows, it's not always 100% reliable. You might not be able to connect, or you might be connecting during the busiest time of the day, when connections are extremely slow.

Unless you're sure you'll have a good connection, you should make contingency plans, such as having available screen shots you've already captured of the more important Web pages.

FIGURE 12.3

You use the Action Settings dialog box to create action links that go to other slides or to the Internet, launch programs, run macros, or play sound effects.

By default, the dialog box displays the Mouse Click tab. The Mouse Over tab is identical to the Mouse Click tab, but the actions on the two tabs occur in dramatically different ways:

- *Mouse click* means you have to click the linked object to make the action take place.
- *Mouse over* means that all you have to do is pass the mouse pointer over the linked object to make the action take place.

The latter method could be quite risky! Save it for things that won't accidentally send you off somewhere else. For example, a mouse over sound might be appropriate, but launching another program using mouse over could surprise both you and the audience if you mistakenly pass the mouse over the action setting.

Let's take a brief look at action settings options. We'll return later to talk about some of them in more depth. Action settings on the Mouse Click tab include the following:

- **None**—This option turns off an action setting if one is already attached to this object.
- *Hyperlink To*—This is perhaps the most commonly used setting. You can use this option to hyperlink, or jump, directly to the following:
  - *Next Slide*
  - *Previous Slide*
  - *First Slide*
  - *Last Slide*
  - *Last Slide Viewed*—The last slide viewed might not be the previous slide if you jumped to this point from somewhere else.
  - *End Show*—This closes the slide show and returns you to PowerPoint.
  - *Custom Show*—This opens a subset of the current show, if you've defined one.
  - *Slide*—This enables you to choose a specific slide in the current slide show to jump to.
  - *URL*—This enables you to jump to an Internet Web address by using a Web browser.
  - *Other PowerPoint Presentation*—This lets you open a different PowerPoint slide show.
  - *Other File*—This enables you to jump to a different document, such as a Word document, and opens the application required to display it.

■ *Run Program*—You can browse to find an application program, such as a game, a calculator, or a word processing program. When you click the object, PowerPoint opens that application.

■ *Run Macro*—If you've defined any macros for the slide show, you can select them from this drop-down list.

■ *Object Action*—If you're linking to an inserted object, such as a sound file, or to a document, this option provides choices for what you want to do with it (for example, play, edit, or open).

Let's take a practical look at two of these action options. Perhaps the most common action settings are to jump to another slide and to jump to a Web site by using a browser. Suppose, for example, that you want to jump to a hidden slide that talks about the company whose logo appears on the current slide (see Figure 12.4). Follow these steps to create an action setting:

FIGURE 12.4

You select a PowerPoint object and then add an action setting to it.

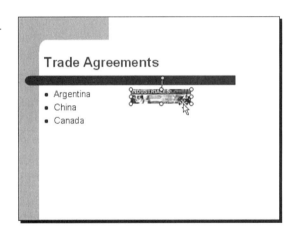

1. Select the object.
2. Choose Sli**d**e Show, **A**ction Settings to display the Action Settings dialog box (refer to Figure 12.3).
3. Click the **H**yperlink To button.
4. From the **H**yperlink To drop-down list box, choose Slide. PowerPoint displays the Hyperlink to Slide dialog box (see Figure 12.5).
5. Click a slide to jump to. The slide number for hidden slides appears in parentheses. The dialog box also shows a preview of the selected slide so you can be sure you're linking to the right one.
6. Click OK and then click OK again to return to the slide editor.

FIGURE 12.5

You can jump to another slide, go to the Internet, or open another file by using Hyperlink To options.

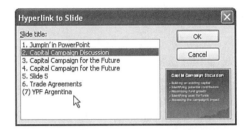

When you play the slide show and arrive at a slide on which you've added an action setting, move the mouse pointer to the object. When the pointer changes to a hand, click the object to jump to the slide you specified.

To add the other common action setting—a hyperlink to a Web site—follow the preceding steps, except that you select URL in the **H**yperlink To drop-down list box in step 4. PowerPoint displays a simple Hyperlink to URL dialog box (see Figure 12.6). Unfortunately, you can't browse to the Web site in this dialog box, so you have to type in the information, including the http:// portion of the Web address. You can, however, use a Web browser to find the Web site and then copy the address from the address toolbar and paste it into PowerPoint's Hyperlink to URL dialog box.

FIGURE 12.6

You can type or copy a Web address in the Hyperlink to URL dialog box.

The following are two other options on the Action Settings dialog box (refer to Figure 12.3) that can be used independently of the other options, or even by themselves:

- *Play Sound*—Select this option to stop a previously playing sound, add a sound effect, or browse to find a .WAV sound file to play. This could be useful in providing auditory reinforcement for an image or text onscreen. For example, you could record a famous quotation, and when you click the onscreen text, you could have the quotation read from the sound file.

  For details on adding sound effects or other sound files, see **p. 210**.

  - *Highlight Click*—This setting is just visual "fluff." Use it if you must, but it doesn't really add much to the slide show other than to show viewers where you clicked.

Creating and Modifying Action Buttons

You can link an action setting to nearly any PowerPoint object, but one object that is easy to create and is also designed for action settings is the *action button*.

An action button is a special AutoShape. After you create one, PowerPoint automatically asks you to specify the action associated with the button. Suppose, for example, that you want a button on a slide that takes you "home," back to the first slide. To create an action button, follow these steps:

1. Determine which slide is to have the action button and where you want to go when you click that button.

2. Choose AutoShapes, Action Buttons on the Drawing toolbar to see a palette of action buttons (see Figure 12.7). You can instead choose Slide Show, Action Buttons, but I like to use the Drawing toolbar because it reminds me that action buttons really are AutoShapes, with a special purpose.

FIGURE 12.7

PowerPoint provides a predefined set of action buttons to which you can add action settings of your choosing.

3. Click a button type. Nothing appears to happen, but as you move the mouse pointer to the slide area, the pointer turns to a crosshairs.

4. Click and drag the shape. Remember that holding down the Shift key while dragging forces the shape to be a square.

5. Release the mouse button to place the button on the slide. PowerPoint displays the Action Settings dialog box (refer to Figure 12.3).

6. Choose an action. For example, choose First Slide under the Hyperlink To option.

7. Click OK to return to the slide. The button remains selected.

8. Use the sizing and rotation handles to size or rotate the button or use the yellow diamond glyph to adjust the button's three-dimensional look (see Figure 12.8).

FIGURE 12.8

You can use the glyph to change the three-dimensional look of an action button.

You can also create an action button and postpone creating the button action by canceling the Action Settings dialog box. You can add the action after you size and position the button or after you decide for sure what action goes with the button. To add or change an action button setting, follow the same steps used to add an action setting to any other object.

Using Hyperlinks

In the domain of the World Wide Web, you're familiar with underlined text that signals a hyperlink to another location in the document, another document, or an entirely different Web site.

Any time you create a link between a PowerPoint object and another place or thing, you create a hyperlink. Indeed, action settings are simply another name for hyperlinks.

Creating Text-Based Hyperlinks

You can create Web page–like links on a PowerPoint slide. Suppose, for example, that you create a bulleted slide that describes the major topics of a presentation. You can create a hyperlink for each bullet to jump to the slide that begins that topic. To create a hyperlink, follow these steps:

1. Select the text that will serve as the hyperlink (for example, the first bullet in a bulleted list).

2. Choose **Insert, Hyperlink** or click the Insert Hyperlink button on the toolbar. PowerPoint displays the Insert Hyperlink dialog box (see Figure 12.9).

The Insert
Hyperlink dialog
box helps you
find and link to
slides, docu-
ments, and Web
sites.

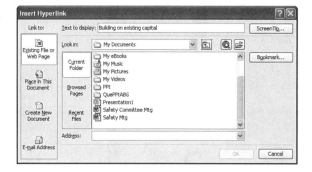

3. Find the location to link to. PowerPoint offers a wide array of link possibilities, and the Insert Hyperlink dialog box makes it relatively easy to browse to
find the link. You can choose from the following options in this dialog box:

   ■ *Existing File or Web Page*—You can search among files in the current
   folder, from Web pages you've recently browsed, or in files you've
   recently opened. You can also browse the Web or your computer's
   hard disk.

   ■ *Place in This Document*—Using this option is an easy way to find a slide
   to link to (see Figure 12.10). As you click a slide name or location, you
   see a preview of that slide, even if it's a hidden slide.

When looking
for slides in the
current slide
show, you also
see a preview of
the slide before
you select it.

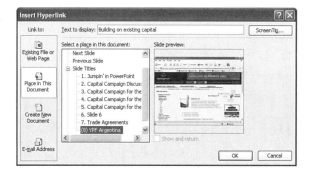

   ■ *Create New Document*—You can specify the name of a document to link
   to and then create it now or later.

   ■ *E-mail Address*—If you think the slide show might be published to the
   Web, you can create email links to where viewers can send email.

4. If you want to display a screen tip when you point at the link during the slide
show, click ScreenTip and then add a custom screen tip. This option is more
useful if you're preparing a slide show to be viewed on the Web than it is for
a live presentation.

5. Click OK to add the link. PowerPoint adds the link and also underlines the selected text and changes its color (see Figure 12.11).

To remove a link altogether, choose **I**nsert, Hyper**l**ink or click the Insert Hyperlink button on the toolbar. In the Insert Hyperlink dialog box, choose **R**emove Link.

I don't know about you, but I find hyperlinked text to be annoyingly distracting. Using underlining goes against all the principles of good textual design, and unless you add hyperlinks to all the bullets on a slide, some are one color and the rest are another, which can be bothersome.

An even more difficult and practical problem is that when you present a slide show slide with hyperlinks, the audience fully expects you to click each link, whether you want to or not. If you're running behind and need to skip over a particular bullet point, someone inevitably asks, "But what about that last bullet?"

Creating Invisible Links

The solution to having ugly visible hyperlinks is to create invisible links that accomplish the same purpose. Trust me. This is a lot easier than it sounds. You simply create a custom action button that covers the text you want to hyperlink and then change the shape's fill to no fill. These are the steps:

1. Choose AutoShapes, Action Buttons on the Drawing toolbar and select the blank Custom action button.

2. Move the pointer to the slide and draw (by dragging) a rectangle that covers the line of text to be hyperlinked. PowerPoint covers the text with a filled blank action button (see Figure 12.12), and immediately displays the Action Settings dialog box (refer to Figure 12.3).

3. If you know the action you plan to use, go ahead and set it now. Otherwise, click Cancel to set the action later.

FIGURE 12.12

To create an invisible link, you first create a visible shape that covers the area to be linked.

4. Double-click the custom action button to access the Format AutoShape dialog box. Figure 12.13 shows this dialog box, with settings being changed.

FIGURE 12.13

You use the Format AutoShape dialog box to turn off fill and line colors.

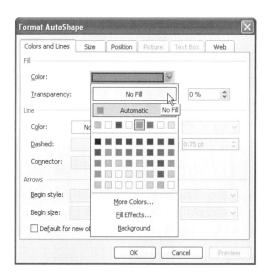

5. Choose No Fill from the Fill **C**olor drop-down list box.

6. Click OK. PowerPoint displays the sizing handles for the invisible, linked action button (see Figure 12.14).

FIGURE 12.14

An invisible object is still an object, to which you can add an action setting.

Invisible links don't clutter the screen with differently colored, underlined links. But when you play the slide show, *you* have to remember where the links are. Moving the mouse pointer to a link displays a hand so you know there's a link (see Figure 12.15). If you click a link, it behaves like any other hyperlinked object.

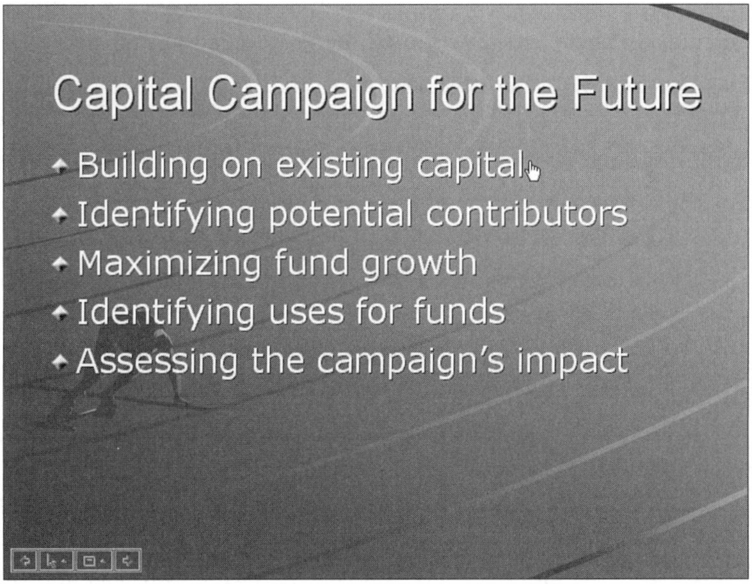

FIGURE 12.15

You find invisible links by moving the mouse pointer until it changes to a hand.

One minor problem with invisible links is that it's hard to find invisible objects to edit or remove the links or the shapes themselves. One way to find invisible links is to move the mouse pointer where you think the object is until you see a four-way arrow. You can also choose **E**dit, Select A**l**l to see where all objects are located. Then deselect them and click just the shape you want.

Creating a Nonlinear Presentation

Creating action settings and hyperlinks provides many advantages to you as a presenter. But perhaps none is so compelling as the ability to create a nonlinear presentation.

If you're presenting anything that might invite input, feedback, questions and answers, or diverging paths of discussion, you don't want to be locked into a strictly sequential slide show. Nor do you want to fumble around trying to find the slide that illustrates the current point of discussion.

Hyperlinks can help you build a *nonlinear slide show*, one in which you can jump from topic to topic as needed, jump to hidden slides that you use only if required, and quickly find your way around the complete corpus of slides.

These are the steps and considerations I try to follow when creating a nonlinear slide show:

1. Create a relatively linear slide show first, using the outlining tools.

2. Determine the segments or modules of the presentation. Ask yourself what parts can stand alone.

3. Create supplemental segments or slides that might come in handy but that you won't necessarily use.

4. Create a menu slide. I like to create a normal title or opening slide, followed by a menu slide with a list of major segments of the presentation.

5. Create an invisible link from each item on the menu slide to the beginning slide of the section of slides that relates to that item.

6. Go to the last slide of the first section of slides and create an action button that returns you to the menu slide. Size and format the button exactly the way you want it to look and position it unobtrusively in a corner of the slide.

7. Select the button and copy it.

8. Go to the last slide of each section of slides or to hidden slides and paste the button. PowerPoint places the button along with its action setting at the same location on the slide each time you paste it.

tip

If you want to create a link to an unusual shape, you can create an AutoShape that matches it, add an action setting or hyperlink to the AutoShape, and then format the AutoShape by changing its fill and line to no fill and no line.

9. If needed, create submenu slides with links to subtopics or peripheral information and then create return links to the submenu and/or the main menu slides.

10. Include links to hidden slides where appropriate.

Linear slide shows are easy to present. Just advance the slide and talk about whatever comes up next. But don't count on making a very flexible presentation this way.

Nonlinear presentations are much more difficult to prepare. They require a great deal of rehearsal so you know exactly where the links are and what will happen when you click them. However, a well-planned and well-rehearsed presentation of this type can be highly effective, appearing natural and spontaneous.

tip

Creating a nonlinear presentation requires careful planning. It often helps to sketch out on paper, like a flowchart, what the various parts of the presentation are and how you might get from one part to another. Then create links in PowerPoint to match the flowchart.

➪ For more information on rehearsing a presentation, see **p. 263**.

THE ABSOLUTE MINIMUM

PowerPoint has huge advantages over a traditional slide show in that it can jump directly to any place in a slide show, or it can link to information and programs outside the slide show itself. In this chapter, you did the following:

- You found out how to use action settings to create a dynamic presentation.
- You learned how to add action settings to nearly any PowerPoint object.
- You explored the use of action buttons.
- You learned how to create links, including invisible links, to text elements.
- You discovered that it's possible to avoid creating a purely sequential, or linear, slide show.

Chapter 13, "Preparing a Slide Show for Presentation," discusses getting a slide show ready for presentation.

PART IV

PREPARING AND PRESENTING THE SLIDE SHOW

13

Preparing a Slide Show for Presentation

To this point this book has focused on the content of a slide show and how to make that content as effective as possible. The time soon comes, however, when you have to make the presentation. This chapter looks at how you can get a slide show ready for a presentation. It focuses on things you can do to entire slides or groups of slides, instead of how you change the content or action of an individual slide.

Using the Slide Sorter

One of the most common last-minute changes people make to slide shows is to rearrange slides here or there to improve the flow of the show. Changing the order of slides is simple and there are two easy ways to do it. Here's one way:

1. Click the Slides tab at the left sides of the screen (see Figure 13.1).

Slides tab

FIGURE 13.1

On the Slides tab of the Normal view, you can drag slides to rearrange them.

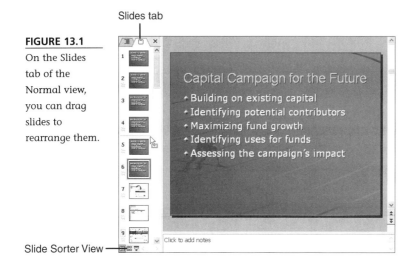

Slide Sorter View

2. Click and drag a slide to a new location. The thin horizontal line that appears between slides shows where the slide will go.

3. Release the mouse button to drop the slide into its new slot.

If you need to move a slide beyond the end of the list that's visible onscreen, just drag beyond the list and wait a second or two until the list begins to scroll. You continue to scroll until you see the target location and then drop the slide there.

A second way to rearrange slides is to use the Slide Sorter view. The advantage of the slide sorter is that it enables you to see more slides at once, making it easier to view their arrangement. To move a slide in the Slide Sorter view, follow these steps:

1. Click the Slide Sorter View button on the Views toolbar at the lower left of the screen (refer to Figure 13.1). PowerPoint displays several slides at once (see Figure 13.2). The number of slides you see depends on your display. You can increase or decrease the number of slides in this view by choosing **V**iew, **Z**oom and changing the zoom percentage.

FIGURE 13.2

The Slide Sorter view displays more slides than the Normal view, making it easier to rearrange or modify them.

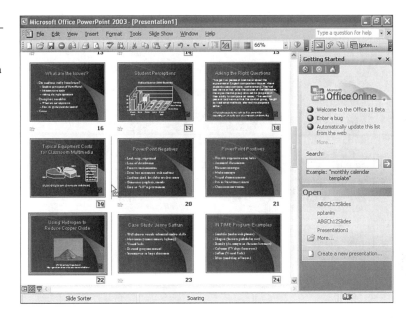

2. Click and drag a slide to a new location. The thin vertical line that appears between the slides shows where the slide will go.

3. Release the mouse button to drop the slide into its new slot. Slides move aside and make room for the newly relocated slide, and slide numbers automatically renumber.

In either the Normal view under the Slides tab or the Slide Sorter view, you can select more than one slide at a time and move them all at once. To move multiple slides, follow these steps:

1. Click the first slide to be moved. PowerPoint places a blue highlighter line around the selected slide.

2. Hold down the Ctrl key and click the second slide to be moved. All selected slides display the blue border (see Figure 13.3).

3. Continue selecting slides and then click and drag the group of slides to their new location.

Note that if you select slides that aren't next to each other, when you drop them in their new slots, they will be next to each other.

Both of these methods really are nothing more than a quick way of cutting and pasting slides. You could accomplish the same thing by cutting a slide and pasting it in a new location. But dragging and dropping slides is much easier and quicker.

However, you can also *copy* and paste slides. Besides the obvious reason that you need a copy in another location, here are a couple of uses for copied slides:

FIGURE 13.3

You hold down the Ctrl key while clicking to select more than one slide.

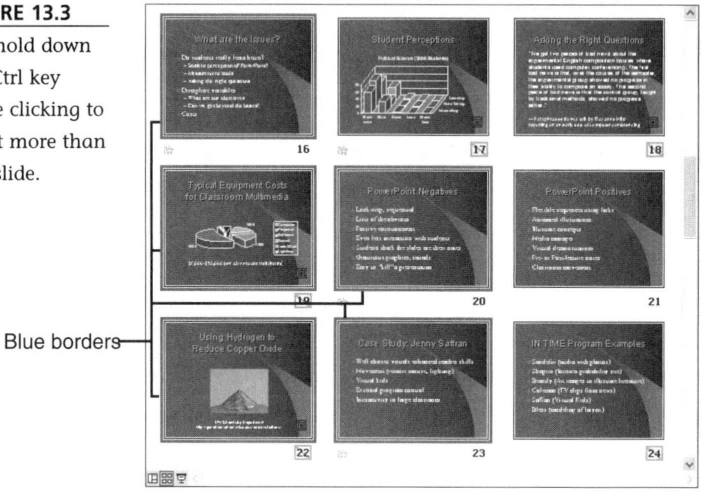

Blue borders

- You want a general title slide to show at the beginning, during introductions, and at the end, during questions and answers. You can create such a slide and copy it to the end of the show.

- You have a self-running show with music. However, you don't want to have to start the Slide Show view with the audience looking on. Therefore, you create an opening slide that you can leave up during introductions and you copy that slide, adding automatic transitions and an embedded sound file. When you click to advance, the audience thinks Slide 2 is still Slide 1, except that the music plays and the show automatically advances to Slide 3 when the time comes.

- You want to create an unusual animation sequence, such as a country that is in the midst of others that grows and gets a red border and a capital, while the other countries remain the original size. You create the first slide, with a title, regular-sized map, color designs, and so on. Then you copy the slide and paste several copies in sequence. Then you simply make the highlighted country slightly larger in each sequential slide (see Figure 13.4). When you play the slides, it appears that the country is growing on a single slide, but in reality you're moving rapidly from one slide to the next.

FIGURE 13.4

A sequence of slides, with rapid automatic transition, can create the illusion of animation.

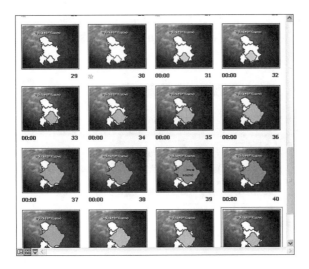

To copy a slide to a new location, you follow these steps:

1. Select the slide or slides to be copied, either in the Normal View Slides tab or in Slide Sorter view.

2. Hold down the Ctrl key.

3. Drag the slide to its new location, indicated by the thin line between the slides. Note that the mouse pointer shows a + beside it, indicating that you're copying.

4. Drop the slide, which becomes an exact copy of the original.

Don't forget that using Undo (Ctrl+Z) can fix any accidental moving or copying.

Hiding Slides

As you consider the slides in a slide show and their sequence, sometimes you find a slide that just doesn't quite fit. You can delete the slide, of course, or you can hide it.

To delete a slide, simply select it, either in the Normal View Slides tab or in the Slide Sorter view. Press Delete or Backspace, and without any warning or complaining, PowerPoint removes the slide. That's a pretty drastic step, especially if you've spent a lot of time creating the content of the slide. If you forget to use Undo, the slide could be gone forever as soon as you save the slide show.

A better strategy might be to *hide* the slide. Although the slide is still in the show, when PowerPoint reaches that slide, it skips right over it to the next slide.

To hide a slide, just select the slide to be hidden, and choose Slide Show, Hide Slide. The slide number is covered by a gray rectangle with a slash through it (see Figure 13.5).

FIGURE 13.5

The hidden slide indicator identifies hidden slides.

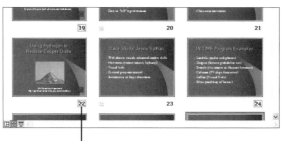

Hidden slide indicator

Later, if you decide to use the slide, you can simply unhide it. To unhide a slide, just select the slide to be unhidden and select Sli**d**e Show, **H**ide Slide.

You can also use hidden slides to hold extra material that you might not use but that's there if you need it. You can jump to a hidden slide while playing the slide show or by linking to it with an action setting. Otherwise, PowerPoint skips over the hidden slide without the audience ever knowing it.

Changing Slide Transitions

Certainly you can consider adding slide transitions to slides as you create them. However, after you've finished creating slide content, when you have everything in the order you want, you need to consider slide transitions in the context of the overall slide show. That's where the Slide Sorter view can be particularly helpful because it enables you to see more of the slide show and to check slide transitions quickly and easily.

You can apply a slide transition to a single slide or to an entire slide show. Usually I find it best to select a transition I like, apply it to all slides for consistency, and then change individual slide transitions only when absolutely necessary.

To add slide transitions to an entire slide show, follow these steps:

1. If you want to view more slides than you do in the Normal view, switch to the Slide Sorter view by clicking the Slide Sorter View button on the Views toolbar. However, the steps outlined here work in either view.

2. Choose Sli**d**e Show, Slide **T**ransition or right-click the slide and choose Slide **T**ransition. PowerPoint displays the Slide Transition task pane (see Figure 13.6).

FIGURE 13.6

You use the Slide
Transition task
pane to change
transitions for a
single slide or
for an entire
slide show.

3. From the Apply to Selected Slides list, select a transition style. PowerPoint previews the transition effect with the currently selected slide.

4. To apply the transition to the entire slide show, click the Apply to All Slides
   button near the bottom of the task pane.

After you apply a transition, PowerPoint displays a transition icon beneath the slide
(see Figure 13.7). You can see how the selected transition looks by clicking the icon.
PowerPoint quickly shows the preceding slide and transitions to the current slide.

FIGURE 13.7

You can view a
slide's transition
by clicking the
slide transition
icon beneath it.

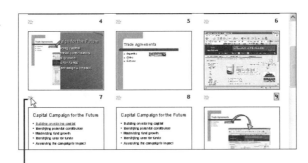

Slide transition icon

Getting just the right transition is almost as much art as it is science. Sure, you can learn about and use any of the transition options, but which of them adds to the effect you want to create? Consider the following:

- No transition can be relatively stark. While it shows a no-nonsense approach, it can also be interpreted as a lack of professional savvy. After all, you do have lots of transitions at your disposal.

- Subtle transitions help viewers move from the content of one slide to the next without feeling a sense of abrupt change. Wipe, cover and uncover, push, and fade are among the effects that create gentle transitions.

- Dramatic transitions can add pizzazz, but they can also distract from a presentation. If yours is a self-running slide show or a high-energy, upbeat presentation that is on the entertaining side, appropriate transitions include blinds, checkerboards, combs, news flashes, wedges, and wheels.

- Random transitions are, in my book, not very useful. However, if you want people to be involved in the entertainment of the show—for example, a series of photos that recapture a team's playing season—changing transitions with each slide might be appropriate.

You also need to consider whether transitions are to be fast or slow. Try them out to see how they look, but also try to imagine how they'll feel when you're making the presentation. For example, you might think a transition needs more time to be appreciated, so you slow it down. But when you make the presentation, you find yourself waiting for the transition, so you need to play it more quickly.

After you find a transition type and speed that works pretty well for the entire slide show, you should look at each slide and see if a change of transition for just that slide is appropriate.

To change a slide transition for an individual slide, simply select the slide you want to change, and from the Slide Transition task pane (refer to Figure 13.6) select a different transition.

The method you use to advance slides is another important choice you have to make. Generally, advancing a slide manually—by clicking the mouse or pressing the spacebar—is the preferred method in a live presentation. However, certain slide sequences might be easiest and more effective if they advance automatically.

To change the method you use to advance a slide, follow these steps while in the Slide Sorter view:

1. Select the slide you want to change.

2. Access the Slide Transition task pane.

3. Click the Automatically After check box and specify the amount of time that should transpire before the slide advances automatically.

4. Click the slide to apply the new setting to the slide. PowerPoint displays the delay time beneath the slide.

If you also uncheck On Mouse Click, you are forced to wait for the automatic timing to move to the next slide. You should leave both checked, so you can advance the slide more quickly if you want to.

For a self-running slide show, such as a memorial tribute with background music, you can use automatic timings to coordinate with the music. In this case, you select a general transition time, such as five seconds, apply it to all slides, and then modify times for individual slides (for example, for rapid-fire effects or to linger on a particular slide).

Changing Slide Backgrounds

When you first start working on a slide show, you usually select a design, which includes a background and coordinated colors and fonts. However, as you prepare the slide show for presentation, you need to assess whether the design and the colors are right. Are you presenting to alumni, and did you mistakenly use background colors that match a rival school's team colors? Are the colors too dark for an already darkened room? Perhaps when you check out the room, you see that the furnishings clash with the colors you've chosen. Or maybe your sense of aesthetics just tells you a change is in order.

note

Setting slide transitions to automatically correlate with a music background is a tricky business. Music always plays at the same speed, but the speed of a slide show's transitions depends on the computer's speed, memory, and hard disk speed and whether other programs are loaded and running at the same time. If you play a slide show on a computer other than the one on which you created it, the timings might be significantly off.

The best you can do is tweak the timings on a specific computer and be sure to use that computer to play the slide show. The extra work you need to put in to create such a slide show usually pays off, with a satisfying and professional-looking presentation.

[Design] You can change the slide show design layer by clicking the Design button on the Formatting toolbar and selecting a new design from the Slide Design task pane. This is a rather drastic step, however, because a change in design also means a change in fonts, default layouts, and color schemes. After you make a design change, you must go through the slide show, one slide at a time, to make sure text fits, that images are positioned properly relative to the background design, and that the change in colors doesn't make anything more difficult to see.

There are several less dramatic changes you can make to slide backgrounds, all of which are easily reversible by using Undo. The first, and easiest, is to simply change the color scheme, leaving the design and slide layouts intact. For example, say you've used the Competition design to convey the idea of racing toward a goal, but the default orange color scheme is just too strong and garish for your taste. To change the color scheme after you've created a slide show using this design, follow these steps:

1. If you're changing a single slide, select that slide. Otherwise, it doesn't matter which slide you're on.

2. Click the Design button on the Formatting toolbar to display the Slide Design task pane.

3. Click Color Schemes at the top of the task pane. PowerPoint displays several color scheme options (see Figure 13.8).

FIGURE 13.8

Each design has several additional color schemes associated with it.

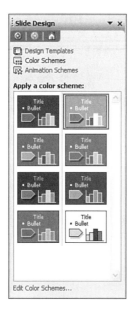

4. Click a color scheme if you want to apply the scheme to all slides, or click the drop-down list box at the right of the scheme and choose Apply to **S**elected Slides to change just one slide.

PowerPoint automatically changes all automatically colored elements of the slide, including the background, text fonts, filled AutoShapes, and even action buttons.

PowerPoint is pretty good at coordinating colors in its various color schemes. Once in a while, however, one color or another just doesn't seem right. If you've got a good sense of color and want to fine-tune an existing scheme or even create your own color scheme, you can do so from the Color Scheme task pane. For now, however, take time to get used to using PowerPoint's predefined schemes. Down the road, you might want to experiment on your own.

Two other changes you can make to the background include changing the background color and omitting the background design. Neither of these changes, however, coordinates with any of the other slide elements. Changing the background color by itself might produce some interesting but unexpected results.

To change just the slide's background, follow these steps:

1. Choose F**o**rmat, Bac**k**ground or right-click the slide and choose Bac**k**ground. PowerPoint displays the Background dialog box (see Figure 13.9).

FIGURE 13.9

You can leave the design alone but change only a slide's background.

2. To remove background graphics, such as a track runner and track, check the Omit Background **G**raphics from Master check box.

3. To change the background color, click the drop-down list box beneath the preview in the **B**ackground Fill group box (see Figure 13.10). Choose an automatic color, select **M**ore Colors for a complete palette of colors, or select **F**ill Effects to select a gradient shading, pattern, texture, or image background.

FIGURE 13.10

You can change a background's color, shading, pattern, texture, or image.

4. Click **P**review to check out the change first, click **A**pply to apply the change to the current slide, or click Apply **t**o All to apply the background to all the slides in the slide show.

What you have learned in this section gives you enough information to get yourself in trouble! Be judicious in changing color schemes and backgrounds. You'll probably be able to go a long time without having to change PowerPoint's predefined designs and color schemes. But you can also impress PowerPoint-jaded audiences with new and different backgrounds and colors, all the while creating an effective presentation.

⇨ For more information on how to choose colors that coordinate properly, see **p. 394**.

Creating Speaker Notes

One preparatory change you are likely to make is one your audience may never see: speaker notes. These are just what their name implies—notes you make to yourself to help remind you of important things to say or details that are too hard to memorize.

To create speaker notes for a slide, simply click in the Speaker Notes area of Normal view (see Figure 13.11). Then type whatever notes you want to make for yourself.

FIGURE 13.11
You use the Speaker Notes area to type notes to yourself.

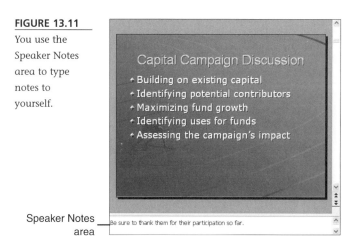

Speaker Notes area

Typically, notes are brief, but if you have a lot of information to refer to, you can expand the Speaker Notes area by dragging the separator line upward (see Figure 13.12). Drag it back down when you're through. This doesn't change the amount of text you can type—just the amount that displays onscreen.

FIGURE 13.12

If you need
more typing
space, you can
drag the separa-
tor line upward.

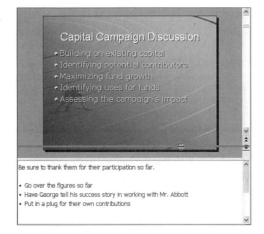

You can use a limited number of text editing tools in the Speaker Notes area. You can right-click some text to see a context menu that includes cutting and pasting as well as use of a dictionary and thesaurus.

You can use speaker notes as you're preparing a presentation, but when you begin the presentation, these notes are not visible. If you want to refer to your speaker notes during a presentation, you need to make a printed copy for yourself.

Speaker notes don't necessarily have to be limited to your own use. If you want to create brief explanations or added details about slides in your presentation, you can print handouts that include a thumbnail view of the slides along with speaker notes. These can often be more valuable than slides printed out by themselves as handouts.

➪   For details on printing speaker notes for yourself or as handouts, see **p. 313**.

Creating Custom Slide Shows

PowerPoint provides a relatively easy way to create custom slide shows that remain within the original slide show. Essentially, you select the slides to include from the master slide show, and then you play just the custom slide show. If you want to explore this feature, you can do so by choosing Slide Show, Custom Shows.

Custom shows can help you quickly create a subset of a slide show, but it's not the end-all answer for customizing a presentation to a particular audience. In particular, you can't modify many of your customized slide controls in a custom show. If you need greater customizing control over a slide show, you can create a new slide show and import the slides you need from the original slide show. Then you can fine-tune the second slide show, including links, transitions, timing, and so on.

⇨ For details on importing slides from another slide show, see **p. 78**.

The Absolute Minimum

Preparing a slide show for presentation involves more than making sure each slide is just right. You must also make sure the overall slide show works in terms of slide order, slide transitions, and color schemes. In this chapter, you did the following:

- You found out how to use the slide sorter to organize and hide slides.
- You learned how to change transitions.
- You explored the differences between manual and automatic slide transitions.
- You learned how to modify color schemes and change backgrounds.
- You saw that it's simple to create speaker notes.
- You discovered that you can create custom slide shows from within a master slide show.

Chapter 14, "Preparing to Make a Presentation," explores getting ready to make a presentation.

14

PREPARING TO MAKE A PRESENTATION

The slides are finished. The slide show's done. Now you have to get yourself ready to make the presentation. Unless you're playing a self-running show, you and the way you interact with your slide show ultimately determine how successful the presentation will be.

This chapter looks at the ways to set up and play a show. It also explores ways to rehearse and plan for unforeseen technical difficulties.

Playing a Slide Show

Playing and stopping a slide show are simple. Just choose Slide Show, **V**iew Show or press F5. PowerPoint automatically jumps to the first slide in the show, and you're off and running. To end a show, play the show to the end or press Esc to stop immediately at any point in the show.

You can also start a show by clicking the Slide Show View button (Slide Show from Current Slide button) or pressing Shift+F5. However, this method starts the show at the current slide, so if you intend to show the entire show, you have to move to Slide 1 before you click the button or press Shift+F5.

If you're making a presentation in which you know there won't be any interruptions, this may be all you need to know. But PowerPoint also provides lots of options to accommodate many different presentation styles and needs.

Setting Up a Slide Show

You can select from among several slide show options by using the Set Up Show feature. Choose Slide Show, **S**et Up Show to display the Set Up Show dialog box (see Figure 14.1).

FIGURE 14.1

You use the Set Up Show dialog box to customize how you play a slide show.

The default show setup assumes that you (or another speaker) will make the presentation using a full-screen display, that you'll play all the slides, and that you'll use a slide's timings, if it has any.

The basic show types include the following:

- ▪ **P**resented by a Speaker—This simply means that you as the presenter have full control over the slide show...at least you hope you do!

- ▪ **B**rowsed by an Individual—This option brings up the slide show in a browser, and by default it also provides a scrollbar to make it easier for an individual to browse the slide show (see Figure 14.2). If you uncheck S**h**ow Scrollbar, it's much more difficult for the viewer to advance from slide to slide. However, if you provide lots of navigation links, such as action buttons and hyperlinks, the show acts like a well-designed Web page, and the scrollbar isn't necessary.

FIGURE 14.2

You can set up a show to be played in a browser, to be navigated by an individual like a Web page.

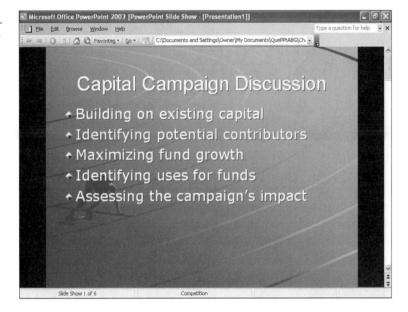

- ▪ Browsed at a **K**iosk—This option assumes that you don't want viewers to interact with the slide show. Instead, the show automatically advances based on slide transition timings. The slide show also loops (that is, repeats) continuously until you press Esc. If you forget to add slide transition timings, the show stops and does not advance.

Other options in the Set Up Show dialog box include the following:

- ▪ Show Options—You can make a slide show loop continuously, even if you're presenting it yourself. If the slide show contains recorded narration or animations, you can suppress either or both. Finally, if you use a highlighter pen during the presentation, you can choose the color. We'll talk about pen options a bit later in this chapter.

- *Show Slides*—By default, you present all the slides in a show. But you can select a range of slides or choose from among any custom slide shows you've defined.

- *Advance Slides*—Choosing **M**anually simply overrides any automatic timings you have added to slide transitions or animations.

- *Multiple Monitors*—Presenters frequently request the ability to see menus and speaker notes onscreen without letting the audience see them. Unfortunately, whatever you see on your computer is also projected to the audience. The Multiple Monitors option enables you to use two monitors—one that the audience sees and one that you see. The details of using this option are beyond the scope of this book. Further, in my experience, this feature is difficult to set up because it depends on having the right combination of hardware and software, besides being able to actually use the feature.

- *Performance*—No, this option doesn't help you do a better job of presenting. But you can use it to improve how well a computer presents the slide show. If you notice serious slowness, jerky transitions, and so on, access the Set Up Show dialog box and click the T**i**ps button. PowerPoint provides a help screen that discusses performance issues in detail. Generally, with today's speedy computers and high-powered graphics hardware, performance issues aren't as common as they used to be.

After you choose setup options, click OK to apply them and to return to the PowerPoint screen.

Navigating a Slide Show

After you begin a slide show, your objective is to move smoothly through the show until you reach the end. If you have no interruptions, make no mistakes, and have a relatively sequential presentation, this shouldn't be too hard. Unfortunately, sometimes you accidentally advance a slide or an animation before you want to, or someone asks a question about the slide you just left behind. Knowing how to back up or go directly to another location can be extremely useful.

An easy way to access navigation options during a slide show is to move the mouse until a mouse pointer appears. PowerPoint can be frustratingly slow at this, especially when you want to back up quickly. But have patience. The mouse pointer eventually appears, along with a semitransparent toolbar at the lower-left corner of the screen (see Figure 14.3).

FIGURE 14.3

You use the onscreen toolbar to navigate a slide show.

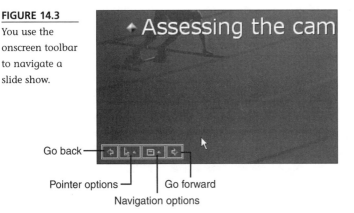

Go back

Pointer options

Go forward

Navigation options

To back up, simply click the Go Back button on the toolbar. Backing up does not always mean that you'll return to the previous slide. If you have animations on the slide, going back steps through those animations one at a time.

If you don't want to wait for the mouse, or if you'd prefer not to have the audience watch as you click to navigate, you can use the keyboard to back up. Press Page Up to back up and Page Down to advance. Quick and easy, clean and simple.

Other types of navigation are a little more involved than backing up and moving forward. If you anticipate the need to jump to a slide out of sequence, consider preparing action settings or links to get there.

For details on using action settings for navigation, see **p. 222**.

You can navigate to nearly anywhere by clicking the Navigation Options button on the toolbar or by right-clicking the slide. In either case, PowerPoint displays a menu of navigation choices (see Figure 14.4). The options on this menu include the following:

- **Next**—This takes you to the next slide or to the next animation, if any.

- **Previous**—This takes you to the previous slide or to the previous animation, if any.

- Last **Viewed**—This takes you to the last slide viewed, even if you jumped to the current slide from somewhere else in the slide show. This can be very useful if you need to backtrack in a nonlinear slide show.

- **Go** to Slide—This displays a list of all the slides in the slide show (see Figure 14.5). You select a slide, even a hidden slide, and PowerPoint takes you directly there. If you become adept at using this option, you can change direction quickly without seriously interrupting a presentation.

FIGURE 14.4

FIGURE 14.4

The navigation menu helps you go directly to anyplace in a slide show.

FIGURE 14.5

The Go to Slide option lists slides in the current slide show.

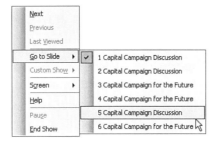

■ *Custom Show*—This lets you jump into a subset of the current show, depending on whether you have defined any custom shows ahead of time.

■ *End Show*—This ends a show and returns you to PowerPoint. It has the same effect as pressing the Esc key.

Navigating by using the mouse is not too complicated. But you can also benefit from learning to use the keyboard, which can be quicker, easier, and less apparent to viewers. For more information on this, see the section "Using Easy Keyboard Shortcuts," later in this chapter.

Using Screen and Pointer Options

If you've ever had to stare into the bright light of a projector while pointing at something onscreen, you'll appreciate PowerPoint's pen and pointer options.

To access the pointer options, click the Pointer options button on the toolbar or right-click and choose Pointer Options. PowerPoint displays a pointer options menu (see Figure 14.6).

One thing you might want to do, especially if you'll be using a lot of pointing or navigation options, is to choose Arrow **O**ptions from the pointer options menu (see Figure 14.7). By default, the mouse pointer disappears automatically after a few seconds of inactivity. Unfortunately, it also takes a few seconds of moving the mouse to make the pointer or the toolbar appear again. If you select **V**isible, the pointer and the toolbar remain onscreen. **H**idden means the pointer never appears, although clicking the mouse still advances slides or transitions. However, if you have an action setting or link to click, you can't see the mouse pointer to do so.

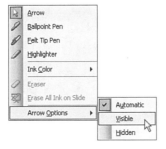

By default, the mouse pointer is simply an arrow. You can use the arrow to point at things onscreen to help the audience see what you're talking about. This is usually better than walking in front of the screen to point with your hand.

You can also change the pointer to a pen, marker, or highlighter, and you can then draw directly on the slide. To draw on a slide, follow these steps:

1. Click the Pointer Options button on the toolbar or right-click the slide and choose P**o**inter Options.

2. From the pointer options menu (refer to Figure 14.6), select the type of pen you'd like to use (for example, **F**elt Tip Pen). PowerPoint changes the mouse pointer to a dot with a color above it.

3. Click and drag the mouse to draw onscreen (see Figure 14.8).

FIGURE 14.8

You use a marker to make drawings or annotations on a slide during a slide show.

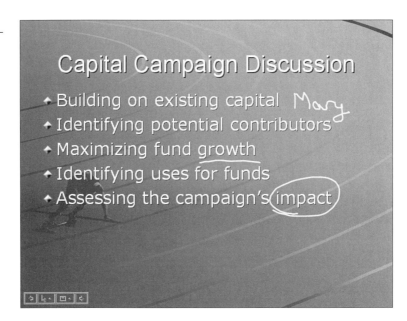

4. When you're through using the pen, click the Pointer Options button on the toolbar and select **A**rrow. Or you can press Esc to turn off the pen.

If you plan to use the pen frequently, you can leave the pen setting turned on and advance the slides by using the Navigation Options button on the toolbar or by using the keyboard.

Drawings onscreen remain there until you erase or clear them, even if you advance to another slide. To erase a drawing, follow these steps:

1. Click the Pointer Options button on the toolbar and choose E**r**aser. The pointer turns to an eraser shape.

2. Click and drag the eraser across a line. The line disappears.

3. Repeat step 2 to erase other drawings.

4. Click the Pointer Options button on the toolbar, turn off the eraser, and select a pen style or an arrow from the Pointer Options menu. Or you can press Esc to turn off the eraser.

To clear all the drawings on a slide, from the Pointer Options menu, choose **E**rase All Ink on Slide.

You can choose the pen's ink color so that it contrasts well with the slide's background. From the Pointer Options menu, choose Ink **C**olor and then choose Automatic or a color from a basic palette of colors.

Finally, when you exit the slide show, PowerPoint asks if you want to keep your annotations so that you can refer to them when editing your slides. If you choose **K**eep the Annotations, PowerPoint displays them on the slide editing screen (see Figure 14.9). These annotations act exactly like AutoShapes in that you can select, move, or delete them. You can also print them if you choose that option when printing. However, they are different from AutoShapes in that they do not display if you play the slide again in a slide show. They're there strictly for your reference so that you can make changes to the slide. When you're through with them, you can select them and delete them.

FIGURE 14.9

Annotations and drawings can remain on a slide and be printed.

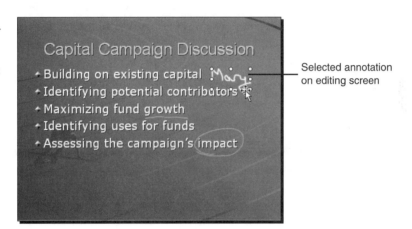

Selected annotation on editing screen

Using Easy Keyboard Shortcuts

Using a mouse while creating and testing a slide show makes sense: You're seated in front of the computer, and you're used to the amount and direction of movement required to accurately move the mouse. When you're standing, giving a presentation, it's harder to use the mouse, especially with any kind of precision.

Using the keyboard can be an easier way to make things happen during a slide show, and indeed there are dozens of keyboard alternatives for mouse and menu options. For example, which is the largest key on the keyboard? Correct. The spacebar is easy to find, easy to hit, and, as luck would have it, it's a key that's used to advance to the next slide or animation. I find it extremely easy to wander over to my laptop while talking, press the spacebar for the next slide and wander away from the laptop, never missing a beat.

To learn about keystroke alternatives, as well as a few unusual mouse click options, you can press F1 in the Slide Show view. You can also right-click a slide and from the context menu choose **H**elp. PowerPoint displays the Slide Show Help dialog box, which provides a long list of options (see Figure 14.10).

You might even want to print this screen. Simply press Alt+PrtSc to copy the window, paste it onto a blank slide or into a Word document, and print the resulting slide or page.

FIGURE 14.10

Using keyboard shortcuts can be quicker and less obvious to the audience than using the mouse.

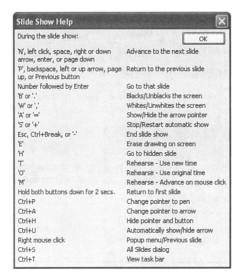

The following are some of my favorite and most useful keyboard shortcuts:

- *Advancing*—You can press the spacebar, Page Down, the right arrow, the down arrow, Enter, or the letter N. Using the spacebar is my favorite method because it's the easiest to find while you continue to talk.

- *Backing up*—You can press Page Up, left arrow, up arrow, or Backspace.

- *Black screen*—Pressing the letter B changes the screen to a blank, black screen. This allows you to force audience attention to you instead of to the screen. Press B again to turn off the black screen.

- *Going to a slide*—Pressing Ctrl+S displays of a list of slides (see Figure 14.11). Move up or down to select a slide, and press Enter.

- *Going to a slide number*—You can type the number of a slide followed by Enter. Of course, you have to know the number of the slide, but if you've memorized a critical slide or two, you can get there quickly by using this method.

Not all keystrokes are useful to you because you use them relatively infrequently. But for actions that you use all the time, learn and practice using keystroke alternatives to save time, or at the very least, to have options as you advance through a slide show.

FIGURE 14.11

The Ctrl+S short-
cut helps you
quickly select a
slide to go to.

Rehearsing a Presentation

Think about the best PowerPoint presentations you've seen. A large part of a presentation's effectiveness is that the presenter makes it all seem natural and effortless; PowerPoint is literally an extension of the person's presenting skills.

Such effectiveness doesn't happen by accident. Skilled presenters rehearse their presentations over and over to make sure they know when and where things happen in the slide show and to practice how they'll deal with changes in direction during the presentation.

PowerPoint can help you practice the timing of a presentation. The Rehearse Timings option keeps track of how long you take with each slide or animation, and it also adds up the total duration of the slide show.

To use this tool, simply choose Slide Show, **R**ehearse Timings. PowerPoint automatically starts the slide show at Slide 1 and displays the Rehearsal toolbar at the upper-left corner of the slide (see Figure 14.12).

FIGURE 14.12

The Rehearsal
toolbar helps
you practice
slide and slide
show timing.

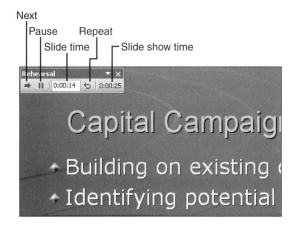

When you use the Rehearse Timings option, you can move through a slide show as you normally do, except that you have to manually advance slides and animations because all automatic timings are turned off. The Rehearse Timings tool keeps track of how long it takes you to present each slide or animation. Besides clicking the slide or using a keystroke to advance, you can also click the Next button on the Rehearsal toolbar to advance a slide or transition. You can also pause—for example, if you get interrupted while rehearsing. If you decide you don't like how you've been presenting the current slide, you can click the Repeat button to start the timing over for the current slide. If you use repeat, the Rehearse Timings tool also subtracts time from the overall slide show time.

When you reach the end of the show, or if you press Esc to stop, PowerPoint tells you the total time of the show and asks if you want to keep the new slide timings to use when you view the slide show (see Figure 14.13). This is a big decision because if you answer yes, all previously set automatic or manual timings are replaced by automatic timings based on rehearsal timings. If you accidentally answer yes but mean no, you can use Undo to reset the original timings. If you want to keep the original timings and also this version with rehearsal timings, you can save the show using a different name.

FIGURE 14.13

You can use new rehearsal timings in place of existing manual or automatic settings.

Exploring Contingency Options

Good presenters know, usually from experience, that not everything goes just the way you hope it will. Some presenters have enough background and expertise to be able to forget the PowerPoint presentation and give a great presentation on their own. The rest of us, however, generally depend on the slide show to make it through the presentation. For us, it's doubly important that we make alternate plans for our presentations in the event that something goes wrong.

What could possibly go wrong? I could make a long list, but these are a few things that come immediately to mind:

- Your laptop computer develops a problem and you can't use it to show the slide show.

- While making a last-minute change, you damage your slide show file or delete it.

- The laptop works fine, but the projector you were promised doesn't show up.

- Everything's working fine until the guy presenting next door blows a circuit breaker, and you lose power.

I could go on, but I think you get the point. Murphy's Law says that things can and will go wrong. A little advance preparation, including options described in the following sections, can help you weather such problems.

Packaging a Presentation for a CD

I never go to a presentation without making a backup copy of my slide show. If my computer fails, I want to be able to play it on another computer if I can find one. I might have to make last-minute adjustments to the slide show, but at least I still have a copy I can adjust!

PowerPoint 2003 has added a powerful tool that enables you to package an entire presentation, or even multiple presentations, and write them to a CD. Because most computers have CD drives, this option means you can play the slide show on other computers. You can even include on the CD a PowerPoint reader, called PowerPoint Viewer, that lets you play a slide show even if the computer you end up using doesn't have PowerPoint installed.

To package a slide show for a CD, you need to make sure you have a recordable CD available and that you have a CD-RW drive in your computer. Then follow these steps:

1. Choose **F**ile, Pac**k**age for CD. PowerPoint displays the Package for CD dialog box (see Figure 14.14).

FIGURE 14.14

You use the Package for CD option to write a slide show to CD.

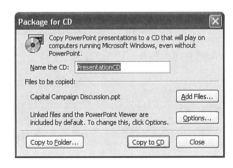

2. Provide a name for the CD.

3. Choose **O**ptions to see what choices you have (see Figure 14.15). They include the following:

FIGURE 14.15

You can include a PowerPoint viewer, slide links, and even the fonts slides use when you package a slide show for CD.

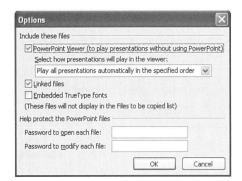

- The PowerPoint **V**iewer option enables you to play a slide show even if the computer used to play the show doesn't have PowerPoint installed.

- If you include more than one slide show on the CD, you can specify whether the shows play automatically and in which order.

- By default, PowerPoint includes on the CD any linked files. This is important if you expect such files to appear when you play the slide show.

- You can embed TrueType fonts if you think those fonts might not be installed on the target computer and if it's important to keep intact the ones you're using.

- You can password-protect the files you copy to CD, either to open the slide show or to modify it. Be aware that this isn't a perfect security solution because after a person opens the slide show, even as a read-only file, he or she can modify it and save it with a new name.

4. After you complete your choices, click OK.

caution

If you think you'll need to depend on the PowerPoint Viewer, try it out first. The viewer has been known to render slide shows, especially animations, differently than the original. You might have to make adjustments to simplify the presentation before you play it with the PowerPoint Viewer.

On the other hand, if the target computer has a recent version of PowerPoint installed, you might be able to play the packaged presentation without any problems.

5. If you want to add more slide shows to the package, click **A**dd Files and browse to find them. After you do, the Package for CD dialog box changes slightly, enabling you to change the play order of the slide shows (see Figure 14.16). Note that you might have greater success including all the appropriate links and graphic images if you first copy all your slide shows to the same folder on your hard disk and package them from there.

FIGURE 14.16

You can pack-
age more than
one slide show
at a time.

6. Click Copy to **C**D to begin the recording process.

You can also package a slide show to a folder—for example, on a network drive or on a zip or floppy disk (if the slide show is small enough to fit). Choose Copy to **F**older and browse to the location to copy to. However, you might be surprised to find that new laptop computers are more likely to have CD drives than floppy drives.

To play a packaged slide show, insert the CD. Depending on the packaging options you selected, the slide shows might play automatically, or you might need to select Start, Run and browse to the CD. To play the viewer, you need to find and run the PPTVIEW program, which automatically displays the names of the PowerPoint slide shows that are packaged with it. Alternatively, you can use Windows Explorer to find the slide shows and open them directly in PowerPoint.

Preparing Overhead Transparencies

Data projectors are expensive and can be hard to come by. But in many businesses, schools, and convention centers, overhead projectors are pretty common. One way to prepare for a possible data projector disaster is to create overhead transparencies of key slides. Then, if you can't use the computer, you can likely find an overhead projector and use that instead.

You need to think about several considerations when preparing slides for use with an overhead projector:

- Color slides may not look good when printed in black and white. One solution is to print in grayscale or pure black and white, which generally removes slide backgrounds. Another is to print in color.

- Animations and media elements obviously can't print. If sequence is important—for example, adding one bullet at a time—you need to create sequential slides. Start by creating the finished slide, and then print, remove a bullet, print again, remove a bullet, and so on.

- Changing transparencies is more difficult than making PowerPoint transitions. It's usually a good idea to limit printing overhead transparencies to a few key slides. This way, you'll have less to fumble with, and you'll be more likely to keep your place and not distract the audience.

To print an overhead transparency, choose **F**ile, **P**rint. The Print dialog box appears.

Choose the options you want, such as **C**urrent Slide, Color/**G**rayscale, and Fra**m**e Slides. Click Pr**e**view to see how the slide will print, and then print the slide when you're ready.

You can print directly to an overhead transparency. However, be sure that you use transparencies that match the type of printer you're using. For example, transparencies for laser printers can withstand high heat without melting. Transparencies for inkjet printers dry the ink quickly so it doesn't smear. These special transparencies tend to cost more than regular transparencies, but if you use the wrong kind, you'll have a mess on your hands.

Using Handouts

Although handing out full-sized copies of each slide as handouts is generally a waste of paper, having handouts of key slides, perhaps in thumbnail or annotated format, could be a way to hedge against technical problems. It's hard to beat a technology that doesn't require electricity!

⇨ For details on printing handouts, see **p. 313**.

THE ABSOLUTE MINIMUM

Creating a good presentation is important. But you also have to make sure you're ready to make the presentation, including ways to run the slide show and backup alternatives in case something goes wrong. In this chapter, you did the following:

- You found out how to set up a slide show for various presentation situations.
- You learned that you can easily jump around in a slide show, even if it's normally a sequential show .
- You explored the use of keyboard shortcuts.
- You learned how to rehearse and time a presentation.
- You discovered how to make backup plans, such as writing a slide show to CD and using overhead transparencies and handouts.

In Chapter 15, "Making a Presentation," you'll learn about making a presentation, including dealing with room conditions and handling unexpected problems.

15

Making a Presentation

If you're new to making presentations in front of a group, you might think you're ready to go. Experienced presenters know, however, that you have to consider many elements before you're truly ready—room conditions, equipment setup, and how and where you can move. You also need to be prepared to handle unexpected problems.

This chapter explores some very practical and real-life conditions that you'll face when making a presentation. Even experienced presenters find that making a PowerPoint presentation brings its own set of challenges. What you learn here just might make or break your presentation.

⇨ A detailed discussion of room and equipment preparation and the mechanics of good delivery is beyond the scope of this book. However, there are lots of good resources out there, including Tom Mucciolo's chapters in Que's *Special Edition Using Microsoft PowerPoint 2002*, Part VII, "From Concept to Delivery."

Preparing the Room

The room in which you present can have a huge influence on the success of a presentation. Unfortunately, we often have little say over the kind of room we present in. If you're lucky, yours will be about the right size for your audience, and it will be clean and attractive so as not to distract from what you're doing.

Several other room conditions, however, *can* be controlled. Unfortunately, too often speakers show up with so little time that they can't take advantage of room features that might help them. To the extent possible, you should try to find out all you can about your room and make adjustments before you begin your presentation.

How's the Lighting?

One of your first concerns should be the lighting because lighting is more critical for a PowerPoint presentation than for traditional ones. You should consider the following:

- Where is the screen located? If you're in a typical convention center, often the screen gets placed right beneath a set of fluorescent lights, which wash out the screen and make it hard to read beyond a few rows (see Figure 15.1). If you can, you should at least turn off the offending lights.

- Does the room have canister or recessed lights that shine directly down and don't spread out toward the screen? If so, you should turn those on and turn off fluorescent lighting altogether. This enables viewers to take notes, see each other, and still clearly see the screen (see Figure 15.2).

- Is there lighting on you so that the audience can connect with you? If you're standing in the dark, it's difficult to take advantage of your ability to smile, gesture, or catch the eye of an audience member.

- Is there enough light to see your keyboard or other equipment you have to operate? You lose precious time and credibility if you have to fumble around in the dark. Even if the room doesn't provide the right kind of lighting, all is not lost: You can purchase miniature lights that plug into the USB port of your laptop to light your keyboard.

FIGURE 15.1
Lights, especially fluorescent lights, can wash out the screen, making slides hard to see.

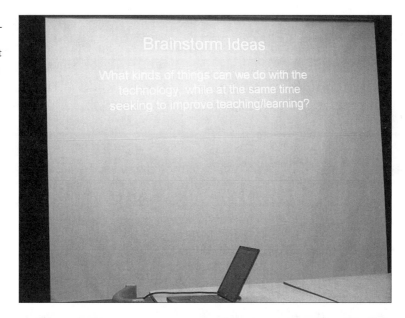

FIGURE 15.2
Canister or recessed lighting is ideal for PowerPoint slide shows.

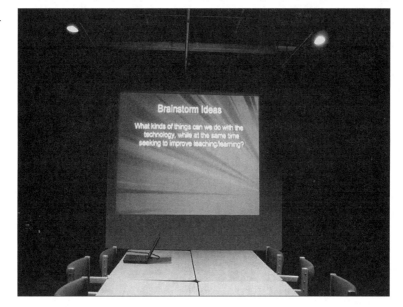

Adjusting Seating

An important concern for presentations is the seating. Often, you have little control over this, but where you do, you should consider the following:

- Try to make sure that seats aren't blocked from clearly viewing the screen.

- If the room is too large, try to cordon off back rows or invite the audience to move closer.

- If the room is too small, try to make sure everyone's seated or at least comfortable before you begin.

- If you want to engender discussion, try to arrange seats such that audience members face each other as well as you.

Determining the Speaker Location

Find out where it's expected that you'll be standing or sitting. Some rooms have specially equipped podiums (see Figure 15.3) where speakers can connect laptops. Unfortunately, you sometimes are nearly forced to stand behind the podium. Like the Wizard of Oz, you secretly maneuver your equipment, but you never step out to be seen by the audience. Later in this chapter you'll learn some ways to overcome such limitations, but you should try to become familiar enough with the setup that you know where you can move and where you can best be seen and heard.

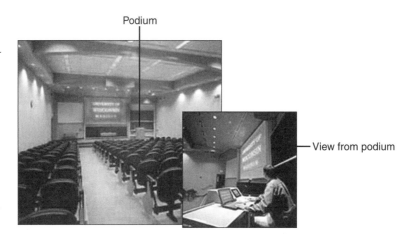

FIGURE 15.3

A presentation podium contains all the necessary equipment in one location, but it can seem like a prison to a presenter who likes to move around.

If you're in a large hall or if you don't have a loud, clear voice, you might need to use a microphone, unless you plan to have your slide show do all the talking! If possible, you should try to arrange to have a wireless microphone so you can move around freely. Even having a handheld microphone with plenty of cord is better than being forced to stand behind a stationary microphone stand.

Don't forget that the computer needs to be heard, too. If you have sound or video clips that are important to the presentation, find out if there's a way to connect your computer to the room's sound system. Typical computer speakers are rarely robust enough for a large room.

Remember that if you've never presented in a room before, you owe it to yourself to check out the room well before your presentation. You might not be able to make many changes to lighting, seating, or speaker location, but at least you'll know ahead of time what you're dealing with and that you've made the best adjustments you can.

Preparing the Equipment

You might be a great presenter, and you also might have prepared a great PowerPoint slide show. But have you forgotten that you'll be using technology to make your presentation? Murphy came close when he said, "Anything that can go wrong will go wrong." Perhaps more accurate is my own corollary: "Anything you haven't prepared for will go wrong, while having prepared adequately at least gives you a fighting chance."

In my experience, many presentations that never seem to make it off the ground are those where technology gets in the way. And more often than not, it isn't really the technology that's the problem, but the presenter's lack of familiarity with it.

Setting Up the Computer

If you've been preparing a PowerPoint slide show on the computer you'll use to make the presentation, you're in good shape. At least you know it works the way you expect it will. However, if you have to move your slide show from your desktop computer to a laptop computer or to a computer that's in the room you're present-ing in, you need to make sure you consider a number of issues, including the following:

- If you copy a PowerPoint presentation to disk or CD, you need to make sure you copy *all* files related to the presentation, including sound files and hyper-linked files. Generally, graphic images are embedded in the slide show itself, but certain other files may not be.

- After you copy the files to the presentation computer, you should play the show through completely to make sure you have all the files you need.

■ Make sure that the version of PowerPoint on the presentation computer matches the version you used to create your slide show. If it's an older version, some of your presentation's features, such as animations, might not work as you expect them to, and you'll have to make last-minute adjustments to your slide show.

■ If you're using sound effects or playing music, you should make sure the computer's sound system is working correctly. You shouldn't assume the worst if it doesn't. For example, the volume might not be turned up or the speakers may not be plugged into the right jack (they might be in the microphone jack, for example).

Matching the Screen's Resolution with the Projector's Resolution

Do you know what your computer's screen resolution is? Is it really that important? Screen resolution is the number of dots (pixels) across the screen, measured horizontally and vertically. For example, older computers used a Standard VGA resolution of 640 across by 480 down (that is, 640×480). Most computers these days use at least Super VGA (800×600) or XGA (1028×724).

To determine the settings for your computer, follow these steps:

1. Right-click the Windows desktop.

2. From the context menu, choose Properties. Windows displays the Display Properties dialog box.

3. Click the Settings tab. Figure 15.4 shows the Settings tab in the Display Properties dialog box on a Windows XP system; yours might be slightly different.

4. Don't change the screen resolution. Just note what it is and click Cancel to return to Windows.

Later, after you become more familiar with your projector, you might need to return to this dialog box to change the screen resolution of your presentation computer.

Turning Off Screen Savers and Power Savers

Screen savers are cute—except when they come on in the middle of a presentation. Likewise, although many laptop manufacturers make sure that power-saving options kick in to help conserve battery power, you don't want the computer dropping into "sleep" mode while you're talking. Your audience can take care of that for you!

FIGURE 15.4

FIGURE 15.4

Use your computer's Display Properties dialog box to determine the current screen resolution.

Well before the presentation, you should check your Windows settings to make sure screen savers and power-saving options are turned off. To change these settings, follow these steps:

1. Right-click the Windows desktop.

2. From the context menu, choose Properties. Windows displays the Display Properties dialog box.

3. Click the Screen Saver tab (see Figure 15.5).

FIGURE 15.5

Turn off screen savers so they don't interrupt your presentation.

4. From the **S**creen Saver drop-down list box, select (None).

5. Click P**o**wer or whatever button tells you to adjust monitor power settings. Windows XP displays the Power Options Properties dialog box (see Figure 15.6), although another operating system might have a slightly different dialog box.

FIGURE 15.6

Make sure the computer doesn't go to sleep during your presentation.

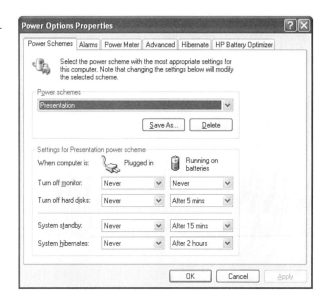

6. From the P**o**wer Schemes drop-down list box, select Presentation or another option that doesn't turn off the monitor, or go into standby mode, even when you're running on batteries. You can also create a custom scheme that leaves the monitor and computer running.

7. Click OK and then click OK again to return to Windows.

Again, your system may vary slightly from the one illustrated here. Take time to become familiar with screen saver and power settings so you can quickly turn them off when using another computer.

Understanding the Projector

The data projector is central to making a good PowerPoint presentation. Fortunately, good projectors are becoming increasingly available. Nevertheless, making sure you have the right projector still requires effort and care.

If you're lucky, you have access to your own projector, and you can make sure you're familiar with it and that it's working properly with your computer.

You're also lucky if the room where you're presenting has a built-in projector, usually ceiling mounted. That means that it's already set up, usually optimally, for the room and that someone at the facility knows how to run it. It might go without saying, but you should take time to find out who that person is.

If you don't have your own projector that you can take with you to the presentation, here are some of the questions you should ask about the one you'll be using:

■ What is the projector's *native resolution*? Although projectors can often display at more than one resolution, only one is the projector's native, or optimal, resolution.

■ What resolutions can the projector display? For example, if its native resolution is 800×600, can it also play at 1028×724?

■ Does the projector have a standard VGA connector, sometimes called a 15-pin D connector? Figure 15.7 shows a standard VGA connector on a laptop computer, which is identical to those found on projectors.

FIGURE 15.7

Video/data projectors and laptop computers use 15-pin VGA connectors to hook up with each other.

■ Does the projector come with a VGA cable? If not, you need to provide your own, and it should have male (pins, not holes) VGA connectors at both ends (see Figure 15.8). If possible, you should have a long VGA cable so you aren't tied too closely to the projector, but be careful you don't bring only an *extender* cable, one that has a male connector at one end and a female connector at the other.

■ Does the projector have a zoom lens? A zoom lens enables you to make the picture as large as possible, while giving you some flexibility as to the distance from the projector to the screen.

FIGURE 15.8

Connecting VGA cables must have male connectors at both ends.

■ Does the projector have keystone correction? *Keystoning* is what happens when the projector has to angle upward, making the top of the picture wider than the bottom (see Figure 15.9). Many projectors allow for digital keystone correction so that the top and bottom are the same width.

FIGURE 15.9

A keystone image, wider at the top than at the bottom, is unattractive and unprofessional looking.

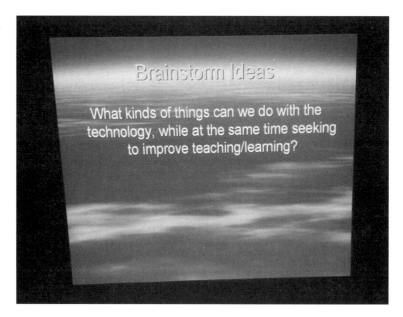

When you connect the computer and the projector, you first need to make sure the projector is actually displaying your computer's screen. If it isn't, try these things:

■ Make sure the VGA cables are connected properly. Sometimes the simplest things cause problems!

■ Use the projector's remote control or manual menu controls to make sure it's using the computer or RGB input instead of video input. Most projectors automatically detect a computer, but some don't.

■ If you're using a laptop and you see a display on the laptop but not on the projector, try these steps:

1. Look on the laptop's keyboard to see if there's a CRT/LCD key or a picture of a monitor. Often it's on one of the function keys (see Figure 15.10).

FIGURE 15.10

You can change your laptop's display output by pressing the Fn key and a Function key.

Display output key

Fn key

2. If the function is colored, look for an Fn key of the same color, usually near the Shift key (refer to Figure 15.10).

3. Press the Fn+function key combination to change the laptop's output to the VGA cable. Wait a couple seconds to see if you get a picture on the projector.

4. If you now get a picture on the projector but not on the laptop, press the Fn+function key again, and you usually get pictures on both the projector and the laptop. Sometimes, however, you get a picture only on the projector, or the laptop, but not both.

After you get a picture, you need to check to make sure the computer and projector resolutions match. You should check the edges of the screen to see if the entire laptop screen displays on the projector. If part of the screen is missing, often this is because the screen resolutions do not match. To fix this, go to the Windows Desktop properties and change the display settings to match the resolution of the projector. (See the section "Matching the Screen's Resolution with the Projector's Resoulution," earlier in this chapter, for details on setting the computer's screen resolution.)

Can you see why it's important to arrive at the presentation room early and to check things out before you try to make a presentation? An otherwise outstanding presentation is dead before it starts if you spend the first five minutes trying to figure out why you can't get a picture.

> **tip**
>
> If you're using a laptop and aren't getting the picture to display, the number-one reason is usually that the laptop has to be told to send the signal through the attached cable instead of only to its own screen. To fix this, you can press the Fn and function key combination that changes that setting to quickly get the display on the projector.

Working with a Remote-Controlled Mouse

I've alluded to the standing-behind-the-podium syndrome several times. There might be some occasions on which this is appropriate, but more often than not, you'll benefit from being able to get out from behind the podium and move around during your presentation.

One simple solution to avoid hiding behind the podium is to get away from using the mouse to advance slides. Instead, you can use the spacebar, which is quicker and easier to use than the mouse. Wandering back to the podium to press the spacebar is at least an inexpensive solution. However, it's still not the most effective solution because you're still tethered to the podium.

Far more effective is to use a remote-controlled mouse. The concept is simple. You set up a receiver and software on the computer, and then you control the slide show with a wireless mouse device from anywhere in the room. For example, you can walk right out into the audience, which promotes greater audience participation.

There are several such devices on the market. One type uses buttons and arrows to control the mouse pointer and to trigger actions (see Figure 15.11). These tend to be inexpensive devices, but they don't let you do much more than simply advance slides. The control works somewhat like an eraser-top pointing device found on some laptop computers.

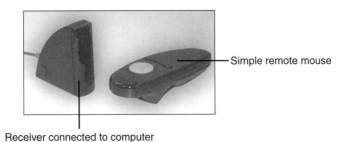

FIGURE 15.11

A simple type of remote mouse is best for advancing slides, not for controlling mouse pointer movement.

Simple remote mouse

Receiver connected to computer

Another device, which I prefer, is the gyro-controlled mouse (see Figure 15.12). As you move the device, gyro-based technology senses your movements and controls the onscreen mouse pointer just like you do with a regular mouse. Such devices are more expensive than the simpler devices, but they work more naturally.

FIGURE 15.12

A gyro-controlled remote mouse helps you use natural movement to move the mouse pointer.

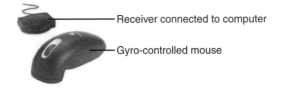

Receiver connected to computer

Gyro-controlled mouse

In any case, if you make more than an occasional presentation, you'll probably find a remote-controlled mouse of some sort well worth the investment.

Using a Laser Pointer

There are several ways to point to things onscreen. The worst, and one you want to avoid if at all possible, is to walk in front of the screen and point with your hand or with a stick pointer.

You can also use the mouse pointer, and if you move slowly enough and the pointer is big enough, the audience can see what you're pointing at. The disadvantage of this, once again, is that you're stuck behind the podium.

An inexpensive and effective solution is to use a laser pointer (see Figure 15.13). Such a device projects a small, brilliant red dot, making it easy for the audience to see what you're pointing at and making it easy for you to point from anywhere in the room. Many projector remote controls also include laser light beams, but you need to make sure such a feature is working before you depend on it.

FIGURE 15.13
Laser pointer devices are available as pens and key chains, making them easy to transport and use.

Choreographing Speaker/Audience Interaction

What? This isn't a dance routine, is it? Technically, no, but the whole idea behind choreography is to plan ahead of time where you're going to move and how you're going to get there. Unless you plan to plant yourself behind a podium, this section's for you.

Using Speaker Notes

You probably think of speaker notes as supplemental information to share with the audience. This might be true, but they're also valuable as stage notes to you, the presenter, to remind you what to do, where to click, when to move, and so on.

For example, consider the slide shown in Figure 15.14. If you've just prepared the slide and practiced the presentation, you probably already know what to do. But if you're returning to the slide show after a few days (or weeks), you might forget that clicking the eagle plays a video clip of an eagle in flight. That's the sort of thing that ought to go in your speaker notes. (Figure 15.14 shows speaker notes below the slide.)

caution

Laser lights have two inherent dangers. The first is that if the beam shines into a person's eyes, it can cause eye damage.

The second, while not physically damaging, can certainly damage a presentation. If you're not careful about how you move the laser pointer, the light flits around the screen, never really settling on what you want to point out. Try to point to something and hold the beam there for a few seconds and then turn off the pointer. Constant pointer movement can be very distracting.

FIGURE 15.14

You can use speaker notes to remind you where hidden action settings are.

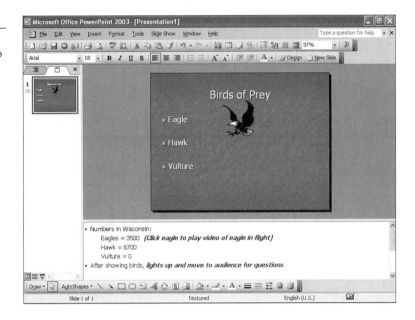

Speaker notes might also include the following:

- A reminder to pause at a particular point and field questions
- A note to tell you to spend only five minutes on questions
- A suggestion to bring up lights and go into the audience for a discussion
- A reminder that if you click an object, you'll jump to a slide that adds to or reinforces the current slide
- The amount of time left in the presentation (for example, 30 minutes), to let you know whether you're moving too fast or too slow

Speaker notes can be anything you need to help you pace yourself or to jog your memory about information or about what you should be doing at any point in the slide show.

How should you access speaker notes? You can view speaker notes while presenting a slide show. However, what you see, the audience sees as well. It might not go over well to show them something like "They're not going to get this, but take a couple questions anyway." Perhaps a better way is to print for yourself either speaker notes or thumbnail pictures of the slides, along with speaker notes.

⇨   For information on printing speaker notes, see **p. 310**.

Moving Around While Presenting

Standing, pacing, gesturing...all these elements have a bearing on whether people pay attention to you and how effectively you communicate with them.

I'm not going to pretend to provide you with hard-and-fast rules here. In fact, quite the opposite. However, please do consider some of the following, just to get yourself thinking about movement:

- If you stand still, people have little reason to watch you. You become like a narrator's voice behind a much more interesting visual presentation. Thus, you lose your powers of nonverbal communication.

- If you move too much or too quickly, you become a distraction. The audience will be thinking more about whether you're going to knock over your laptop computer or fall off the edge of the stage than about your presentation.

- You should find an *anchor point*, a spot to which you always return. If you don't have a remote-controlled mouse, that doesn't mean your laptop has to be the anchor. In fact, your computer's location should only be somewhere you go to and come back from.

- If you do use a remote-control device, you should practice advancing slides from various locations to make sure the computer picks up the signal. You don't want to be standing there saying that you know your blankety-blank mouse was working last night. In fact, if you choreograph slide advances properly, the audience will hardly know it's you that's moving the slides.

- You should try to avoid blocking the view of the screen. Yes, you might want the audience members to watch you, but if you block their view, they'll ask why you even bothered to bring your slides.

- The closer you are to the screen, the easier it is for audience members to move back and forth between you and the slide. If you're presenting a slide with a lot of detail, you should move closer to the screen so the audience doesn't have to make a choice between watching the slide and glancing at you.

- The farther away you are from the screen, the more likely it is that audience members will watch either you or the screen, but not both. With a simple slide, you can get the audience to look at you much more easily. To force people's eyes off the screen, press the B key to black the screen. Press B again to turn it on.

With some of these ideas in mind, you should also observe effective presenters. How do they move, what position are they in when they want your attention, and how natural does it all seem?

Finally, practice does indeed make a difference. If you can, gain access to the room you'll present in and try walking around a bit to get a feel for the distances and the obstacles. Practice using your mouse or otherwise advancing slides. Look for ways you can get up close with the audience and where you can go when you want to minimize attention on you and maximize attention on the slides. All this can go a long way toward giving you a more comfortable, home-court-advantage type of feeling.

Handling Unexpected Problems

What can go wrong? Nearly anything. You could lose power, or your computer could lock up on you. You might have someone break a chair and fall on the floor. You might be interrupted by jack-hammering outside the presentation room's window. You can practice and plan all you want, but you can't avoid everything that might go wrong.

What you *can* do, however, is have a backup plan ready to go. A short anecdote or joke can help diffuse tension that comes from interruptions. A visual handout could help in the case of a loss of power. For the most serious interruptions, you have to decide whether it's worth continuing. If you're not in charge, the decision might be made for you, but if you are, you should consider postponing or pausing until the source of disruption ends. It's hard enough to communicate when you're in control, but fighting against outside disturbances is a losing battle.

You should also remain calm. Getting upset, cursing at the equipment, and yelling at the tech support person who shows up don't make the show go any better or faster and serve to alienate the audience. Getting the audience back on your side becomes doubly difficult. However, if you show the audience members calmness under pressure, they'll likely be willing to listen to you when the problems are solved.

Finally, and most importantly, take seriously the suggestions offered in this chapter to minimize potential problems. I've had my share of unexpected problems, but when I've followed my own advice, I have been lucky enough to make some perfectly smooth presentations. And you can, too!

The Absolute Minimum

In this chapter, you have learned about the requirements for adequately preparing the room and equipment for making a presentation. In particular, you did the following:

- You found out how important lighting is and ways to make it work for you.
- You learned how to set up equipment properly.
- You explored ways to make a presentation more natural, including the use of a remote-controlled mouse.
- You learned how to move around a room so as to make the presentation more effective.
- You looked at ways to deal with unexpected problems.

Chapter 16, "Learning the Elements of Effective Presentations," reviews and brings together all the important elements of an effective presentation.

IN THIS CHAPTER

- Find out ways to size up an audience
- Learn the importance of objective-driven content
- Explore ways to grab and keep an audience's attention
- Learn how colors and fonts are part of the message
- Discover ways to assess the impact of a presentation

16

LEARNING THE ELEMENTS OF EFFECTIVE PRESENTATIONS

An effective presentation is one that achieves its objectives of communicating ideas, teaching concepts, or convincing or motivating listeners. This book presents PowerPoint features and procedures with an eye toward helping you create successful presentations. But all that has come in bits and pieces. This chapter brings together some of the key ingredients in creating and presenting effective presentations.

However, you should also know what this chapter doesn't do. It does not provide a comprehensive treatment of public speaking, learning theories, motivational psychology, or the like. There are plenty of other books out there that can do a much better job with those topics, partly because their authors are experts in those areas and because they've got a lot more pages to cover the topics.

So does that mean you've got a rookie here, trying to tell you what to do? Not at all. I've got plenty of teaching and presenting experience. Take what you can from these pages, and, like I do, continue to observe other presenters. Some day you'll be able to compile your own list of what makes an effective presentation.

Understanding an Audience

Some time ago I spent two years in Argentina. I've always loved to tell jokes, especially those that involve puns. I found that my Argentine friends often wouldn't laugh at my jokes but would instead try to correct my Spanish. I had to explain that I knew what I was saying and that what I said was a pun. By that time, of course, the moment was lost. The problem wasn't that my Spanish was bad or that I was saying anything wrong. It was that I didn't understand that the listeners didn't expect me, a newcomer, to have the ability to play with words the way I could.

As a presenter, you also have to determine who it is you're speaking to and what kind of "filters" they have as they listen to you. How do you determine who your audience really is? The following are some considerations:

- *Age*—Are you presenting to children, teens, young professionals, or seasoned veterans? Speaking down to young adults can be as disastrous as speaking over the heads of children.

- *Experience*—What experience do members of the audience have with what you'll be talking about? If it's a technical presentation, how much background do you have to cover before the audience can understand? How much "shorthand" (terminology that assumes prior knowledge) can you use?

- *Interest*—Why are the audience members there? Are they eager students or lumps of unmotivated humanity? Are they team members interested in success or skeptical outsiders looking to be convinced?

- *Motivation*—What's in it for the audience members? Do their grades depend on what you say? Does their financial future rest on the quality of the information you give them? Will chances for their success be enhanced by your presentation?

- *Technology background*—Are they from the old school, expecting verbal presentations more than snazzy charts and pictures? Or have they experienced lots of visual programs and therefore expect the quality of your presentation to match their experience? Are they, as some have called them, the "MTV Generation"?

■ *Familiarity*—Are these people you know, and might they cut you some slack as a result? Or are they total strangers, who may or may not be willing to give up their time unless what you have to say is really worth it? Conversely, are they so familiar with you that they don't afford you the courtesy you deserve, feeling free to interrupt or divert the presentation?

■ *Your background*—Are you the kind of expert or authority who commands respect even before you start? Or are you an unknown who has to establish your credibility before the audience will put stock in what you say?

As you can see, this partial list underscores the complex nature of determining who your audience is. One type of presentation definitely won't work for all audiences. Understanding your audience determines what and how you prepare and is a key factor in your success or failure.

Audiences usually have mixed backgrounds. You might find young and old, experienced and inexperienced, motivated and disinterested all in the same group. Finding a way to reach all of them is a seemingly impossible task. Nevertheless, you have to try if you want to communicate with them. Here are a few ideas that might work:

■ Ask the person who invites you to speak to tell you something about the audience. Ask what the audience expects, what audience members' backgrounds and expertise are. You, too, have filters, and when you're asked to speak on a certain subject, you tend to assume that you know what the audience wants to hear. Take time to clarify what's expected first, and you'll be much more likely to make a successful presentation.

■ Spend a few moments getting to know the audience. Ask survey-type questions, such as "How many of you have been to an off-shore drilling site?" or "How many of you have degrees in chemical engineering?" Nonthreatening, general questions like this can do two things: They can help you find out about the audience, and they can let the audience know that you care who they are and what they know.

■ Take a moment to tell the audience about yourself. An anecdote or a bit about your background can help audience members adjust their preconceived notions about you before you begin, making it easier for them to accept you for who you are. Before I begin a workshop on computer software, I tell them I'm highly qualified because I have a Ph.D. in Latin American literature, and that if I can do it, anyone can.

■ Do a little research on your own before you begin. Find out something about the company where you're speaking or the organization to which you're presenting. Recently my professional organization invited a NASA astronaut to speak to us. Although we were meeting in Houston, near the Space Center, the astronaut wisely determined that we were much more interested in how astronauts learned and used foreign languages in pressure situations than we were in the mechanics of a space mission.

■ Make midcourse corrections if necessary. Ask questions that help you determine if you're headed in the right direction. Observe people's faces. Are they giving you blank stares or are they asleep? Be careful, however, not to let one or two people overly influence your assessment of the entire audience. A vocal complainer or a sleepyhead, for example, may not be speaking for everyone.

The bottom line is that you have to find ways to know who you're presenting to. If you don't, all the other elements in preparing and presenting will be of little value.

Getting the Content Right

Knowing your audience is a step in the right direction. You might think that content is the next step, but you'd be only partially right. Before you can determine what to present, you have to establish your objectives. In other words, you have to start with the end in mind (see Figure 16.1).

FIGURE 16.1

An effective presentation consists of over-lapping ele-ments, anchored by understand-ing your audi-ence and having clear objectives.

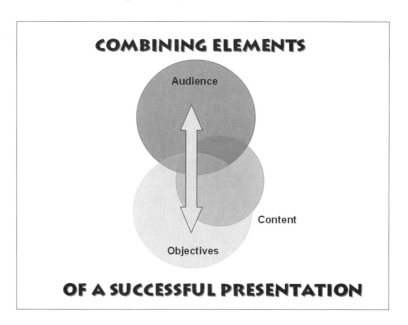

For example, if your objective is to merely entertain, your content could be nearly anything, from sports to politics to television. If you want audience members to understand the complexities of a valve assembly, you better think about what steps can help them reach that understanding.

Having your objective in mind helps you select, organize, and present the right kind of material. At each step along the way, you can ask yourself, "Will this help me reach my objective?" If it doesn't, you probably need to consider eliminating it, no matter how interesting it is to you personally. That doesn't mean you eliminate supporting material altogether. Like an experienced tour guide, you need to keep your objective in mind, but you also need to know when it's appropriate to take a little side trip. Nevertheless, you should always make sure you return to the main road.

PowerPoint's outline feature helps you organize the textual content leading to the final objective. But you also have to focus on visual content. Does a clip art image or a photograph really help the audience understand better? Or have you found an interesting image and you've bent your presentation to make it fit? Does that nifty sound effect or video clip really help the viewers understand the final objective? Or does it distract from or overwhelm what you're trying to accomplish? Can you get your awestruck tourists back on the bus?

Enough browbeating. You know your content, and you know what the audience needs to know. Make sure you use PowerPoint to assist you in the process. Don't let PowerPoint become the main attraction.

Capturing and Maintaining Interest

That's why the opening of your presentation is so important. Although you don't want to spend too much time on the preliminaries, you need to find a way to capture the audience's interest before you launch into the rest of your presentation.

Opening "hooks," or attention grabbers, can include anecdotes, jokes, controversial statements, current events, and interesting facts. But these hooks must be related to your presentation. A joke by itself does little to get the audience thinking, unless it's to wonder why you told the joke and wasted their time.

For example, I work for a dean who has an uncanny ability to get a room full of department chairs to leave a budget meeting with smiles on their faces, determined to make do with resources that have just been reduced. Inevitably, he starts with a story, a cartoon, or a joke that helps everyone realize that he's in this right along with us, defusing the us–them mentality under which most budget discussions are conducted.

Whatever it is you do, you want the audience members to start thinking about the objective. If they need to cut their budgets, get them thinking about how they can do it, not whether they want to do it. If it's a sales presentation, you want them to begin thinking about why they should buy your product. If it's a lecture on tomatoes, you want them to feel the need to understand, appreciate, and maybe even eat tomatoes.

When the excitement from the opening bell wears off, a presentation needs some timely prodding to maintain its pace and interest. What can you do to keep things going and to maintain audience interest? Facts, figures, and information may be interesting in and of themselves, but a presentation can suffer from too much sameness. Look for ways to vary what you present. For example, instead of bulleted lists of information, use graphic images. Instead of descriptions, use diagrams or charts. Instead of written quotes, use recorded sound or video quotes.

Returning to the tour bus analogy, consider when it's time to make a brief stop. A well-timed break may help audience members catch their breath, get their blood circulating again, or use the bathroom. You shouldn't assume that just because you can keep going, they all can. They'll thank you by coming back to the presentation with greater attention and focus.

Memorable tours also include interesting side trips and unexpected bumps in the road, but remember that these are not the tour themselves. In a like manner, you can use attention grabbers, or hooks, to maintain interest in a presentation. Once again, these could include stories or anecdotes, examples or analogies, opportunities for interaction such as questions and answers, a statement or visual image that challenges the audience to think, a sound effect, or an unusual animation.

These activities should in some way relate to the topic, but they can come from anywhere. In fact, the more unexpected they are, the more likely it is that they'll accomplish your objective of grabbing the audience's attention once more. Be careful, however, not to take the audience so far off the beaten path that it's hard to get them back. Again, always keep the end in mind.

Making Color, Font, and Font Size Work for You

One often-overlooked element of successful presentations is the use of colors and fonts. If you're just starting out, it's likely that you've been using PowerPoint's predefined designs and color schemes. That's actually a good idea because the creators of PowerPoint have built their designs with good color and font combinations in mind.

You'll soon discover that you can control nearly every aspect of a PowerPoint slide show, including color schemes, fonts, and font sizes. However, because these visual elements can be nearly as important as text and graphic content in conveying your message, you should be aware of some of the guidelines that can help you use these effectively. You at least need to know the rules before you can break them!

Anyone can show you color charts and explain theories about primary and secondary colors, complementary and analogous colors, and so on. But the real test as to whether colors work well together is how the audience sees them and reacts to them. In particular, can the audience see and read the text, and do the colors add to the mood or feeling you're trying to create? I can't give this subject a comprehensive treatment, but here are a few suggestions:

- Try using PowerPoint's color schemes before branching off on your own. If you like the effect one of these schemes provides, it's quite probable that your audience will too. Ask an office colleague or a friend what they think to get someone else's take.

- White and very light colored backgrounds often give the best contrast for text or graphic images. However, such backgrounds are awfully bright, especially in darkened rooms, making it hard for the audience to look at them for a long period of time.

- Darker colors can be used to set a mood. Blue is soft and soothing, while red and orange suggest passion or action. Green is life-giving and positive. Of course, color can't do all the work. You can use a bright yellow background and still put people to sleep with a lifeless presentation.

- Gradient shades and textured backgrounds can add a touch of professionalism to a slide and can be more pleasing to the eye than a solid-color background (see Figure 16.2).

FIGURE 16.2

Gradient or textured backgrounds provide a soft backdrop for text and other content.

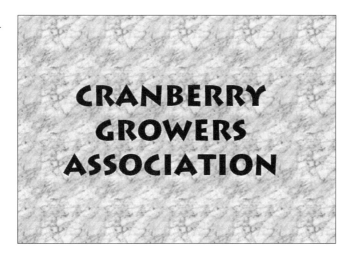

- Be particularly careful with solid-color backgrounds and colored text to make sure it's readable. For example, red on dark blue or green is very difficult to read.

- Be aware that many people have some form of color-blindness, red/green being the most common. Avoid color combinations that depend on these colors for contrast. In fact, avoid anything that depends totally on color contrasts. Use the Color/Grayscale button to preview a slide in gray tones to see if there's enough contrast without color.

Many rules exist regarding fonts and font sizes. When it comes right down to it, however, all you need to do is find a font and font size that's easily readable, not only by someone in the front row, but also by those in the back row.

As for fonts, consider the following:

- Try to limit the number of fonts used in a slide show. Select one or two basic fonts and stick with them. Try to be consistent in terms of style, color, and size.

- Serif fonts, those that have little feet on them, like the type in this book, are easier on the eyes than sans-serif fonts when used in printed text. However, they tend to be harder to read than sans-serif fonts when used on a PowerPoint slide. If you use a serif font, such as Times Roman, make sure the text is large and that there's not much of it (see Figure 16.3).

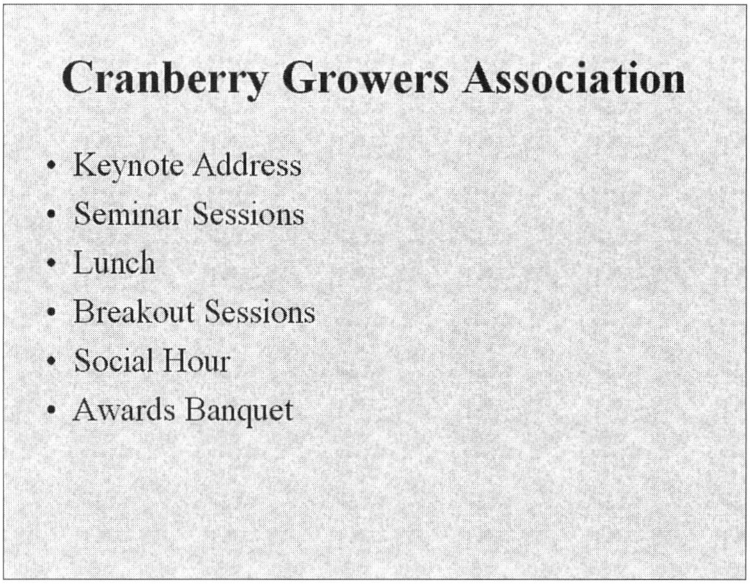

FIGURE 16.3

Serif fonts are harder to read than sans-serif fonts on a PowerPoint slide.

Cranberry Growers Association

- Keynote Address
- Seminar Sessions
- Lunch
- Breakout Sessions
- Social Hour
- Awards Banquet

■ Sans-serif fonts, such as Arial and Tahoma, are usually easier to read than serif fonts on a PowerPoint slide, especially for the small text sizes typically used in lists, bullets, and quotes (see Figure 16.4).

FIGURE 16.4

Sans-serif fonts are easier to read than serif fonts on a PowerPoint slide.

Cranberry Growers Association

- Keynote Address
- Seminar Sessions
- Lunch
- Breakout Sessions
- Social Hour
- Awards Banquet

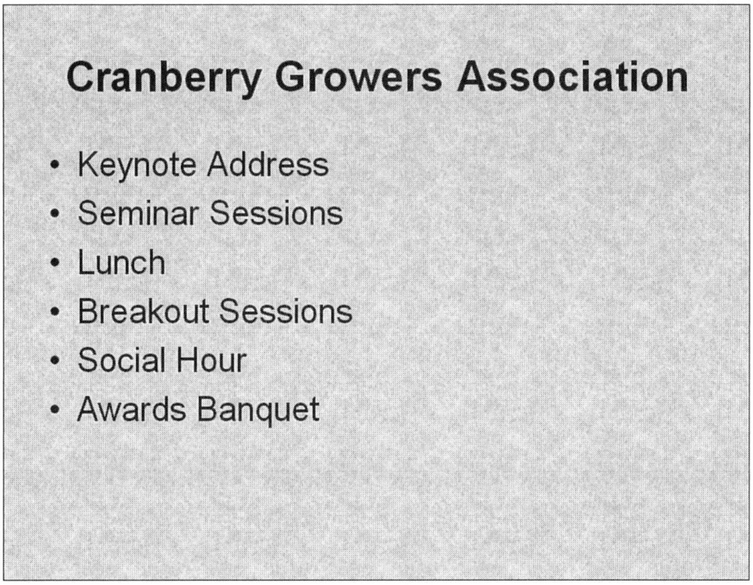

■ Traditional fonts, such as Arial and Times Roman, are considered *neutral* fonts in that they're common enough that they don't attract undue attention.

■ Fancy fonts, such as cursive or theme fonts, should be limited to very specific situations, where the font lends to or supports the meaning of the slide. Otherwise, the font is merely distracting (see Figure 16.5).

Choosing the right size of text involves using something that's large enough to be read easily. Fonts are measured in such a way that I can't just give you specific point sizes. A 44-point font in Arial might be perfect, but in a script font it might be too small (see Figure 16.6).

If you're not sure if your text can be read by those in the back row, try it out yourself. If you can read it comfortably from a back-row distance, the text is large enough.

One problem we all face some time or another is that we try to cram too much text onto a single slide. In the case of text and PowerPoint, less is more. Make your bullet points succinct, and keep them to only a few per slide (refer to Figure 16.4). If you find yourself needing more space, create a new slide instead of cluttering one slide with too much information (see for example, Figure 16.7).

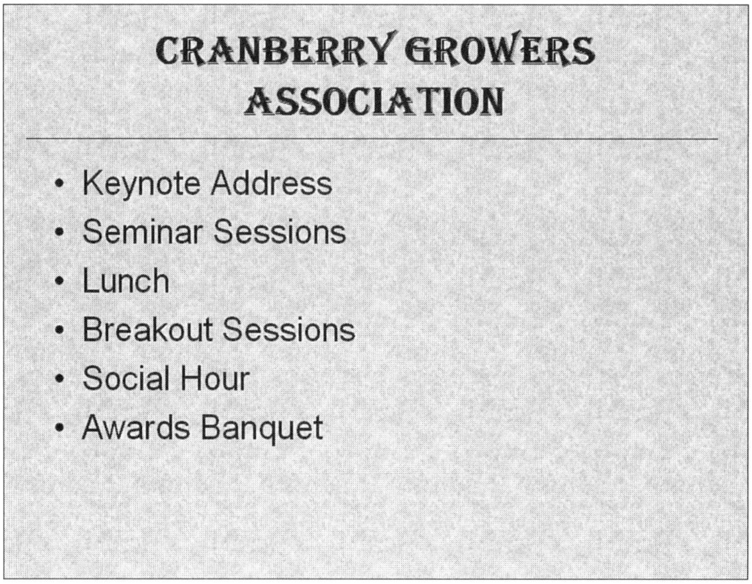

FIGURE 16.5

Fancy fonts are hard to read and should be reserved for slide titles or other large font text.

CRANBERRY GROWERS
ASSOCIATION

- Keynote Address
- Seminar Sessions
- Lunch
- Breakout Sessions
- Social Hour
- Awards Banquet

FIGURE 16.6

Point size doesn't mean much on a PowerPoint slide; both of these fonts are the same point size (44 points).

Cranberry Growers
Association

Cranberry Growers Association

Another problem that often occurs when you're experimenting with color schemes is that text is very readable on one part of the screen, but if it crosses a graphic image or a different color on the background, it becomes hard to see. An easy solution is to add a shadow style to the text that contrasts with the text color. For example, light text with a dark gray or black shadow is legible on nearly any kind of background (see Figure 16.8).

CRANBERRY GROWERS ASSOCIATION
• Keynote Address by Senator Oscar Lacayo
• Seminar Sessions (see your schedules for room assignments, speakers, and topics
• Lunch (be sure to have your tickets with you)
• Breakout Sessions (choose three of the five sessions available)
• Social Hour (cash bar and hors d' ouvres)
• Awards Banquet (see program for dinner menus and program entertainment)

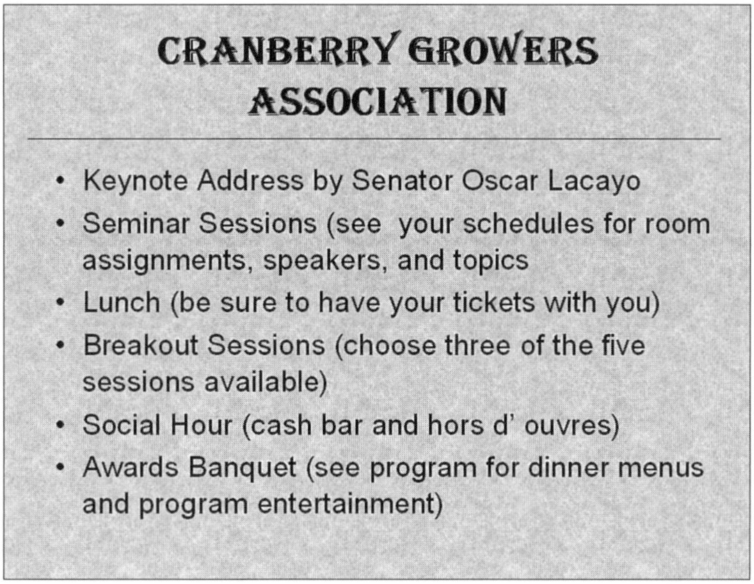

FIGURE 16.7
Too much text forces text to be smaller and less readable.

CGA
Cranberry Growers Association

FIGURE 16.8
You can add shading to text to contrast with all backgrounds.

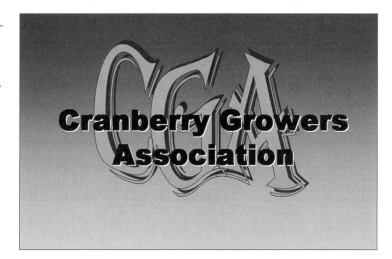

Getting Results from a Presentation

All your attention and hard work to create the perfect slide show is bound to pay off. Or is it? Just how do you know whether your presentation is successful? If people avoid eye contact with you after the presentation, that's one clue. But even if people tell you how much they enjoyed the presentation, how do you know if it was effective?

One way to get good results from a presentation involves helping audience members know what it is that they've learned, in three phases:

1. At the beginning of the slide show, tell them what you're going to tell them. For example, using an introductory overview slide, you tell them "We're going to explore several methods that can improve cranberry crop production."

2. Tell them what you told them you would. Don't promise them one thing and give them another. You might find the side roads interesting, but keep your focus on the objectives.

3. Tell them what you've told them. A summary slide can help recap what they've learned.

Another way to assess effectiveness is to establish activities that let audience members tell you what they've learned. Review your objectives and determine how you can measure whether you've met them. You might have to rephrase your objectives so that you can assess observable behavior. Here are some examples:

■ Avoid using immeasurable objectives. *Understand, comprehend, appreciate,* and *know* are difficult to assess without seeing something more observable.

■ Try to establish measurable objectives. For example, "Audience members will write down two procedures they will use to enhance their cranberry crop this year." Or, "Given a case study, audience members will suggest ways a grower can improve yield."

Not all situations lend themselves to this kind of assessment. But often they do. If you never find out how well you've communicated with the audience, chances are the next time you make the presentation, you'll repeat the mistakes you make this time. On the other hand, if you're the kind of presenter that I suspect you are, you'll find a great deal of satisfaction in seeing action as a result of what you present.

In short, creating a successful presentation doesn't happen by accident. You start by assessing the audience and your objectives, and then you add content and other elements that meet those objectives (see Figure 16.9). Throughout this book you'll learn that there are lots of other things that can enhance your presentations, but with these basics, you'll be off to a good start.

FIGURE 16.9

Various key elements combine to make an effective presentation, but of these, the audience and your objectives are probably the most important.

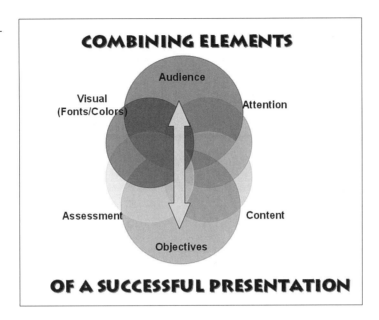

THE ABSOLUTE MINIMUM

In this chapter, you explored several key elements in effective slide show presentations:

- You found out ways to better understand to whom you're presenting.
- You learned how to organize and prepare content so that you work toward well-defined objectives.
- You explored ways to capture and maintain interest.
- You learned the importance of choosing color combinations that help communicate your message.
- You looked at how fonts and font styles can improve readability.
- You learned that it's important to build in assessment activities so that you know whether you've been effective.

Chapter 17, "Printing a Presentation," looks at a variety of ways to make a slide show available other than through a face-to-face presentation.

PART V

MAKING THE SLIDE SHOW AVAILABLE IN PRINT AND ON THE WEB

IN THIS CHAPTER

- Find out why it's not always a good idea to print a slide show

- Explore effective uses for printing slides

- Learn how to print speaker notes

- Discover how to create useful handouts

- Learn ways to print overhead transparencies or to make 35mm slides

17

PRINTING A PRESENTATION

You might not realize this, but PowerPoint was originally created to help produce better-looking overhead transparencies. As computers and data projectors became more capable and more readily available, we've all but forgotten that information you create for a visual, electronic presentation might also be useful in printed formats.

This chapter explores some of the various ways you can put your presentation in print. It also helps you determine when printing makes sense and when it doesn't.

Printing Slides

Have you ever attended a PowerPoint presentation where, as you enter, you're handed a thick sheaf of pages that contain every slide that will be in the presentation? Often, you sit down, thumb through the slides, and wonder why you bothered to come. Then, to make matters worse, the presenter gets up and reads through the bullets for you.

I'd like to say I'm exaggerating, but unfortunately, this scenario is all too common. There has to be a better reason for printing than to give everyone copies of all your slides. Indeed, there are a number of good reasons to print slides. Consider these possibilities:

- You have 3 slides out of 20 that contain critical information. One is a data chart, another is a table, and the last is a summary list of action items. You make printed copies of only these slides for your audience members to take with them.

- You've used PowerPoint to create an announcement or a flyer. You print a copy for duplication.

- You print a draft copy of your entire slide show to proof as you ride the train to work. Because you're not able to make changes to the slides in PowerPoint, you make notes and mark changes on the printouts. This helps you keep perspective. Later, you apply your changes.

- You print your title slide in color and post a copy at each entrance so attendees know they're in the right session.

- You've created an artistic rendering for a printed t-shirt, and you print the slide in reverse onto special iron-on paper.

- You add notes or mark up slides during your presentation, and now you want a printed record of those notes.

You can probably come up with more ideas. The point is, however, that wasting paper by printing full pages of slides as handouts isn't a good reason for printing. In fact, there are also better ways to create handouts than by simply printing slides.

Assuming that you've found a really good reason for printing a slide or slides, you follow these steps:

1. Choose **F**ile, **P**rint or press Ctrl+P. PowerPoint displays the Print dialog box (see Figure 17.1).

2. Make sure the proper printer is selected. Change printers if necessary from the **N**ame drop-down list box.

3. Select which slides you want to print: **A**ll, **C**urrent Slide, or Sl**i**des (to print specific slides; see the sample page ranges given in Figure 17.1).

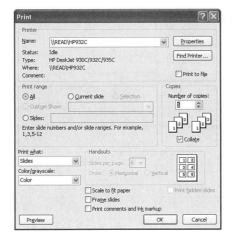

4. Set the number of copies, and choose how you want multiple copies stacked.

5. By default, PowerPoint prints all the slides in the slide show in their natural color if you have a color printer or in *grayscale* (shades of gray) if you don't. You can force color slides to print in grayscale or pure black and white by choosing from the Color/**G**rayscale drop-down list box.

6. Click OK to print your selection.

The preceding steps are the basics, designed to get a slide or slides printed quickly. However, you have several options that also might come in handy:

■ Perhaps the most useful option is Print Pre**v**iew, which enables you to see the results *before* you waste time and money printing on paper. This also lets you try out various print options ahead of time. For example, if you change the paper size, you might need to see how the slide prints on that particular size. Some changes, however, such as mirrored printing, do not display in Print Preview.

■ If you're printing a proofing copy, you can save ink and time by changing your printer's properties to print in draft mode. Click the **P**roperties button, and PowerPoint displays a dialog box that matches the capabilities of your particular printer (see Figure 17.2, which shows options for a color inkjet printer). For example, if you want to print in photographic quality, you could choose Photo Paper and change the quality to Best. Or perhaps you don't want to waste color ink for this draft copy. You could choose to print in black and white. Advanced options, if available, might include the ability to mirror the image (for example, to print it backward on iron-on transfer paper).

FIGURE 17.2

This Properties dialog box enables you to take advantage of your printer's unique capabilities.

- You can scale the slide to fit the size paper you've chosen as best it can.

- You can add a frame—a thin black border—around a slide's content (see Figure 17.3), by choosing Fra**m**e Slides. Especially with overhead transparencies, this can add a touch of professionalism.

- You can print slides along with markups or annotations you made while making the presentation by choosing Print Comments and In**k** Markup. For example, you could make annotations while practicing the show and then print those out and solicit comments from colleagues. You could then make corrections or changes before making the final presentation (see Figure 17.4).

▷ For information on making annotations or comments on slides while playing a slide show, see **p. 258**.

note

You cannot print all the way to the edge of the paper, regardless of its size. Printers have certain margin limits built into them that force you to leave at least a small margin.

tip

A handy way to keep track of minutes, discussion, or action items is to make annotations on a slide show. When you stop playing the slide show, tell PowerPoint to keep the annotations. Then print the slides that have annotations as a permanent record or reference.

FIGURE 17.3
Frames help printed slides stand out.

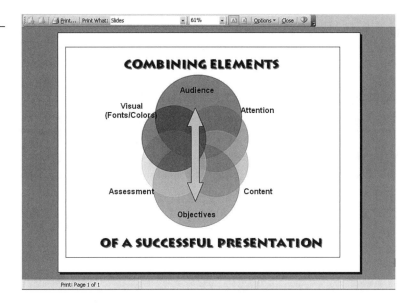

FIGURE 17.4
Markups and annotations you make while playing a slide show can be saved and printed.

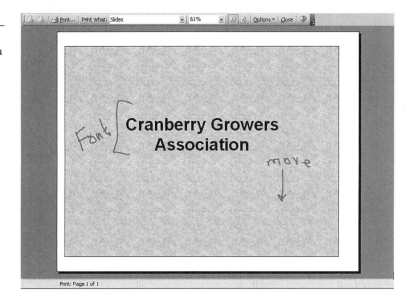

Printing Notes

Speaker notes can be used for a variety of reasons. One obvious purpose is to provide the speaker with reference material, or cues about what to say or do during a slide presentation. Another, however, is to provide written comments intended for the audience. Because notes don't display during the presentation, you provide them in printed format.

PowerPoint assumes that you want to provide notes along with the slides they describe. This makes sense, but it also limits your flexibility in how you print them out. By default, PowerPoint prints one slide and its notes per printed page.

To see quickly what a notes page looks like, choose **V**iew, Notes **P**age. PowerPoint shows a whole-page view, including the slide, the notes, and a page number (see Figure 17.5). To return to the Normal view, click the Normal View icon or choose **V**iew, **N**ormal.

FIGURE 17.5

The Notes view shows what printed notes look like.

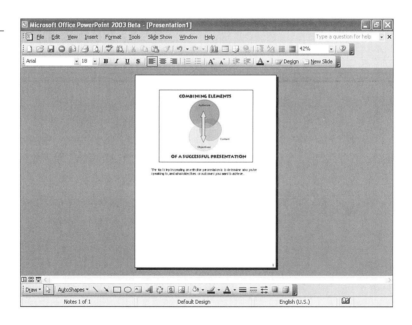

When you access the Print dialog box (refer to Figure 17.1) under Print **W**hat you can choose Notes Pages. However, that gives you only one slide and set of notes per page, which is the same as what you see in the Notes view.

Within PowerPoint there really is no way to print a list of speaker notes, without slides, or combine several notes on a page. However, you can do better than one per page by sending a slide show to Word. Follow these steps:

1. Save the slide show. What you're about to do opens Word and therefore brings the possibility of program crashes and lost data.

2. Choose **F**ile, Sen**d** To, Microsoft **W**ord. PowerPoint displays the Send to Microsoft Word dialog box (see Figure 17.6). You have two options for formatting notes:

FIGURE 17.6

Sending a slide show to Microsoft Word provides flexible formatting options that are not available in PowerPoint.

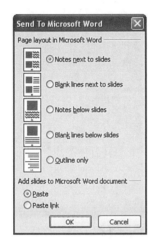

- The third option in the dialog box, Notes Below Slides, is the same as the one you find in PowerPoint's Print dialog box—half the page contains the slide, and the bottom half contains any notes.

- The first option, Notes Next to Slides, places a small version of the slide at the left, with notes at the right. This is a better use of paper and is typically easier to manage when you use notes during a presentation.

3. Choose a notes format, such as Notes **N**ext to Slides, and click OK. PowerPoint opens Microsoft Word, creates a three-column table, and places a slide number, slide, and its notes on each row (see Figure 17.7).

One advantage to sending a slide show to a Word document is that you can edit the results in Word. For example, if you choose the one-slide-per-page option, in Word you can then delete slide images and page breaks, thus leaving a numbered list of speaker notes (see Figure 17.8).

FIGURE 17.7

If you want small printed slides along with notes, you can send a slide show to Microsoft Word.

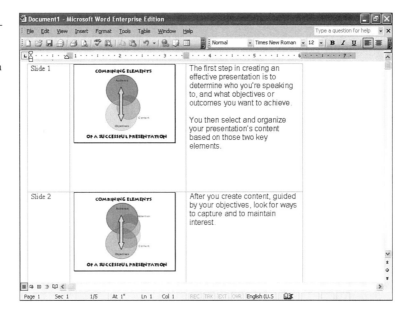

FIGURE 17.8

In Microsoft Word you can delete slide pictures, leaving just the slide numbers and printed speaker notes.

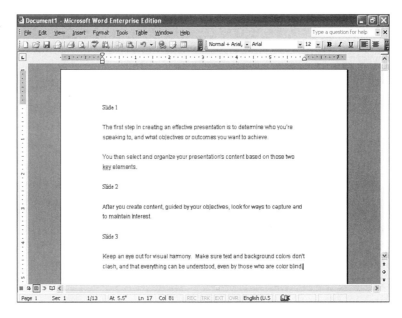

Creating Handouts

If you're bound and determined to provide your audience with printed handouts of your slides, you can at least conserve resources while helping viewers be actively involved by taking notes. Try these steps:

1. Choose **F**ile, **P**rint to access the Print dialog box.

2. From the Print **W**hat drop-down list box, choose Handouts (see Figure 17.9).

FIGURE 17.9

You can print multiple slides per handout to conserve paper or to provide note-taking areas.

3. Choose 1, 2, 3, 4, 6, or 9 in the Slides pe**r** Page drop-down list box and preview the effect in the Handouts preview box. Note that choosing 3 slides also provides lined spaces for viewers to take notes.

4. Choose **V**ertical to make slide numbers increment down the columns or Hori**z**ontal to increase them across rows.

5. Click Pr**e**view to see a larger view of the printout (see Figure 17.10). Here you can also click the Landscape button on the toolbar to get a different arrangement of slides and notes areas (see Figure 17.11). Note that the notes areas are left blank and do not include your speaker notes.

If you want a little more editing control over the printout, you can also send the slide show to Word by using the Send to Microsoft Word feature (refer to Figure 17.6). This way you can use Word to add a comment or two and still leave room for viewers to take their own notes (see Figure 17.12).

FIGURE 17.10

Choosing three handouts per page also gives lined spaces for viewers to take their own notes.

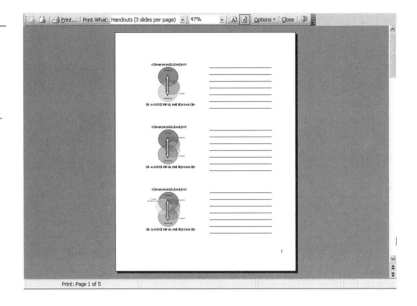

FIGURE 17.11

You can print handouts in landscape as well as portrait orientation.

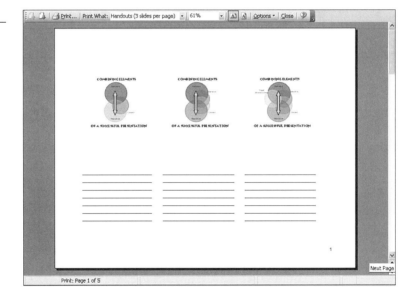

FIGURE 17.12

By using
Microsoft Word,
you can cus-
tomize note-
taking
handouts.

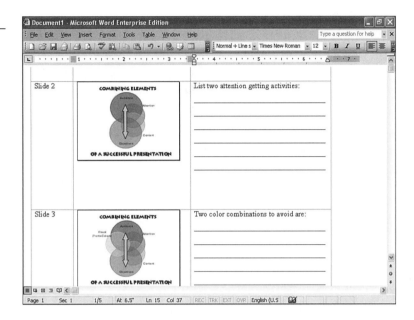

Creating Overhead Transparencies or Film Slides

PowerPoint slide shows are cool, but sometimes reality steps between you and what
you'd like to do. Laptop computers and data projectors are fairly expensive.
Sometimes you're forced to consider less expensive alternatives, but that doesn't
mean you have to abandon PowerPoint altogether.

A simple and inexpensive alternative is to create a slide show and print it on overhead transparencies. The advantages are obvious: Overhead projectors are cheap
and usually readily available. The disadvantages are also clear: Images on transparencies are static, and transitions between slides are more clumsy. In the end,
however, audiences appreciate the professional look of overheads created using
PowerPoint.

You print overhead transparencies the same way you create paper printouts of slides.
Use the Print dialog box to select the printer, print quality, color or grayscale, frame,
and so on. However, consider the following:

■ Preview slides before printing or print a draft paper copy. Paper is usually
  much cheaper than overhead transparencies. Also, print one test transparency before printing your entire slide show.

■ Decide whether you need all the slides you would have used in an electronic
  format. If you have slides that don't add significantly to the presentation,
  consider not printing them.

■ If a slide contains animations, such as progressive bullets, that clearly add to the slide's effectiveness, consider preparing several transparencies to simulate an animation sequence. For example, the first transparency shows the title and the first bullet, the second shows the title and the first two bullets, and so on. If the animations can be eliminated, print a static picture of the slide as it appears after the animations are completed.

■ If you use color on slides to distinguish meaning—for example, segments of a diagram (refer to Figure 17.3) or bars of a data chart—and you plan to print in black and white, consider changing color fills to pattern fills (see Figure 17.13) to make the distinctions clearer.

FIGURE 17.13

Fill patterns can help distinguish meaning when you're printing in black and white.

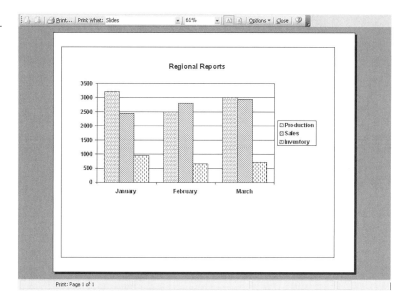

Besides the preceding, one of the most important considerations is to make sure you print on the proper medium. Overhead transparency film comes in a variety of types. The kind you buy to use with transparency markers does *not* work with printers.

For laser printing, purchase transparencies clearly designated for use with laser printers. If you're not sure about your particular printer, consult your owner's manual to determine exactly what you need. Transparencies designated for use with laser printers can withstand the heat generated by laser printers, whereas traditional film melts and sticks to the inside of a laser printer. Having been forewarned, you can purchase the right kind of transparency and avoid this costly mistake.

For inkjet printing, an even more expensive, specially coated film is used that dries quickly and evenly. Printing to normal transparency film won't damage your printer, but the ink *never* dries and will smear even days later. However, printed correctly, color transparencies are often worth the extra cost because of the professional look they provide.

Back in the day, we judged a presentation's professionalism by whether the speaker brought a slide show. You remember, the kind with 35mm slides and a carousel slide projector? Even today, slide projectors are relatively easy to borrow or rent, and they certainly cost less than a computer and projector.

Fortunately, you can easily convert a PowerPoint slide show into 35mm slides by contracting with any of a number of professional slide bureaus. Prices can range from $2 a slide to $5 or more. But if your professional reputation rests on making a quality presentation, creating a slide show in PowerPoint and purchasing slides could well be worth a $50 investment. Besides, just think of all the graphic artist time you *don't* have to pay for! However, if you make lots of different presentations, it might be more cost-effective to purchase your own data projector.

Some of the same considerations apply to slide conversion as to printed overhead transparencies. In particular, you need to consider which slides are most important and how to work around animation sequences. Then, simply save your slide show and send it to the company that is doing the slide conversion work. Depending on the company's procedures, you could have your slides back within a day.

THE ABSOLUTE MINIMUM

In this chapter, you explored various ways to get a slide show into printed form:

- You found out that printing every slide as handouts may not be the best reason for printing.
- You learned several effective uses for printing.
- You explored ways to create speaker notes.
- You learned about various types of printed handouts.
- You found out how to create overhead transparencies.
- You learned that you can have a slide show converted into traditional 35mm slides.

In Chapter 18, "Publishing to the Web," you'll learn how to avoid the use of paper altogether by publishing a slide show to the World Wide Web.

18

PUBLISHING TO THE WEB

It seems these days that you can find nearly anything on the Web—important news, facts and information, and even Billy Wilson's third-grade dinosaur report. In fact, the Web has possibly done more to spur the information revolution than any other single computer development.

This chapter looks at how you can contribute to the Web by making presentations available online. It also looks at how publishing to the Web is different from presenting before a live audience.

What Is a Web-Based Presentation?

If you've learned nothing else from me throughout this book, hopefully you've remembered my complaining about how too much paper is wasted by presenters who insist on providing printed handouts of their slides. With the Web, you now have a paperless method of making slides available. Consider these situations, for example:

- Prior to an important meeting of the board of directors, you post a bare-bones version of your presentation, including key questions and information. At the meeting, you build on what board members have already thought about, fleshing out the presentation with additional slides and discussion.

- You've concluded a terrific speech to your professional organization, and several people ask if they can get copies of your slides because they missed writing down several key details. You provide them with a Web address and invite them to view the slide show there.

- You make a slide show available to students the day before class so that those who want to can print slides to use as an outline on which they can take in-depth class notes.

- You present the findings of your research at a conference, but the audience is relatively small. You want to disseminate your work more widely, so you post your presentation on the Web, along with links to your bibliographies, data, and so on.

As you can see, the Web can be a great way to make your work available to nearly anyone, quickly and cheaply.

Along with this tremendously liberating ability to publish come some serious, and perhaps limiting, responsibilities. Here are some examples:

- What you publish becomes publicly available unless you take specific steps to restrict access to it. Further, automatic indexing programs constantly search the Web for Web pages just like yours and add content indexing to their search engines. Programs such as Google, Yahoo!, and Lycos can make it easy for anyone to find your work, even if you don't want them to.

- Information you present on the Web doesn't have the benefit of your presence to answer questions. What you publish might be interpreted incorrectly or taken out of context.

- Material that you use in face-to-face teaching might be legal under the fair-use provisions of the copyright law, but publishing the same material publicly on the Web might infringe on someone else's copyright.

- Some teachers wonder if students will bother to attend class if they make notes available on the Web. Depending on how effective you are in the classroom, this might or might not be a problem.

- You have control over the type of computer and hardware you use when you make a presentation, but you can't control what your Web viewers use. For example, if you use large video clips, will those who have only dial-up access to the Web be able to view them?

Despite these caveats, publishing a presentation to the Web offers so many advantages that you'd really be missing out if you didn't learn how to do it. Besides, with PowerPoint, publishing to the Web is easier than you could ever imagine.

Modifying a Presentation for the Web

Before you publish a slide show to the Web, which in and of itself is quite simple, you first need to consider whether the presentation needs modifications to make it more useable in a self-instructional setting. Because you won't be there to guide, direct, or answer questions, you have to put more of those elements into the slide show itself. In fact, Web-based and live slide shows really are two very different kinds of presentations. You don't just simply "put a slide show on the Web"—at least not if you expect it to be effective.

Consider, for example, the slide in Figure 18.1. If you were viewing this on the Web, what would you do? Unless you know something about PowerPoint slide shows, you might stare helplessly at the screen, wondering what comes next.

FIGURE 18.1

When you view PowerPoint slides on a Web site, nothing tells the user how to advance to the next slide.

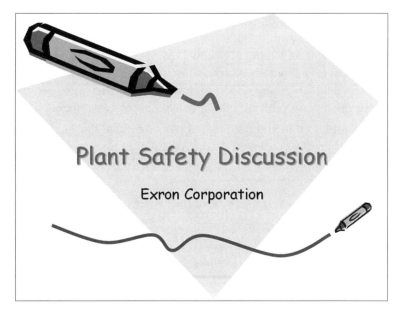

Figure 18.2, however, includes an action button and simple text directions, making it much easier for the viewer to know how to proceed.

Three key differences between audience-based and Web-based presentations have to do with explanation, navigation, and fancy features, as described in the following sections.

Explanation

Having lots of text in a slide show that is presented live is counter-productive because it requires too much reading, too fast, and because you're there to fill in the details. On a Web page, however, viewers have more time, are closer to the screen, and can read larger amounts of text more easily. They also need the additional information you would provide verbally in a live presentation.

You might find that you need to add slides here and there with full pages of narrative; for example, you might need to create links from bullet points to pages that develop or amplify the topic. Or you might need to add narrative to slides that are dominated by visual images (see Figures 18.3 and 18.4).

In short, you need to consider what the viewer is missing by not having you there and what kind of textual information is required for the slide show to make sense.

FIGURE 18.3

This pie chart works for a live presentation because you're there to explain it.

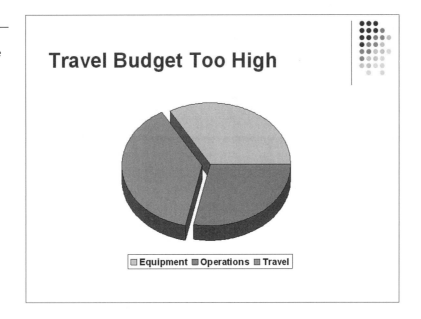

FIGURE 18.4

For a web-based presentation, you should add textual explanations to slides where graphics alone don't communicate the whole message.

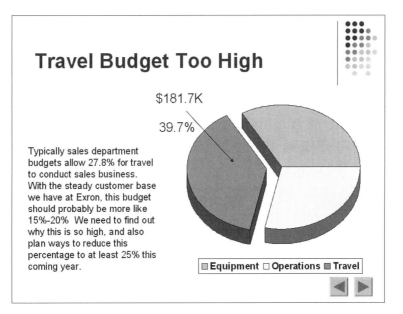

Navigation

When you make a presentation, you're in control of which slides you show and in which order. Even if the Web version of a slide show is intended to be strictly sequential, you need navigation tools to help viewers make it through the presentation. At a minimum, you should make sure the slides contain something the viewer can click to advance or back up in the slide show (refer to Figure 18.4).

If a slide show is not sequential, but *modular* (the viewer can jump to various sections, nonsequentially), you should provide even more navigational assistance. For example, you could create a table of contents or menu slide toward the beginning of the slide show, with obvious, Web-type links to the various "chapters" or sections of the show (see Figure 18.5). Throughout the slide show, you could add action buttons or links that return the viewer to the main menu.

FIGURE 18.5

A menu slide, with links, can help viewers navigate a non-sequential slide show.

Basically, you have to think of a slide show as a Web page. What do *you* expect when you visit a Web page? Would you find it difficult to navigate your own slide show? You should add the tools viewers need to successfully view and benefit from your presentation.

Fancy Features

You need to keep in mind that when you're in control, you can use or skip the piz-zazz, and you can get people back on track if they get distracted. You have no such control on the Web, and what might be interesting for one person might turn another person off. Further, fancy animations or multimedia elements might not work on many browsers, so if you depend on animations, sounds, or video to convey information or meaning in a live presentation, you need to find other ways of accomplishing this on the Web. Video and audio clips are particularly troublesome on the Web. Some viewers see them perfectly, and others don't even know they're there.

On the other hand, if one of your fancy elements really is important, go ahead and use it, but provide an alternative in case it doesn't work for everyone. For example, say you want viewers to hear Martin Luther King, Jr.'s "I have a dream" speech. You could place a graphic photo of Dr. King, with an action setting to play the sound clip, and also a link beneath the picture that takes the viewers to a page that shows the printed speech (see Figure 18.6).

FIGURE 18.6

You should con-sider providing alternative ways for viewers to access informa-tion when multi-media elements alone might not work.

Working with Hyperlinks

In Chapter 12, "Letting Action Settings Work for You," you learned that you can create Web page–like links on a PowerPoint slide. You also learned that you can create invisible links that look better than Web-style links in PowerPoint presentations. However, visible hyperlinks have a distinct advantage in Web-based presentations because viewers are conditioned to click such links.

⇥   For details on creating hyperlinks, see **p. 229**.

You should also be aware that creating hyperlinks intended for a Web presentation can present these difficulties:

- If you create links to files on your local computer, those links might not work when you move the presentation to a Web server. It's safer to use links only to Web pages or to graphic or multimedia files found in the same folder as the presentation. They can then be transferred to the Web server along with the presentation.

- If you create a link to another location entirely—for example, to another Web site—viewers might not know how to return to your slide show, and thus you lose them after they click the link. One way to help is to place information near the link: "Clicking this link takes you to another Web site. Click your browser's Back button to return to this presentation."

Saving a Presentation As a Web Page

Saving a Web version of a slide show is quick and simple. Getting it just right for all the different Web browsers out there can be a bit tricky. Let's start with the easy part.

You can simply save a PowerPoint presentation as a Web page, in *Hypertext Markup Language (HTML)* format. HTML is the basic language used for nearly all Web pages. Although you rarely see this language, it's the common basis on which Web pages are built and controlled. Even better, you can open an HTML PowerPoint presentation in PowerPoint, edit it, and save it again without having to convert it back to the PowerPoint presentation format.

By default, PowerPoint saves Web pages in a recent variation of HTML called *Mime-encapsulated HTML (MHTML)*. The advantage of this format is that instead of creating the several pages normally required to publish an HTML page, MHTML does it all in a single page. A disadvantage, however, is that MHTML file sizes can be relatively large and thus quite slow for those who have slow connections to the Internet.

Although PowerPoint's default is the MHTML format, I suggest that you learn to save or publish presentations by using standard HTML. It's nearly as easy, and the resulting files are more likely to be viewable by more users and more Web browsers.

To save a presentation in HTML, follow these steps:

1. Choose **F**ile, Save as Web Pa**g**e. PowerPoint displays the Save As dialog box. (See Figure 18.7, which shows Save as **T**ype already selected, as described in step 2.)

FIGURE 18.7

Converting a presentation to a Web page is as simple as saving it in a Web-based format.

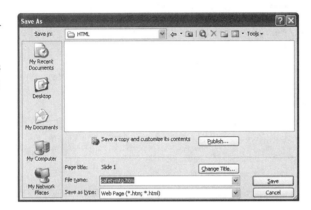

2. If necessary, change the Save as **T**ype drop-down list box to Web Page (*.htm, *.html).

3. Click **C**hange Title. The Set Page Title dialog box appears. Type the title you want to appear in the title bar of browsers when viewers open this page (see Figure 18.8, which shows a changed title). Click OK to return to the Save As dialog box.

FIGURE 18.8

Try to make Web page titles short but descriptive.

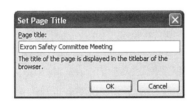

> **tip**
>
> Unlike Windows, many Web servers are picky about the use of uppercase or lowercase filenames. If you try to open WebPage.htm in your browser by typing webpage.htm, your browser might tell you that the file can't be found. To save yourself a lot of grief, you should always use lowercase filenames when saving PowerPoint presentations as Web pages.

4. If you want, you can change the filename. By default, PowerPoint adds .htm to whatever filename you choose.

5. Click **S**ave to convert the presentation to an HTML-formatted document.

In addition to the basic HTML format, you can save files in the following formats, each of which has a specific purpose:

■ *Single Web page*—This is PowerPoint's default format for saving a presentation as a Web page, using the MHTML coding format. This simply means that the entire presentation is encoded into a single file on your computer. Such files are self-contained, thus making it easier to send them by email or to move or retrieve them from a network. You also can open and edit these single Web page versions directly in PowerPoint. If you make such pages available on a Web server, persons viewing the file must also have PowerPoint installed on their computers.

■ *Web page*—This is the traditional HTML format, which can be opened directly into PowerPoint. The main difference is that with this format, you create a basic Web page along with a folder that contains all the additional files needed to make the page viewable in traditional Web browsers.

■ *PowerPoint show*—The .PPS format can be served from a Web server, and it goes directly into play mode when accessed. However, viewers must have PowerPoint installed on their computers for this format to begin playing. Such files also can be downloaded and opened in PowerPoint for editing.

■ *PNG graphics format*—This is one of several graphics formats you can use to create static images of slides. Other formats include GIF, JPG, TIF, BMP, and WMF. You view such files in whatever graphics program you use, or you can insert these images into regular Web pages, using a Web page editor such as FrontPage.

■ *PowerPoint presentation*—If you open a Web page version of a slide show, such as HTML or MHTML, you can save the page back into a native PowerPoint format by choosing Presentation (*.ppt).

> **note**
>
> If you choose the standard Web page (HTML) format, PowerPoint creates one file with the name you specify (for example, `yourfile`) and also a folder based on that filename (for example, `yourfile_files`). In this folder PowerPoint places several supporting files, including graphic images, sound clips, navigation pages, and more. All these files, together, are required for editing or for publishing to a Web server. The main advantage to using standard HTML is that viewers with slower connections don't have to download a entire presentation before viewing it. They download smaller bits and pieces as they need them.

When you view HTML or MHTML Web pages in a browser, by default you see several frames, including one with an outline that is used as a table of contents, one for the slide, and another for speaker notes (see Figure 18.9). If you're using Internet Explorer 4.0 or later, you also see navigation controls and a button that enables you to see the slide show in full-screen mode, as if it were playing in PowerPoint. If you're using Netscape or Mozilla, you *might* be able to view the slides, but more likely than not slide formatting will be seriously distorted.

FIGURE 18.9

Just by saving a slide show as a Web page, you create fully developed, frame-based Web presentations.

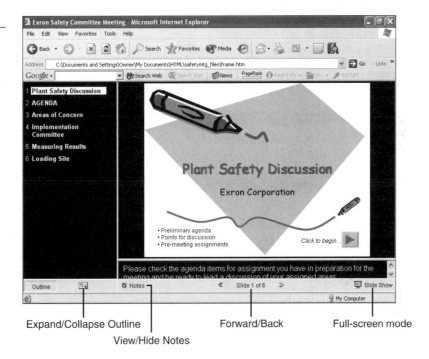

Expand/Collapse Outline   Forward/Back   Full-screen mode

View/Hide Notes

However, to a certain extent, you can change these defaults to accommodate the needs of those viewing a Web page with other browsers. You might have to sacrifice animations or multimedia effects, but at least those using something other than Internet Explorer can see your slides.

To customize a Web page, simply click the **P**ublish button. PowerPoint displays the Publish as Web Page dialog box (see Figure 18.10).

Here you find more options than you probably care to know about. These are a few of the important choices you can make in this dialog box:

FIGURE 18.10

The Publish as Web Page dialog box gives you control over many of the details of a Web-based presentation.

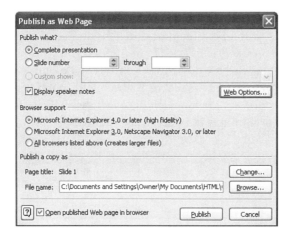

- You can publish the entire slide show or only a selected sequence of slides.

- You can also choose to display your speaker notes along with the slides, although this option works best in the most recent Web browsers. This option can be handy if you need to add extra information for those viewing the slide show on the Web but you don't want to modify the original slide show that you use for a live presentation.

- Probably the most promising, yet the most disappointing, option involves choosing which browsers can view your slides. Choosing the second or third options means that you *might* be able to see *some* of the slides in both Internet Explorer and Netscape. But the reality is that Microsoft has done a decent job of creating output that works with Internet Explorer while basically ignoring other browsers.

- When you click the **W**eb Options button, the Web Options dialog box appears, offering many fine-tuning options (see Figure 18.11), some of which seem to work better than others. You should click through the options just to see what's there. The following are the items you're most likely to use:

caution

Unless a slide show is very basic, not using animations or special graphic elements such as charts or diagrams, those viewing it on the Web with anything but a recent version of Internet Explorer are going to be disappointed at best and frustrated or upset at worst.

If you plan to make a slide show available on the Web and you also want to include animations or multimedia elements, you should consider informing potential viewers that your site requires the use of Internet Explorer and help them know what they need to do to download, install, and use this browser, if they don't already have it.

FIGURE 18.11

Use the Web
Options dialog
box to adjust a
Web page for
different
browsers and
other technical
requirements.

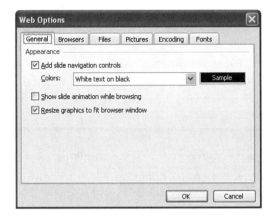

- On the General tab you can change text and background colors. By default, PowerPoint uses white text on a black background (refer to Figure 18.9).

- Also on the General tab, you can choose to show animations while the viewer is browsing the slide show. If the viewer plays the slide show as a full-screen presentation, animations already play automatically.

- On the Browsers tab, you can optimize for even more recent versions of Internet Explorer, which affords even more compatibility with the original slide show. Ironically, choosing a later version of Internet Explorer also makes the slide show slightly more compatible with the latest versions of Netscape.

- By default, choosing Publish as Web Page means you save the file as a standard HTML file, along with a folder of all its supporting files. This simply means that non-Microsoft browsers at least have a fighting chance to view the slides.

You have to decide how much compatibility you want with the wide array of browser programs and versions that are out there. If you are relatively sure most folks will visit your Web page using a recent version of Internet Explorer, publishing Web pages is quick and easy. If you have to worry about making pages compatible for everyone else, you have a lot of experimenting and testing to do, and you probably have to modify your presentation to include only basic, static information.

Transferring a Web Page to a Web Server

Creating or publishing a Web version of your presentation is only the first step in making it available to the world via the Web. The second step involves transferring your Web page files to a Web server. Then, when someone wants to view your Web page, he contacts that Web server, which "serves" your Web pages to the person so he can view them in a browser.

The precise details of transferring files to a Web server are beyond the scope of this book. However, here are a few things you need to consider:

- You should contact your network administrator or technical support person early in the process to determine whether you have access to a Web server. If your company or school has such a server, this person can show you exactly what to do.

- The first couple times, getting pages to the Web server can take some time, so allow plenty of time to learn the process. After a while, you get more comfortable with the procedures and you can transfer your Web pages in a matter of seconds.

- If you use the typical HTML-formatted page, don't forget that you must also transfer *all* the supporting files, which by default are kept in a subfolder. That same file relationship (main file with subfolder of supporting files) must also be established on the Web server.

- If you use the MHTML or PPS formats, users must have newer browsers and also have PowerPoint installed on their computers. If they don't, they won't be able to view the files.

- After you transfer your files, be sure to thoroughly test the slide show to make sure everything works as you expect it to. Check to make sure that graphic images, fonts, and links are all there and working properly.

- If you want a wide audience to view your presentation on the Web, you need to test it using as many browsers and computers as possible. For example, besides using Internet Explorer on a PC running Windows XP at XGA resolution, you should try it using Windows 98 or SVGA resolution, or for real fun, you could give it a whirl on a Macintosh using Netscape. That way you can determine whether to leave the slide show as is or modify it so more people can view it.

THE ABSOLUTE MINIMUM

In this chapter, you learned about methods for publishing a presentation to a wider audience by using the Web. In particular, you did the following:

- You found out that there are good reasons for and good reasons against putting a slide show on the Web.
- You learned what it takes to get a slide show Web ready.
- You reviewed how to use hyperlinks in a slide show.
- You learned which slide show formats work well in a Web environment.
- You found that not all browsers can view Web slide shows equally well.
- You learned how to go about getting a slide show on a Web server.

In Chapter 19, "Adding Multimedia Elements," you'll explore the world of multimedia and find how to integrate sound and video into your presentations.

PART VI

BEYOND THE BASICS

19

ADDING MULTIMEDIA ELEMENTS

Media are simply formats in which information is communicated, and each medium takes advantage of one of our five senses. PowerPoint doesn't do touch, taste, or smell—unless your presentation really stinks!—but it does use a variety of visual and auditory approaches. Visual examples include text, pictures, animations, and video. Auditory examples include your voice, sound effects, music, and video sound tracks. *Multimedia* means that you're adding sound or visual elements to an otherwise normal slide presentation.

This chapter explores some of the powerful ways you can integrate multimedia elements into presentations.

Understanding the Uses for Multimedia

Each individual learns differently. Some people like to read. Others like to be told how something works. Still others need to see a picture. When you make a presentation, the more different ways you can communicate information, the more people you're likely to reach.

The ways in which multimedia elements can be used are seemingly endless. You'll discover that there are some limitations, such as those imposed by technology or legal requirements. But if you use your creative imagination, you'll soon find that you can do some incredible things in PowerPoint. Consider these examples:

- Sound effects for objects onscreen, such as animals or machinery

- Sound effects that support a mood or feeling, such as danger, disaster, happiness, or applause

- Recorded sound clips that provide a narration to text onscreen or in support of a slide's message

- Sound clips that help viewers learn to hear and understand a foreign language

- Music as a bridge from one section of a slide show to another

- Music as a background to an entire slide show

- Video clips to illustrate a complicated procedure

- Video clips that give the audience a better sense of who someone is or what the person has done

- Video segments to help teach historical or cultural events

caution

Although this chapter intends to encourage you to use multimedia elements, be aware that you can spend huge amounts of time and effort adding them to your presentations. You should always keep in mind what your objectives are. If the audience can understand through a simple text bullet or a comment from you, then leave it at that. If the audience needs the kind of help that only a video presentation can provide, then going the extra mile might be worth it.

All in all, it's your call. It's what's called the point of diminishing returns—at some point your presentation's effectiveness doesn't increase significantly enough to merit additional effort. As a professor once told me, "I finally learned, at 2 a.m., that good enough is good enough."

The list goes on, and on, and on. Now that you're convinced that multimedia elements are useful (you are, aren't you?), how do you use and control them so that they support, rather than dominate, a presentation? You want to be in control of your media elements, and PowerPoint helps you establish exactly when and how sound or video clips are played.

Adding Sound Objects

A common—and sometimes overused—use for sound is the addition of simple sound effects that play during slide transitions or as action settings that play when you click an object. PowerPoint comes with several such clips, including applause, bomb, breeze, explosion, and whoosh. You can also find many free sound effects by searching Clip Organizer or the Internet.

To add a sound effect as an action setting for an object, follow these steps:

1. Select the object.
2. Choose Slide Show, **A**ction Settings to display the Action Settings dialog box.
3. Choose **P**lay Sound and then select a sound from the Play Sound drop-down list (see Figure 19.1).

FIGURE 19.1

PowerPoint comes with several basic sound effects that can be played through the action settings feature.

4. Click OK to associate the sound with the selected object.

At the bottom of the list in step 3 is Other Sound. Selecting that option opens the Add Sound dialog box (see Figure 19.2). You can use this dialog box to browse to find a sound clip, select it, and click OK twice to return to your slide.

FIGURE 19.2
You can use the
Add Sound
dialog box to
browse for and
find sound files.

When you play the slide show and click the object, PowerPoint plays the sound clip.

Sound clips come in many formats. The most common, and the one that always works in PowerPoint, is the WAV format. When you browse for Other Sound, by default PowerPoint looks only for this format. Other formats, such as the popular MP3 format, usually can be played, but not as action settings. Instead, you can create a hyperlink to an object by following these steps:

1. Select the object.

2. 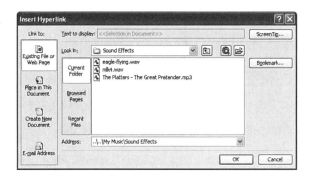 Choose **I**nsert, Hyper**l**ink or click the Insert Hyperlink button on the toolbar. Note that if the object already has an action setting sound associated with it, PowerPoint displays the Action Settings dialog box (refer to Figure 19.1). Deselect the **P**lay Sound check box and click OK before starting this step again.

3. PowerPoint displays the Insert Hyperlink dialog box (see Figure 19.3).

FIGURE 19.3
You can browse
and hyperlink to
a sound file.

4. Browse and select a sound file.

5. Click OK.

When you play the slide show and click the hyperlinked object, PowerPoint uses whatever method is set up on your computer to play that particular sound file. For example, to play an MP3 music file, PowerPoint might launch the Windows Media Player or some other MP3 music player, which covers the slide show. If you're intentionally playing the piece and want to control it (start, pause, rewind, and so on), you can easily do so. If you don't want the player to appear, you need to minimize it as soon as it starts playing.

Another method for inserting sound clips is to insert the sound directly, creating a sound file icon. To do so, follow these steps:

1. If you have a specific file in mind, choose **I**nsert, Mo**v**ies and Sounds, Sou**n**d from File. You can also search for a sound not only on your local computer but also in several Web collections by choosing **S**ound from Clip Organizer, which searches not only your local computer but also several Web collections.

2. Browse to find a sound file in the Insert Sound dialog box, which is identical to the Add Sound dialog box (refer to Figure 19.2), or if you're using the Clip Organizer, find a file in the Clip Art task pane (see Figure 19.4, which shows a completed search for a sound clip).

FIGURE 19.4

You can also find sounds clips by using the Clip Art task pane of the Clip Organizer.

3. Select the sound file and insert it in the slide.

4. PowerPoint asks how you want the sound to start in the slide show. You have two options:

■ *Automatically*—When this option is selected, as soon as the sound's turn comes up in the animation sequence, the sound begins to play. If it's the first or only such object on the slide, the sound begins as soon as the slide appears.

■ *When Clicked*—When this option is selected, you click the sound speaker icon to start the sound.

5. PowerPoint places a small sound speaker icon in the middle of the slide (see Figure 19.5).

FIGURE 19.5

The sound speaker icon shows where to click to activate an inserted sound when you're playing a slide show.

Sound Speaker icon

You can also play sounds or music directly from an audio CD, by following these steps:

1. Insert the audio CD in your computer's CD drive. If an audio player starts automatically, close it.

2. Choose **I**nsert, Mo**v**ies and Sounds, Play **C**D Audio Track. PowerPoint displays the Insert CD Audio dialog box (see Figure 19.6).

FIGURE 19.6

You can select CD tracks or parts of tracks by using the Insert CD Audio dialog box.

3. Choose from these options:

- *Clip Selection*—You can specify at which track and at what time on that track to begin. You can also specify the ending point. If you're not playing an entire audio track, you might have to time the CD track and experiment a bit to get the timing exactly right.

- **L**oop Until Stopped—If you want the selection to repeat over and over until you stop it, check this option. If you want the selection to continue playing when you advance the slide, you also have to change the selection's custom animation, as described later in this section.

- *Sound* **V**olume—If, for example, you want a music track as background where other sounds might be used, turn the volume down. Note, however, that sound volume depends more on your computer's volume settings than on PowerPoint's volume setting, which controls WAV files but little else.

- *Hide Sound Icon During Slideshow*—If you choose to have the audio track start automatically (see step 5), you can also hide the icon. Otherwise, the icon always appears.

4. Click OK.

5. Choose Automatically or When Clicked to specify how the audio track starts when its turn comes in the slide's animation sequence.

Finally, you can customize how multiple sound clips play and interact with each other. To do so, choose Sli**d**e Show, Custo**m** Animation to display the Custom Animation task pane (see Figure 19.7).

FIGURE 19.7

Media clips automatically appear in a slide's animation list to show the order in which they play, even if a clip itself is not animated.

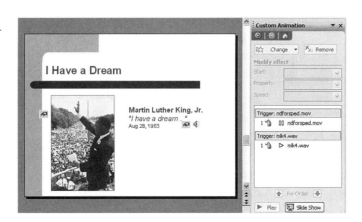

Each media clip appears in the list, even if no animation is currently associated with it. What each clip does have, however, is a timing and play order. Right-click a media element and choose from the options listed on the menu (see Figure 19.8). For example, if you choose Start **W**ith Previous, that clip begins at the same time as the clip above it.

You can also select a media element and use the Re-Order arrow buttons at the bottom of the task pane to change its play order.

If you want a sound to continue, for example, as a background, you have to change the way it stops, which by default occurs when you click the mouse. Even if you loop a sound to play over and over, as soon as you click or advance to the next slide or animation, the clip stops. To allow a sound to continue, follow these steps:

1. Choose Sli**d**e Show, Custo**m** Animation to display the Custom Animation task pane.

2. Right-click the clip and choose **E**ffect Options. PowerPoint displays the Play Sound dialog box (see Figure 19.9).

3. In the Stop Playing section, choose A**f**ter and the number of slides after which the sound should stop playing. If you enter a high number (for example, more than the number of slides in the presentation), the sound continues to the end of the show.

4. Make other changes as desired and click OK to return to the slide editor.

FIGURE 19.9

Access the Play
Sound dialog
box to choose
options to con-
trol the length
and timing of a
sound clip.

With a little creative fiddling around, you can create elegantly orchestrated sound
effects, music, and sound clips to enhance a slide show's effectiveness.

Adding Video Objects

Video is a powerful tool for communication. Just take a look at the MTV Generation
and others who sit spellbound for hours in front of the television. Video clips, which
appeal to both the auditory and visual senses, can also be useful in PowerPoint
presentations.

To insert a video clip into a PowerPoint slide show, follow these steps:

1. Choose **I**nsert, Mo**v**ies and Sounds, Movie from **F**ile. (We'll talk about the
   Clip Organizer later in this chapter.) The Insert Movie dialog box appears.

2. Browse for a video clip, typically an .avi file. MPEG (.mpg) and QuickTime
   (.mov or .qt) are other movie types you might use.

3. Click OK. PowerPoint asks whether you want to play the movie automatically
   or when clicked. Usually, you want to click the object, but it's your choice.

PowerPoint places the movie on the slide, displaying its first frame (see Figure
19.10). When you play the slide show and click the object, it plays in place until you
click or move to the next slide or animation. If you click the video clip itself, the
video pauses until you click it again.

Typically, video clips are quite small, and when you play them at full screen, image
quality seems to degrade dramatically. However, if you back away from the screen,
as your audience does, the picture quality often doesn't seem so bad. On the other
hand, if you leave a video clip at its initial small size, the audience is likely not to be
able to see it clearly.

FIGURE 19.10
An inserted movie clip appears onscreen as a picture, showing the clip's first video frame.

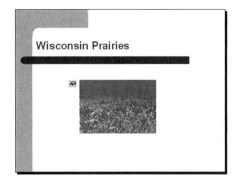

You can make PowerPoint automatically play a video clip at full-screen size. To do so, right-click the video clip image and choose Edit Movie Object. PowerPoint displays the Movie Options dialog box (see Figure 19.11), where you choose Zoom to Full Screen.

FIGURE 19.11
You select Zoom to Full Screen to have PowerPoint automatically enlarge a video clip while it's being played.

If you choose **I**nsert, Mo**v**ies or Sounds, **M**ovie from Clip Organizer, PowerPoint's Clip Organizer looks for animated graphics as well as video clips. These animated GIF files are like cartoon videos but don't include sound. They're also typically very brief and loop continuously. To preview what an animation can do, right-click the clip in the task pane and choose Previe**w**/Properties. PowerPoint displays and plays the animation (see Figure 19.12).

➡ For more information on inserting graphic images, such as GIF images, see **p. 113**.

note

When you insert a video clip, PowerPoint does not include it in the slide show itself but creates a link to it. When you play the slide show, PowerPoint looks for the video clip on your computer's hard drive. If you move the slide show to another computer, you must also copy any linked video clips. The same is true for large audio clips (those over 100KB). If you're not sure whether clips have become part of a slide show, copy all your media clips along with your PowerPoint file.

FIGURE 19.12

Animated images are considered movie clips and can be previewed in the Preview/Properties dialog box.

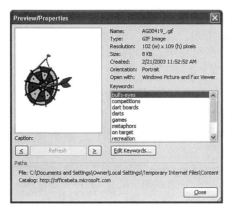

Using PowerPoint As a Multimedia Manager

In the days before PowerPoint, if you wanted to use video, audio, and slides, you had to set up three different pieces of equipment to play all three types of media. The hassle to accomplish this meant that you rarely used more than one type of media.

PowerPoint provides a means of integrating multimedia elements so that you use only one set of equipment—computer and projector. If you're lucky enough to have access to a classroom or conference room that has a projector and sound system, all you have to do is prepare your presentation and bring your computer with you.

> **tip**
>
> Don't assume that you can use only one media clip at a time. Depending on your computer's capability, you might be able to play more than one sound or video clip at a time. For example, you might want to play a sound clip, such as your own narration, as background to a muted video clip. Use your imagination!

Making Sure You Have the Proper Equipment

The first step in using PowerPoint as a multimedia manager is to determine what kind of hardware and software limitations or capabilities you have. Consider the following:

- Do you have your own computer (for example, a laptop computer) that you can use for the presentation? This is the ideal situation because it enables you to test your slide show ahead of time. At the presentation site, all you have to do is connect to the data projector and sound system.

- If you have to rely on someone else's computer (for example, one at the conference room or lecture hall), you have to find time to test your presentation thoroughly to make sure everything is working the way you expect it to. With multimedia elements, this is hardly a given.

- A presentation computer that also incorporates multimedia needs a little more horsepower than the average laptop. Consider the following:

  - Hard disk space needs to be bountiful to accommodate typically large video and sound files.

  - Memory (RAM) makes a huge difference in how smoothly multimedia presentations play. I usually recommend at least 256MB, although 512MB is even better. If you have graphics-intensive slides and are trying to synchronize music, you want as much memory as possible.

  - The computer's video card should also have plenty of memory, preferably not shared memory. Gaming computers typically have the fastest video cards because they require maximum video speed.

  - The computer's sound system should be powerful. Some sound cards, for example, easily handle multiple audio channels, whereas others barely handle one.

  Most recent laptop computers can easily handle multimedia presentations. Try your slide show first. You might find that it can handle anything you throw its way. If not, scale back your multimedia requirements or talk yourself into getting a newer computer!

- Make sure you have all the software programs required to play your sound and video files. More recent versions of Windows and Windows Media Player tend to be able to play a greater variety of media types. But you might find that upgrading software actually renders a multimedia file unplayable, or that it causes a file to play differently. If you do upgrade, be sure to test everything before standing up in front of the audience.

Checking the Hardware and Software

In addition to having the necessary hardware and software, you must make sure they are installed and set up properly. Each system is different, so a step-by-step procedure isn't possible here. However, here are a few things to consider:

- Sound files require the right software in order to be played. Windows has built-in capabilities for playing WAV files, but other sound file types might require a full version of Windows Media Player or a QuickTime or MP3 player.

- A common problem in getting sound to play is that the volume has been muted or turned down. You can check this quickly by clicking the speaker icon in the Windows system tray and making sure volume is up and sound has not been muted. Double-click the icon to open the complete sound control panel and make changes there as necessary. For example, the system volume may be up, but a particular sound option may be turned off.

- A common video problem is that you can see the slide show on your laptop but not on the screen via the data projector. Typically you can solve this problem by pressing your laptop's Fn key and finding the corresponding LCD/CRT or video key (usually a function key across the top row of the keyboard). This determines what goes to your screen and what goes to the projector.

- If the projector displays a slide but the place where a video should be showing is only a black box, try using the Fn+LCD key combination. When you do this, you might be able to see the slide show only on the projected image, not on your laptop, but at least your audience can see the video image.

- Sound and video files also require the necessary codecs to play properly. *Codecs* are coders/decoders that translate digital files so that they can be played. Fiddling with codecs is a last resort, but if they're damaged or missing (you'll probably get an error message saying so), they might need to be reinstalled.

You have undoubtedly heard it many times: "Try it out ahead of time." Even if it sounds obvious, or perhaps unnecessary, it's still a good idea. That way, if you need technical assistance, you have time to find someone who can help.

Getting Materials into Digital Format

All this talk about using multimedia sounds good, but where do you get the digital materials you need? You might easily find basic sound effects or even sample video clips on Internet Web sites. But if you want exactly the right thing, you might have to create it yourself.

The process for creating digital materials is similar for both audio and video, although the latter is more challenging. The steps for each involve the following:

1. Identifying the source of the original material (for example, live performance or material found on tape, CD, or DVD).

2. Using a digital conversion process to change analog recordings into digital files that can be played on your computer.

3. Compressing the resulting digital files to conserve space and to increase playing speed and smoothness while retaining as much quality as possible.

Let's look at a few examples. Nearly every computer has built-in sound capabilities, either through a sound card installed in the computer or through hardware found on the computer's system board. Look on the back of your computer, and you should find small jacks—like those found on a typical personal CD player—that can accommodate a mini-phone plug for speaker/headphone output, microphone input, and line-in input:

- The speaker output is used to take the sound from the computer and play it through headphones, a speaker system, or a room's sound system.

- A microphone input requires some sort of microphone. You can spend a lot of money on high-quality microphones, or you can begin small with an inexpensive one ($10–$20). You can then experiment with recording your own voice.

- Line-in allows you to connect another device to your computer (for example, tape player, radio, CD player).

To make a voice recording, you have two built-in options in Windows and PowerPoint. The first is the Windows Sound Recorder, which you can usually find by selecting Start, Programs, Accessories, Entertainment. With a properly installed microphone, you can use this simple program (see Figure 19.13) to record up to 60 seconds of sound. You can also edit the recording by trimming off the beginning or end. Files created with the Sound Recorder are saved in .wav format and can easily be integrated with a PowerPoint slide show. You can also find a simpler version of the Sound Recorder in PowerPoint, by choosing **I**nsert, Mo**v**ies and Sounds, **R**ecord Sound.

FIGURE 19.13

You can use the Windows Sound Recorder program along with a microphone to record simple sound files.

The second option for making a voice recording is to use PowerPoint's Record Narration feature, which enables you to record a narration that also adds slide timings and synchronizes the recording with the slide show. Imagine—you could record an entire lecture and never show up for class! To use the Record Narration feature, follow these steps:

1. Make sure the slide show is complete, saved, and ready to present.

2. Choose Sli**d**e Show, Record **N**arration. PowerPoint displays the Record Narration dialog box (see Figure 19.14).

FIGURE 19.14

You can record the narration for a complete slide show.

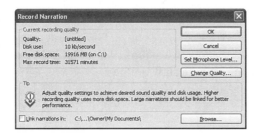

3. Click Set **M**icrophone Level to display the Microphone Check dialog box (see Figure 19.15), where you can test your microphone and set its volume level. Click OK.

FIGURE 19.15

The Microphone Check dialog box lets you know if your microphone is working properly and lets you set recording quality.

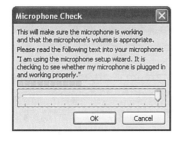

4. Click **C**hange Quality to display the Sound Selection dialog box (see Figure 19.16). Adjust the quality and the size of the recorded file, from CD to telephone quality. For example, 16-bit CD-quality stereo files are considerably larger than 8-bit Mono files. However, when you listen to these files, you might find little difference in quality, especially for a typical PowerPoint presentation. Click OK.

FIGURE 19.16

Higher-quality recorded sounds create larger sound files than lower-quality recorded sounds.

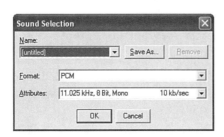

5. Adjust your microphone and click OK to begin recording.

6. Go through your slide show as you do during a regular presentation, advancing slides and animations as you narrate the slide show.

7. When you finish, either by ending the show or by pressing Esc, PowerPoint tells you that the narrations have been saved with each slide and offers to save slide timings as well. If you click **S**ave, PowerPoint creates a self-running, self-narrated slide show (see Figure 19.17, which shows the slide show in Slide Sorter view, along with slide timings).

FIGURE 19.17

A recorded narration can synchronize automatically with slide timings to create a completely self-running slide show.

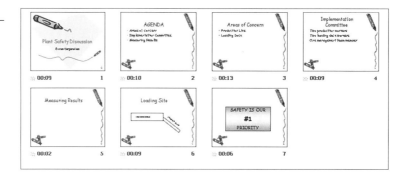

Just put a dummy of yourself in the boardroom chair, and the audience will never know you're out playing golf! If you don't save slide timings, you have to stick around to advance the slides yourself. Self-running slide shows can also be useful for displays, trade show booth demonstrations, or self-directed training.

Finally, you can convert other prepared recordings for use in PowerPoint. Usually, this requires extra software that you can obtain commercially or through shareware. For example, CD *ripping* software (such as CDex from `www.cdex.n3.net`) enables you to convert CD tracks to WAV or MP3 files. Other software, such as Sound Forge, takes sound from the line-in jack of your sound board and converts it to any of a number of sound formats. It might take some time to learn how to control such digitizing processes to come up with acceptable quality and efficient file sizes. But the payoff is access to a whole world of recorded sound that you can use to bring life to your presentations.

Don't forget that many such converted materials are still copyrighted. Be sure you're protected by fair use provisions of the copyright law or that you have permission to use media that belongs to someone else.

Digitizing video is more complex than digitizing sound, primarily because hardware and software requirements are greater but also because you have to worry about video quality as well as audio quality.

When you're digitizing video, you need to consider the following:

- You need a device to convert analog video to digital video, such as a video capture board. As of this writing, virtually no computers are equipped with such boards, but the boards are readily available for a few hundred dollars. You can also find external conversion devices that connect to any computer equipped with USB 2.0 or Firewire connectors.

- A convenient alternative to a video capture board is a digital video camera. Prices are falling fast, and purchasing a digital camera instead of a standard analog tape camera might be a wise investment—at least that's what you can tell your spouse!

- Newer digital cameras also have composite inputs (those yellow, red, and white connectors) that enable you to digitally record from a VCR, DVD, or TV.

- To get digital video to your computer, you need a very high-speed connection, typically a *FireWire* connection (the IEEE 1394 standard). Not all digital cameras or computers have such connections, but recently they are fairly standard on cameras, and they're increasingly common on computers.

- Your computer should be a recent model, with a high-speed processor, lots of memory (RAM), and lots of hard disk space. Video files take up huge amounts of space and require intense computing to process.

- When a digital video file is on your computer's hard drive, you need editing software to mix, edit, and save the video clips in a format that ensures good enough quality and small enough file size.

I've warned you about keeping video and audio clips short. After you experiment with video clips, you'll understand even better that long video segments (more than a couple minutes) just aren't practical for use in a PowerPoint slide show.

Using Player Controls

The simple act of creating small, manageable clips of important audio or video information goes a long way toward helping you create a slide show that manages your multimedia elements. When you want to play a video clip, you go to the slide that contains it and you play it. No fumbling with a VCR or a videotape.

However, if you need to play parts of a clip or repeat short segments of a clip, you have to insert audio and video differently. Otherwise, PowerPoint plays the entire segment, allowing you only to pause and restart until the clip finishes. The easiest way to provide yourself with player controls is to follow these steps:

1. Create or select an object that you'll click to start the media clip, such as a Sound or Movie action button (see Figure 19.18).

⇨ For information on creating action buttons, see **p. 228**.

FIGURE 19.18

Sound or Movie action buttons can be hyper-linked to sound or video files, allowing you to use media programs and controls with such files.

2. Access the Action Settings dialog box for the object and choose **H**yperlink to, Other File.

3. Use the Hyperlink to Other File dialog box to browse for a media clip.

4. Click OK to return to PowerPoint.

When you play the slide show and click the hyperlinked object, PowerPoint starts the application that plays the media clip (for example, Windows Media Player). By using that application, you have the ability to stop, start, rewind, and otherwise fully control the media clip (see Figure 19.19, which shows a typical sound control panel).

FIGURE 19.19

With a media control panel, you can stop, start, rewind, and otherwise fully control how a sound or video clip plays.

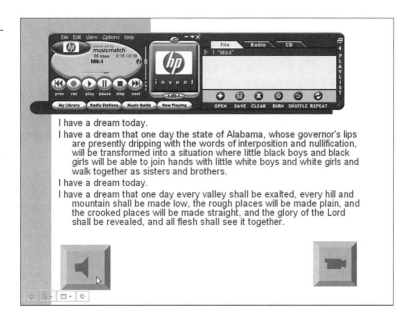

THE ABSOLUTE MINIMUM

In this chapter, you explored the possibilities and procedures for using multimedia elements in a slide show:

- You found out that multimedia really means audio and video clips added to a PowerPoint slide show.

- You learned how to insert and play sound effects and sound clips.

- You learned how to add video segments to a presentation.

- You found out what's required to create your own digital media clips.

- You discovered that PowerPoint can help you manage and control media clips during a presentation.

In Chapter 20, "Customizing PowerPoint," you'll find out how to customize PowerPoint by changing settings and preferences to better match the way you work.

IN THIS CHAPTER

- Learn how to create and save custom design templates
- Explore useful PowerPoint options settings
- Find out how to customize menus and toolbars

20

CUSTOMIZING POWERPOINT

If you're a long-time PowerPoint user, chances are there are things about PowerPoint 2003 that you just don't like, largely because they work differently from what you're used to. If you're new to PowerPoint, you might think everything you've learned is "just the way it's done," but in some cases you might wonder if there's a better way.

This chapter explores ways to customize PowerPoint, including how to create customized PowerPoint templates. You'll learn what options you have and ways to change them, and you'll explore what makes sense to change and what's better left alone.

Creating Custom Templates

One of the first questions I hear from new PowerPoint users is, "Can I make my own design templates?" The answer is, "Yes," but that's usually followed by, "But wait awhile, until you have a better grasp of PowerPoint before you try it." You've waited long enough. Let's try it.

Downloading Design Templates from the Internet

You've used, overused, and gotten bored with the design templates that come with PowerPoint. But before you spend a lot of time creating something new, you should try finding already-made templates at the Microsoft Web site or elsewhere on the Internet. You just might find something that's fresh and also that fits the presentation you want to make.

To locate and download a design template, make sure you have an active Internet connection and then try these steps:

1.  Choose F**o**rmat, Slide **D**esign or click the Slide Design button on the toolbar to display the Slide Design task pane.

2. Scroll to the bottom of the Available for Use templates and select the item Design Templates on Microsoft.com. PowerPoint opens your browser and takes you to the Microsoft Office Online Web site (see Figure 20.1). The list of templates you see varies, depending on what's currently posted and how the Microsoft site filters your request.

FIGURE 20.1

Microsoft's Office Online Web site can be a good source for fresh new design templates.

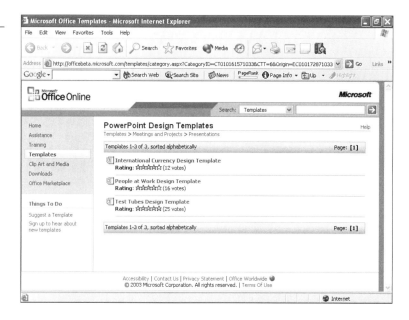

3. Click a template to see what it looks like. Figure 20.2 shows an example of what you see next.

FIGURE 20.2

At the Office Online Web site you can preview a design template before you download it to your computer.

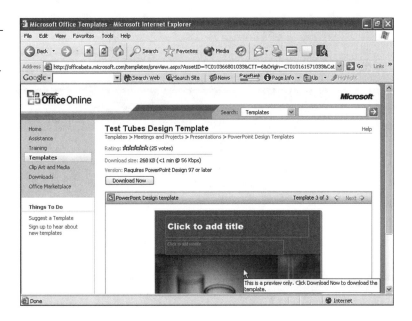

4. Click the Download Now button to download the template to your computer.

Depending on your computer's setup, you might be asked to install download-assistance programs, to swear you'll use the download legally, or to answer other questions designed to confuse you. If you're not sure you want to let Microsoft install this software, answer no and skip this section. Otherwise, follow the prompts. Eventually, you see the template in your current PowerPoint slide show (see Figure 20.3).

The downloaded template applies only to the current slide show, unless you save it as a template. To save the template for future use, follow these steps:

1. Choose **F**ile, Save **A**s. The Save As dialog box appears.

2. From the Save as **T**ype drop-down list box choose Design Template (*.pot). PowerPoint automatically jumps to the `Templates` folder (see Figure 20.4).

3. Rename the template (for example, `fancystuff.pot`) and click **S**ave. The `.pot` extension on the filename identifies the file as a PowerPoint template.

The template is now saved, and in the future when you access the Design Template task pane, the template also appears in alphabetical order in the Available for Use section. Note, however, that new templates do *not* appear in the task pane until you exit PowerPoint and start it again.

FIGURE 20.3

Downloaded templates work like any other design templates, but they initially apply only to the current slide show.

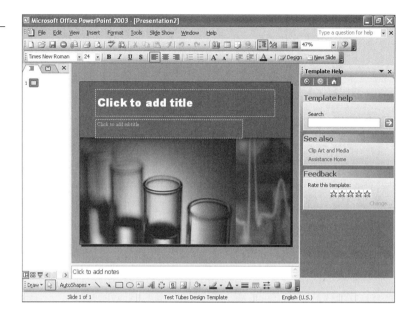

FIGURE 20.4

If you save a slide show as a Design Template (*.pot) file, only the design portion is saved, making it available for future use.

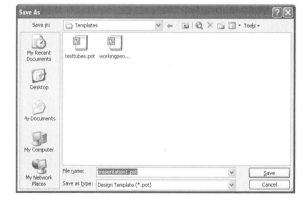

Creating Design Templates

You really do want to create your own design or customize a template yourself, don't you? The steps for doing so are quite simple, although you need to bring to bear many of the skills you've learned in this book, such as how to create backgrounds, add graphic images, and so on.

Each template is controlled by a slide master. Instead of customizing each individual slide, you customize the slide master, which then automatically modifies all slides in the slide show. Modifying a slide master also modifies other masters, such as the notes master.

To modify a slide design template, follow these steps:

1. Apply a slide design to a slide. For the purposes of this exercise, we'll start with the default design, which is plain and simple.

2. Choose **V**iew, **M**aster, **S**lide Master. PowerPoint displays the slide master and a floating toolbar to assist you in modifying the master (see Figure 20.5).

3. Make changes to the master, such as background, color scheme, fonts, and font sizes. You can also add graphic images, such as a background image, a company logo, and drawing images. Remember that the changes you make apply to all slides in the slide show.

> **tip**
>
> Although you want to be bold and go where no one else has gone before, before you build a design template from scratch, you should consider starting with a template that's close to what you're looking for. Then customize that template as described in this section. You can save a lot of time and effort by building on the work someone else has already done for you.

FIGURE 20.5

You can modify design template information by viewing the slide master.

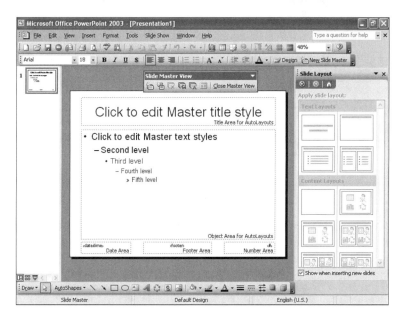

4. Move, size, or delete placeholders. If you delete a placeholder, you can add it again by clicking the Master Layout button on the Slide Master View toolbar and then selecting from the Master Layout dialog box a placeholder to add.

5. After you design the slide master, view and modify the title master by clicking the Insert New Title Master button on the Slide Master View toolbar. PowerPoint inserts a title master and shows the slide master and the title master as being linked (see Figure 20.6).

FIGURE 20.6

The title master is based on the slide master, and the two are a linked pair.

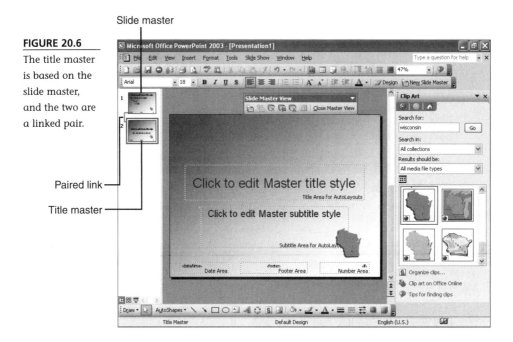

6. Make changes to the title master. Remember, however, that changes you make to one slide master aren't replicated automatically in the other. Changes should be specific to only the title master.

7. Click **C**lose Master View on the Slide Master View toolbar to return to the slide show.

The template you create is used only in the current slide show, but it can be applied to any or all slides. If you want to save the template for use with other new or existing slide shows, follow the steps outlined earlier in this chapter, at the end of the section "Downloading Design Templates from the Internet."

Slide masters also include placeholders for footers, page numbers, and dates. You modify their location, fonts, and so on in the Slide Master view. To activate and use these placeholders, follow these steps:

1. Choose **V**iew, **H**eader and Footer. PowerPoint displays the Header and Footer dialog box (see Figure 20.7).

FIGURE 20.7

Use the Header
and Footer dia-
log box to select
which elements
should appear
on slides.

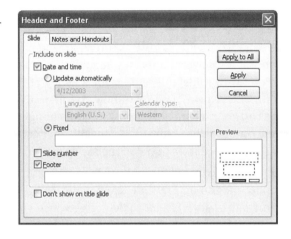

2. Change what appears on the slides by using these options:

   ■ *Date and Time*—You can turn this option off or on by clicking the check box. You can also select Fi**x**ed to use the date or time that you type in the box, or you can select **U**pdate Automatically to have PowerPoint automatically update the date and time in a variety of date/time formats and even in other languages, if they are installed on your computer.

   ■ *Slide **N**umber*—This option enables you to display page numbers in the page number placeholder. In the Slide Master view, the number placeholder contains <#>, and you can add information around that, such as Page <#>, or -<#>-.

   ■ *Footer*—This option lets you place anything you want on the slide, such as a company or university name or the title of the presentation.

3. If you don't want the content of these placeholders to appear on the title slide, select Don't Show on Title **S**lide.

4. Click **A**pply to apply these changes to only the current slide, or click Appl**y** to All to apply them to the entire slide show.

tip

You can edit header and footer information—date and time, slide number, and footer placeholders—in the Slide Master view. This can save you some time because you format and arrange the placeholders, and then you choose **V**iew, **H**eader and Footer to specify which ones are to be displayed on your slides. Also, changes you make in the Slide Master view automatically apply to all slides in the presentation.

Setting PowerPoint Options

Beyond templates, there are scores of options you can change to make PowerPoint behave the way you want it to. However, I usually suggest that PowerPoint users, new or not, use PowerPoint with its default settings for a period of time before seeking to change those settings. That way, you learn how PowerPoint's designers thought features might best be implemented, and you gain enough knowledge to know whether something ought to be changed. If you still can't get used to something, and there's a way to change it, then by all means do so.

Several PowerPoint options are scattered throughout PowerPoint's menus—for example, the Set Up Show options found on the Slide Show menu. Many options, however, can be found in one place—the Options dialog box—which you access by choosing **T**ools, **O**ptions (see Figure 20.8). PowerPoint offers options for eight broad categories, each with its own tab. You're smart enough to figure out most of these options, so I don't want to bore you by going over everything. Instead, the following sections look at each category and talk about the options that might be most useful or that might not be clear. You'll also learn about the AutoCorrect options.

FIGURE 20.8

The Options dialog box enables you to set option preferences in eight broad categories.

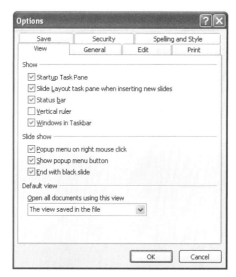

Setting View Options

View options (refer to Figure 20.8) relate to the way PowerPoint is viewed onscreen. For example, if you don't like having the task pane start automatically, you can turn it off. If you use the ruler, you can choose to display the vertical ruler along with the horizontal one. When you select the Windows in Taskbar check box, each

PowerPoint presentation you're working on displays as a separate icon on the Windows taskbar, making it easy for you to switch from one presentation to another.

One slide show option that you might want to change is whether the menu buttons appear. If you're used to right-clicking and choosing from a pop-up menu, the onscreen buttons may be redundant and distracting. Another handy option is ending with a black slide, so you don't accidentally return to PowerPoint's editing screen at the end of a slide show.

Finally, when you save a PowerPoint presentation, it normally opens again in the last-used view (for example, the Slide Sorter view). You can choose a specific view for slide shows that you open.

Setting General Options

General options (see Figure 20.9) include the ability to link, rather than embed, large sound files. Video files link automatically, helping keep the size of a presentation small. Linking large sound files is also a good idea, although you have to remember to copy all linked sound files along with your presentation if you move it to a different computer or to the Web.

FIGURE 20.9

You can use the General options tab to limit the size of embedded sound files.

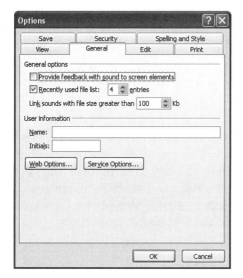

Setting Edit Options

Edit options (see Figure 20.10) affect the way you select text and how you cut and paste. An important option here is the ability to change the number of undos. Be careful, however. Undos disappear whenever you save your work. An unusually large number of undos might encourage you to save less frequently. Instead, you should use undo quickly and save more frequently.

You can also disable some of PowerPoint's newer options. If you're collaborating with someone who doesn't have the latest version of PowerPoint, you might want to disable features that person can't use so that you don't accidentally use them yourself.

Setting Print Options

By default, print options you select in the Print dialog box are *sticky*—that is, they remain in effect the next time you access the Print dialog box, until you exit PowerPoint. If you don't like that, and you prefer that the default print options or settings you choose always appear, you can select Use the Following **P**rint Settings on the Print tab of the Options dialog box and specify the options you want to keep, even after you exit and restart PowerPoint (see Figure 20.11).

Setting Save Options

Two important save options (see Figure 20.12) are the format in which files are saved and where you save your presentations. By default, PowerPoint saves files in its native format, but you can also save in Web page format or in formats compatible with earlier versions of PowerPoint. This latter option disables features that are not compatible with earlier versions.

FIGURE 20.11

You can use the Print options tab to set print options that reset themselves each time you use the Print dialog box.

FIGURE 20.12

The Save options tab enables you to specify where and in what format to save slide shows.

You can also change the default location where PowerPoint files are saved. To do so, type the entire path to the new default location (for example, c:\docs\pptfiles).

Setting Security Options

If you want to protect a file from being opened or modified by others, you can add a password (see Figure 20.13). If you want others to be able to open, but not modify, a file, you can add a password to modify. PowerPoint users have requested this feature for a long time. PowerPoint users often make their files available to others via email or the Web, and this feature helps people protect the integrity of the presentations that bear their names.

FIGURE 20.13

You can set passwords on the Security tab of the Options dialog box to prevent others from opening or editing a slide show.

Setting Spelling and Style Options

Some people don't like the distraction of automatic spelling corrections. If you're one of them, you can turn off any of the listed features you don't like (see Figure 20.14).

FIGURE 20.14

You can use the Spelling and Style tab of the Options dialog box to specify how PowerPoint assists or doesn't assist in correcting spelling and style problems.

PowerPoint's style checker is a powerful tool. If you have the Office Assistant turned on, it constantly checks to make sure your styles fall within certain predefined guidelines. For example, if you capitalize a title incorrectly, a light bulb appears onscreen. If you click the light bulb, the Office Assistant appears, giving you several options: change to the suggested style, ignore it this time, ignore it always, or go to the Style Options dialog box to change the style's settings.

Click the Style Options button on the Spelling and Style tab to display the Style Options dialog box (see Figure 20.15). In this dialog box you can set the type of case and punctuation you use for text. On the Visual Clarity tab (see Figure 20.16), you learn some guidelines for good slides and have the option of overriding these guidelines. If you make a lot of changes and forget what you started with, you can click the Defaults button to restore PowerPoint's original style settings.

FIGURE 20.15

Use the Style Options dialog box to establish a method for consistent case and punctuation.

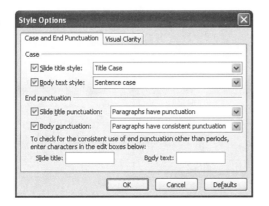

FIGURE 20.16

The Visual Clarity tab of the Style Options dialog box offers excellent guidelines for good slide composition.

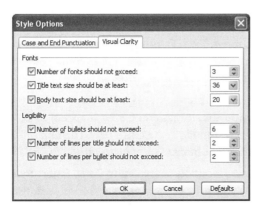

Setting AutoCorrect Options

AutoCorrect is a feature whose options aren't found in the Options dialog box but are often asked about. Generally, this tool can be helpful in correcting typographical errors. The feature also automatically formats certain combinations, such as replacing a fraction with a fraction character (for example, 1/2 becomes ½).

You access the AutoCorrect dialog box, shown in Figure 20.17, by choosing **T**ools, **A**utoCorrect Options.

FIGURE 20.17

You can fine-tune or turn off AutoCorrect options in the AutoCorrect dialog box.

Besides being able to turn off corrections you don't want made, you can create exceptions. For example, if you type `Joseph Smith, Jr.`, you don't want to capitalize the next word just because it follows a period. Also, some words *should* begin with two capital letters (for example, TVs). Finally, you can create your own AutoCorrect options; for example, you can have the shortcut *ppt* become *PowerPoint*.

The AutoFormat As You Type tab provides several stylistic options. One that is especially useful is the ability *not* to change font size automatically if there's too much text in a title or text box. You sometimes don't even realize that PowerPoint has made the font smaller to accommodate the extra text. Turning off this feature forces you to reduce the amount of text instead of reducing the font size.

The last tab in the AutoCorrect dialog box is Smart Tags. Smart tags enable PowerPoint to automatically insert and format such things as dates and names of people from your Outlook database, and so on. Most people find these annoying and are glad the default is not to use them. If you find a use for these, you can turn them on here.

Customizing Toolbars and Menus

One of the strengths of a graphical user interface (GUI) such as Windows is that it gives you several choices for accessing a single feature. You can use text-based menus, use keyboard shortcuts, or click visual icons or buttons. A useful feature in PowerPoint is the ability to customize toolbars and menus so that you can access features you need even more easily.

For example, you can choose **V**iew, **T**oolbars, **C**ustomize and add, remove, or relocate toolbar buttons or menu commands. The following sections touch on a couple of the methods for customizing toolbars and menus that you're most likely to find useful.

Customizing Toolbar Locations

One way to customize a toolbar is to change its location onscreen. By default, PowerPoint's major toolbars appear at the top (Standard and Formatting toolbars), at the bottom (Drawing toolbar), and at the right (Task Pane toolbar). Others pop up as floating toolbars when needed. To move a toolbar, move the mouse pointer to the four vertical dots at the left side of the toolbar. When the pointer turns to a four-way arrow, click and drag the toolbar to any side of the screen or to the center. As you drag the toolbar, you see how it looks in its new location. Release the mouse button to reposition the toolbar. You can't undo toolbar movement except by dragging the toolbar back to its original position.

> **caution**
>
> Just because you can remove or reposition toolbar buttons or menu commands doesn't mean you should. If you don't use a button or command for a while, or if someone else tries to use your modified version of PowerPoint, you'll both have a hard time finding what you're looking for.
>
> Generally, it's better to add commands or buttons to menus or toolbars than to remove or reposition them. The more choices you have, the easier it is to find a command. If you remove those choices, you could waste a lot of time later on, trying to find them again.

Customizing Menus

A practical use for customizing menus can be found on the Options tab of the Customize dialog box (see Figure 20.18). Many of the options really are just personal preferences, but you can also modify PowerPoint's method for displaying menus.

By default, PowerPoint displays only a basic set of commonly used features, along with a double-arrow at the bottom of the menu. You have to click that arrow or wait a few seconds for less-commonly used menu items to appear. Microsoft designers think this is helpful, but some people find it very confusing because they think they remember using a feature but don't find it immediately. After you use a feature, it appears by default on the menu, but not until then.

FIGURE 20.18

One useful custom option is to allow PowerPoint to always display full menus.

These are two useful options in the Customize dialog box:

- **R**eset Menu and Toolbar Usage Data—Clicking this button sets menus and toolbars back to the default lists and buttons so that once again you don't see certain features.

- Show F**u**ll Menus After a Short Delay—If you deselect this check box, PowerPoint displays menus the same way as any other normal Windows program—all menu items appear at once.

And now here's what you've been waiting for: You can even change menu animation to determine how menus appear—unfolding, sliding, or fading. Aren't you glad you read all the way to the end of this chapter? Okay, so this feature isn't very important. In fact, many of the options you've read about in this chapter really aren't all that critical. However, PowerPoint's many options allow you to configure PowerPoint to work the way you want it to, not the way an anonymous software designer thinks it should work.

THE ABSOLUTE MINIMUM

In this chapter, you found that you can customize PowerPoint to match your own preferences. Here's what you've done:

- You learned how to acquire additional design templates.
- You learned how you can create and save your own design templates.
- You explored many of PowerPoint's option settings.
- You found that you can customize PowerPoint's toolbars and menus.

Chapter 21, "Looking Beyond the Basics," takes a quick look at some of the advanced features that aren't covered in this book and suggests resources you can go to for more information.

IN THIS CHAPTER

- Explore some of PowerPoint's advanced features
- Find out how to add special programs to enhance PowerPoint
- Learn how and where you can find more information about PowerPoint, from basic help to advanced features

21

LOOKING BEYOND THE BASICS

As you've learned throughout this book, PowerPoint is a powerful and wonderfully flexible communication tool. Nearly everything covered in this book can be accomplished quickly, easily, and with the software and tools you have at hand.

But this is an *Absolute Beginner's Guide*. Beyond what you've learned already, there are also many other useful features and capabilities that you can use in or with PowerPoint. In some cases, this book doesn't cover them because they're not often used or their use is very specific and limited. However, some very useful additional features are advanced because they require special network setups, the acquisition of additional software or hardware, or subscription to specialized services.

This chapter explores some of these features, describing what they do, what's required to use them, and some suggestions about where you can find additional help or resources.

A Survey of Advanced PowerPoint Features

The following sections describe various types of feature groups—although the treatment of these groups is by no means exhaustive. Most of these features are well beyond the scope of this book, so you need to seek help or information elsewhere. Nevertheless, these features can give you a sense of some of the power left for you to unlock in PowerPoint.

Note that the figures shown in these sections are intended to illustrate rather than teach you how to use these advanced features.

Online Meeting Services

A whole group of advanced features have to do with online collaboration. Imagine, for example, that you're connected through the Internet with colleagues around the world and you want to work on a presentation together, or you want to play a slide show for everyone and conduct a Web-based discussion of the presentation. If you have the necessary network setup, these are some of the things you can do:

■ *Meet now*—Online meetings are accomplished by using NetMeeting, an intriguing and extremely valuable service that is used for conducting meetings over the network and for sharing, viewing, annotating, and commenting a slide show that everyone sees. (See Figure 21.1, which shows a NetMeeting chat in progress.) This feature requires an Internet locator service (ILS) set up on a server that knows about and can connect you to other users who are running NetMeeting and are connected to the same ILS server. The ILS server, in turn, must be set up on a Windows 2000 or later recent domain, and it must be running the Microsoft Internet Information Server (IIS) Admin Service. If you are in a company or school that has or can have this type of resource, you should ask your network administrator if you can take advantage of this or other network-related features.

■ *Web discussions*—This feature enables you and your colleagues to attach comments to a Web page or to any document that can be opened with a browser, such as PowerPoint slide shows saved in the Hypertext Markup Language (HTML) or Mime-encapsulated HTML (MHTML) format. As comments are added, they can be viewed in a discussion task pane, threaded so that you can see who responded to whom. This feature requires a Web-based discussion server.

■ *Shared workspace*—A shared workspace is an area, hosted by a Web-based discussion server, where you and your colleagues can share documents and information, monitor the status of given projects, and so on. This new feature in PowerPoint 2003 also requires Microsoft's SharePoint services.

FIGURE 21.1

Online meetings can include chat sessions where you type questions and answers while viewing a PowerPoint screen.

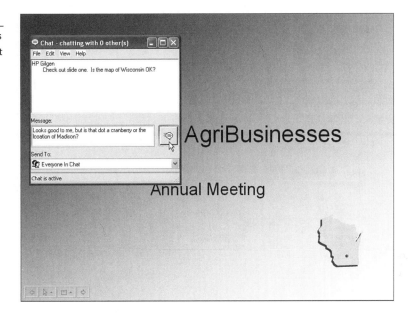

- *Subscription notification*—Along with SharePoint services and Web discussions, you can receive notification of any changes made to a Web page via email notification. You can subscribe to an individual Web page or to an entire folder on a Web site.

- *Information rights management (IRM)*—This feature, which is new in PowerPoint 2003, enables you to make documents available to others but also to restrict who can use them, when they can use them, and what they can do with them while they have them checked out. IRM requires you to download and install the Microsoft Windows Rights Management client and also to subscribe to Microsoft's .NET services, which enables you to generate your own authentication certificate and to respond to requests for licenses and keys to work with your documents.

Research Services

Another group of advanced features is research services, which involve the ability to look up words, get reference information, and even translate from one language to another.

You can select a word or phrase and choose **T**ools, **R**esearch to display the Research task pane (see Figure 21.2).

FIGURE 21.2

Research serv-
ices enable you
to do much
more than look
up words in a
dictionary.

PowerPoint can search for information in its own dictionary and thesaurus, or if
you're connected to the Internet, it can search several online research, business, and
financial sites. You simply select the service or group of services you want and see
what kind of results you get.

Special Characters

You can insert special characters individually, but if you're working extensively with
a foreign language, or if you're using mathematical equations, that approach is
tedious and inefficient.

PowerPoint, indeed the entire Office suite of applications, enables you to install support for any of a number of languages, including common European languages and
those that use non-Roman characters or that read right to left, such as Russian,
Japanese, and Hebrew.

You must be running a recent version of the Windows operating system, such as
Windows 2000 or Windows XP, both of which have built-in language support. In
addition, you can select or create keyboards that enable you to input foreign characters more naturally (see Figure 21.3). If you're using characters that require multiple
keystrokes for each character, such as Japanese, you also must install and use an
Input Method Editor (IME) for that specific language.

Equations are handled a bit differently from the way you insert foreign language
characters. Although you can insert as text some of the same characters and symbols used in equations, formatting them to look like equations is nearly impossible.

Instead, you insert an equation object by choosing **I**nsert, **O**bject, Create **N**ew and choosing Microsoft Equation from the list of object types. If you did not install the Equation Editor when you installed Office 2003, you must do so before you can select this option from the list.

FIGURE 21.3

You can set up languages by using keyboards and characters from many different countries.

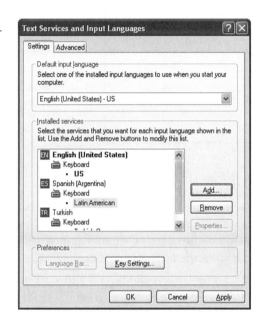

PowerPoint then opens an equation editor in a separate window, and you use it to create and format an equation (see Figure 21.4). When you click OK, the equation editor closes, and PowerPoint inserts the equation in a slide as an object (see Figure 21.5). You can move, size, and otherwise manipulate the equation box. To edit the equation, double-click it to return to the equation editor.

FIGURE 21.4

Microsoft's Equation Editor is a powerful tool for formatting equations.

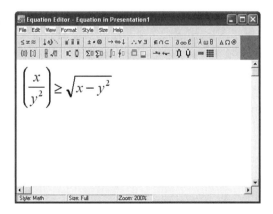

FIGURE 21.5

Equations appear as objects in a PowerPoint slide, and they can be moved or sized.

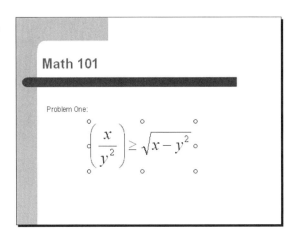

Features That Automate Difficult or Tedious Tasks

If programming can be used to create a program such as PowerPoint, it stands to reason that even more programming can add to or modify how PowerPoint works. PowerPoint, along with the rest of the entire Office suite and Windows, enables you to use programming techniques in the following features:

- *Macros*—A macro at its most basic is simply a recorded sequence of keystrokes or actions that can be played back by typing a simple keystroke or attached to an object as an action setting. However, you can take macro programming way beyond simple macro recording to accomplish some rather complex and amazing feats.

- *Visual Basic*—This object-oriented programming language can be used to edit recorded macros or to create entirely new macros (see Figure 21.6). If you already have programming skills, learning to program in Visual Basic isn't very difficult. Indeed, anyone wanting to learn to program in this language can learn quickly with the help of a self-study book.

  The challenge comes in learning to use Visual Basic to hook into things that PowerPoint already does and modify the process or add capabilities that aren't already there. The satisfaction comes from getting PowerPoint to do exactly what you need it to do, even if it's not designed that way.

- *Script editing*—PowerPoint files can be saved as Web pages, which makes it easy for others to view them by using a browser. PowerPoint also allows you to open Web versions of a slide show and edit directly in PowerPoint. Nevertheless, Web versions of PowerPoint slide shows are written using HTML and its variations, and they can be viewed and edited directly in that language.

FIGURE 21.6

You can use
Visual Basic
Editor (VBE) to
edit or program
macros and
other
PowerPoint
controls.

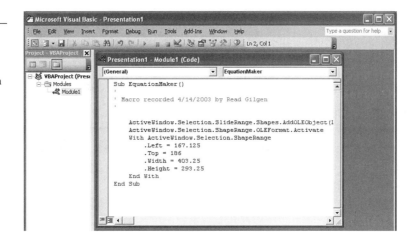

If you choose **T**ools, **M**acro, Microsoft Script **E**ditor, PowerPoint opens the
Microsoft Script Editor, displaying HTML code in the center of the editor, with
a variety of tools for editing (see Figure 21.7). Chances are that you'll find
this approach less than appealing. However, if you're experienced in working
with HTML code, and if you need to get behind the scenes and tweak that
code to make something specific take place, you can do so by using the
Microsoft Script Editor.

FIGURE 21.7

PowerPoint's
Microsoft Script
Editor enables
you to edit
HTML code
directly for
Web-based
presentations.

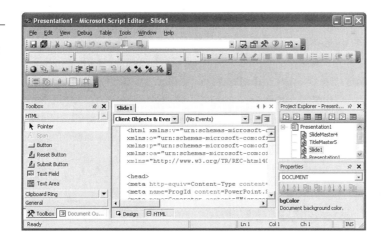

Add-ins

Add-ins are special supplemental programs, usually provided by third-party sources, to extend and enhance the capabilities of PowerPoint. Add-ins range from programs that add multimedia capabilities to those that simply enhance PowerPoint's default menus or toolbars.

Some add-ins are free; others you have to pay for. You can even write your own custom add-in programs by using the VBE. Also, you can find many add-ins on the Web. Look at the Microsoft Web site for the ones that are provided by Microsoft or do a Web search for *addins* and *PowerPoint* to find possible PowerPoint enhancements elsewhere on the Web.

You can easily add add-in programs by choosing **T**ools, Add-**I**ns, **A**dd New and browsing to find the filename of the add-in you want, one that ends with `.ppa`.

caution

Because virtually all add-ins contain macros, you should be careful when using an add-in from an unknown source. If you're not sure you can trust the source, it's best not to use the add-in.

Commercial Programs and Services

You can purchase third-party add-ins, templates, and graphics to add variety and interest to presentations. Packages of animations, templates, and add-ins can cost anywhere from a few dollars to a couple hundred dollars. With a little research, you can often figure out which ones offer the best value. If you get to the point where you create lots of presentations, an investment in commercial programs might well be worth it.

You'll also find that certain PowerPoint features really are a conduit to commercial services, or that in order to use a feature, you have to invest in other programs or hardware. Examples include PowerPoint's Fax service and its collaboration features, such as NetMeeting, SharePoint, and Web discussions. The next section shows you how to get information and reviews on products and services so you don't waste time and money.

Additional Resources

As good as this book has been for getting you started with PowerPoint, there's a lot more information and help available to enrich your experience and to take you to the next level. The following sections do not offer an exhaustive treatment of additional resources, nor are these resources necessarily the best or most recommended. However, they can point you in the right direction for getting additional help and information.

Advanced Topic Books

If you're ready to move to the next level, you should consider acquiring an advanced book such as Que's *Special Edition Using Microsoft Office PowerPoint 2003* or *Special Edition Using Visual Basic*. How do you decide which of the many books out there are right for you? After deciding whether you really need some sort of book to help, you should do two things:

- Scan the table of contents. Does the book seem to cover the features or procedures you're interested in learning?
- Choose a sample chapter and begin reading it. Does it speak to you? Is it clear? Does it pack a lot of information?

If you're comfortable with these criteria, the book just might work for you.

Presentations Magazine

You can also learn a lot from professional journals or magazines. My favorite, and one that I find extremely helpful for beginner and experienced PowerPoint users alike, is *Presentations*. Because the magazine is supported by advertising, you can receive a free subscription. Each month's issue is chock full of ideas, basic presenting how-to, tips and tricks, and software and hardware reviews. Even the commercial advertisements give you a sense of what can be done in and what's available for PowerPoint.

For more information, and to get a sample of what this magazine has to offer, go to www.presentations.com.

Microsoft's PowerPoint Newsgroup

Newsgroups can be a rich source of information. This is especially true of those that focus on specific subjects, such as the PowerPoint newsgroup, which is hosted by Microsoft but entirely managed by volunteer, non-Microsoft employees. This is a "no-question-is-too-dumb" discussion group where everyone shares freely with everyone else (see Figure 21.8).

Information on how to join the PowerPoint newsgroup can be found at www.rdpslides .com/pptfaq/FAQ00024.htm.

Several of the group's moderators also offer their own Web sites, with a variety of free and commercial add-ins, tutorials, graphics, animations, and more. The following are their sites, along with other sites you may want to visit:

- Steve Rindsberg's RDP Slides site, at www.rdpslides.com
- Sonia Coleman's site, at www.soniacoleman.com

FIGURE 21.8

The Microsoft PowerPoint Newsgroup is a great place to ask questions, to find answers, and to learn all about PowerPoint.

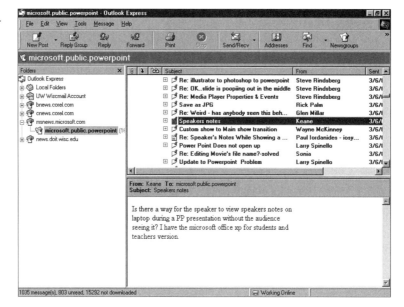

- Echo Swinford's site, at www.echosvoice.com
- Kathryn Jacobs's site, at www.powerpointanswers.com
- Shyam Pillai's site, at www.mvps.org/skp

The following story, which introduces the PowerPoint newsgroup moderators, is both fun and informative. It was written by one of the PowerPoint newsgroup moderators, Austin Myers, and it can be found at www.rdpslides.com/pptfaq/FAQ00094.htm. As a conclusion to this book, the story helps summarize in an allegorical way the evolution of PowerPoint and its increasing complexities:

> There was a caveman by the name of Brian (Reilly) that started it all with some really crude drawings on the wall of his cave. Actually the drawings weren't that bad but his ability to speak and point at the drawings was somewhat limited.
>
> He asked his friend Steve (Rindsberg) if there wasn't someway to jazz up his presentation and Steve said sure, hold this burning stick up by the drawing you want people to look at, and darkness will hide the rest of the drawings. We believe this was the first attempt at a "Custom Show".
>
> Enter agrarian Austin (Myers) who was the one who made all those drums and voices audible and the funny flickering moving pictures visible. He was the one who daily climbed the hill and yelled "CODEC - - MCI - - QT - -

MPEG!!!!!!" Everyone wondered about the new words he had invented. They are, to this day, still trying to de-code them, but Austin's voice from the hills cannot be suppressed. Now there were three.

One day Kathy (Huntzinger) came walking by and asked the guys what they were doing. At first she thought they had lost their mind but after an explanation she could see what they were trying to do. Naturally she wanted to improve on the situation and suggested they add drum sounds to the presentation. While the three guys thought it had possibilities they didn't want her to be seen so they made her sit off to the side out of sight. (That's why we drag the Icon off the slide to this day.)

When Kathy began beating the drum the guys noticed a sound that was almost a duplicate but sounded fainter and far away. Steve asked Brian, do you here that? Brian said of course, it's Echo (Swinford). Hey, did someone call my name said the woman with the strangely colored hair as she came walking into the cave.

She looked over what everyone was doing and said that while the pictures were nice, what was needed was some text to go with it. No one had any idea what she was talking about so she showed them by making squiggly marks beside all the drawings. Everyone thought it was a big improvement but the problem was that everyone looked at the squiggly lines before looking at Brian's drawings.

Not a problem at all said Echo. Just cover the text with a bear skin and then take it off when you shine the burning stick on it. Should make a nice "transition". Just remember to cover them back up or they won't look right the next time you show it to anyone. Now there were five.

With all the improvements cavemen and women came from miles around to see the presentation. But alas, after all the local folks had seen the presentation it became obvious that they needed a way to take the entire thing on the road so they might show it to others. What to do, what to do?

Fortunately for our friends there was a woman that lived next to the big water hole who claimed she could transport anything. Her name, Sonia (Coleman), was spoken only rarely but all knew who she was. The group convinced her to look over the problem and asked for her help.

After much study and concentration Sonia hit upon an idea. We will "burn" copies of everything on my new invention the wheel. That way we can simply roll the presentation to the next cave and everyone can see the show. Problem solved! Now there were six.

Things went along well for the gang, but you know how people are and they soon started complaining about not having enough tools to make drawings, text, and sounds with. Complain as they might, there just weren't any better tools available. That is until the day they met a traveler from far, far away by the name of Shyam (Pillai).

Because he was a decent sort of fellow he agreed to help out and had soon produced many new tools. Sharp sticks for text, wide sticks with all sorts of berry juices on the tip for drawing, and he even made a better set of drums for sounds. He was immediately invited to live in the cave and now there were seven.

Things just couldn't get any better and these folks found a life long calling explaining how to make presentations to others.

The Absolute Minimum

In this chapter, you've been nudged toward the next level. Here's what you've done:

- You learned about some of PowerPoint's advanced features.
- You learned that some advanced features depend on having additional software, hardware, or special servers.
- You explored several additional resources where you can find help and advanced information.

In the next chapter....Oops, there is no next chapter. In fact, I am delighted to officially certify you as no longer being an absolute beginner! Happy presenting!

Index

C

How can we make this index more useful? Email us at indexes@quepublishing.com

How can we make this index more useful? Email us at indexes@quepublishing.com

How can we make this index more useful? Email us at indexes@quepublishing.com

How can we make this index more useful? Email us at indexes@quepublishing.com